WHAT DID JESUS MEAN?

RON RHODES

HARVEST HOUSE PUBLISHERS
Eugene, Oregon 97402

Cover by Koechel Peterson & Associates, Minneapolis, Minnesota

WHAT DID JESUS MEAN?

Copyright © 1999 by Ron Rhodes
Published by Harvest House Publishers
Eugene, Oregon 97402

Library of Congress Cataloging-in-Publication-Data

Rhodes, Ron.
    What did Jesus mean? / Ron Rhodes.
       p.   cm.
    Includes bibliographical references and indexes.
    ISBN 0-7369-0049-7
    1. Jesus Christ—Teachings—Miscellanea.   I. Title.
BS2415.R47   1999
232.9'54—dc21   98-42006
                                                  CIP

Printed in the United States of America.

99 00 01 02 03 04 / BC / 10 9 8 7 6 5 4 3 2 1

To Tom and Alpha Rhodes

ACKNOWLEDGMENTS

As always, I want to give a special thanks to my wife Kerri. There is no way I could have completed this book in a timely fashion without her able assistance and encouragement. Each year that passes I thank God anew for putting me together with this gem of a woman!

I also want to acknowledge my two children—David and Kylie. David deserves special mention because he is the one who came up with the idea for this book in the first place. (Sometimes at the dinner table my kids turn the topic of discussion to the question, "What book should daddy write next?") Thanks, David! You have played a special role in the development of this book. Your enthusiasm for this project has been a constant source of motivation for me. And Kylie—thanks for all your little acts of encouragement during the writing of this book, especially your great drawings. You are a joy.

I treasure all of you!

CONTENTS

"TRULY I SAY TO YOU"

Jesus' teachings were always presented as being ultimate and final. He never wavered in this stance. He unflinchingly placed His teachings above those of Moses and the prophets—and in a Jewish culture at that!

Jesus always spoke in *His own* authority. He never said, "Thus saith the Lord . . ." as did the prophets; He always said, "Verily, verily, *I say* unto you. . . ." He never retracted anything He said, never guessed or spoke with uncertainty, never made revisions, never contradicted Himself, and never apologized for what He said. He even asserted that "heaven and earth will pass away, but my words will never pass away" (Mark 13:31), hence elevating His words directly to the realm of heaven.

The teachings of Jesus had a profound effect on people. His listeners always seemed to surmise that these were not the words of an ordinary man. When He taught in Capernaum on the Sabbath, the people "were amazed at his teaching" (Luke 4:32). After the Sermon on the Mount, "the crowds were amazed at his teaching, because he taught as one who had authority, and not as their teachers of the law" (Matthew 7:28,29). When some Jewish leaders asked the temple guards why they had not arrested Jesus when He spoke, they responded, "No one ever spoke the way this man does" (John 7:46).

One cannot read the Gospels long before recognizing that Jesus regarded Himself and His message as inseparable. The reason Jesus' teachings had ultimate authority was that He was and is God. *The words of Jesus are the very words of God!* We would be wise, then, to give heed to what He says. To ignore Him is to invite peril.

But as both believers and critics have noted since the first century, some of Jesus' statements are hard to understand. Some seem harsh and even cruel. What are we to make of such statements? *What did Jesus mean* by such statements?

Bridging the Culture Gap

Part of the problem we encounter in seeking to interpret Jesus' words is that His culture was entirely different from ours. This is such an important point that I want to illustrate it with an example a bit closer to home. Let us suppose that a person from another country decides to move to the United States. This person is rather rusty on the English language and is completely unfamiliar with most American figures of speech. He thus finds it difficult to fully grasp the meaning of people's words.

As he flips through a magazine one day, he comes across a chronicle of a child's soccer game held at a local park. A father is with his son, and before the son engages in play, the father says to him, "Son, break a leg. Knock 'em dead." The son replies, "Don't worry, dad, we'll kill'em. It'll be a piece of cake."

This person begins to ponder the meaning of such words. Surely the words are not to be taken literally, for they portray a young boy being instructed by his own father to break the legs of his youthful opponents, and even kill them, and somehow this is all related to eating cake. *Very strange!* Soon after, though, the man finds a sympathetic ear at a neighbor's house, and the neighbor, after having a good laugh, enlightens the man on the meaning of the strange words.

Perhaps this is an extreme example, but you get my point: A little understanding of English figures of speech clears everything up. And so it is with some of the hard sayings of Jesus. A little understanding of first-century Jewish culture and Jewish figures of speech goes a long way in making things much clearer.[1]

The interpreter of Scripture must step out of his Western mindset and into a first-century Jewish mindset, seeking to understand such things as Jewish marriage rites, burial rites, family practices, farm practices, business practices, the monetary system, methods of warfare, slavery, the treatment of captives, and religious practices.[2] Armed with such detailed information, interpreting the hard sayings of Jesus becomes a much easier task.

Jesus' Use of Parables

Though Jesus' teachings take a variety of forms, a full third of them involve the use of parables.[3] The word *parable* literally means "a placing alongside of" for the purpose of comparison.[4] A parable is a teaching tool. Jesus would often tell a story from real life (involving, for example, a woman who lost a coin, or a shepherd watching over sheep, or a worker in a vineyard) and use that story to illustrate a *spiritual* truth.

By taking such a story and "placing it alongside" a spiritual truth, the process of comparison helps us to understand Jesus' spiritual teaching more clearly. For example, Jesus' story of the good shepherd helps us to understand that Jesus watches over us and guides us, just as a shepherd watches over and guides sheep.

It is important to understand that there are several kinds of parables in the New Testament. Understanding a little about these different forms helps us to interpret Jesus' intended meaning more accurately.

Some parables take on the form of a simile. These involve a likeness that employs the words "like" or "as." An example is Matthew 10:16, where Jesus said, "I am sending you out *like* sheep among wolves. Therefore be *as* shrewd as snakes and *as* innocent as doves" (italics added).[5]

Some parables take on the form of a metaphor. In this type of parable there is an implied likeness of some sort. An example is John 10:7, where Jesus said, "I am the gate for the sheep."[6] This metaphor teaches that Jesus is the way of salvation.

Some parables take on the form of a similitude. In this type of parable, Jesus illustrates a particular spiritual truth by citing something common in the everyday natural world. Jesus takes what we *already know* in the natural world and uses it as a word picture to teach us some new spiritual truth. We see this in Matthew 13:33, where Jesus said, "The kingdom of heaven is like yeast that a woman took and mixed into a large amount of flour until it worked all through the dough." Here Jesus refers to yeast to illustrate the growth of the kingdom of heaven and the penetrating power of the gospel.[7]

Some parables take the form of a story. This was Jesus' most common type of parable in teaching His followers. In such a parable, Jesus would tell a story about a person in order to teach an important spiritual concept. For example, in Luke 15:11-32 Jesus told a story of a man who had two sons, one of which was the "prodigal son."[8] Through this story Jesus taught that God always has His arms wide open to receive into fellowship those who repent and come to Him in contriteness.

Interpreting Jesus' Parables

Earlier I mentioned the importance of understanding first-century Jewish culture. This is especially important when it comes to seeking to understand Jesus' parables. Jesus lived in ancient Palestine among Jewish people, and all His parables are drawn from that cultural backdrop. In fact, most of the parables are drawn from material that would be familiar to a poor, agricultural Jewish peasant living in the first century.[9]

In interpreting Jesus' parables, then, it is necessary to understand the cultural context in which they were originally spoken.[10] One cannot understand the parable of new wine in old wineskins, for example, unless one first understands the process of making wine in Christ's day. We cannot discover the truth contained in a parable by superimposing our modern culture on Christ's first-century culture. We must instead become thoroughly conversant with biblical history, geography, culture, and customs.[11]

In addition, it is critical to understand that Jesus' parables were never spoken in a vacuum. Indeed, every time He spoke a parable, He was seeking to answer some question or address a problem His hearers were facing.[12] Hence we find great help in properly interpreting the parables by consulting the verses before and after each parable. We often find clues in the context as to what the main point of each parable is.

Further, consulting the broader context of all of Scripture is beneficial when interpreting Christ's parables and hard sayings. We must keep in mind that the interpretation of a specific passage must not contradict the total teaching of Scripture on a point. Individual verses do not exist as isolated fragments, but as parts of a whole. The exposition of these verses, therefore, must involve exhibiting them in right relation both to the whole and to each other. *Scripture interprets Scripture.* As J. I. Packer put it, "If we would understand the parts, our wisest course is to get to know the whole."[13]

Why Did Jesus Teach Using Parables?

In Matthew 13, Jesus is portrayed as being in front of a mixed multitude comprised of both believers and unbelievers. He did not attempt to separate the believers from the unbelievers and then instruct only the believers. Rather, He constructed His teaching so that believers would understand what He said but unbelievers *would not*, and He did this by using parables.

After teaching one such parable, a disciple asked Jesus, "Why do you speak to the people in parables?" (Matthew 13:10). Jesus answered, "The knowledge of *the secrets* of the kingdom of heaven has been given to you [believers], but not to them [unbelievers]" (verse 11, italics added).

The Greek word for *secret* in this passage means "mystery." A mystery in the biblical sense is a truth that cannot be discerned simply by human investigation, but requires special revelation from God. Generally this word refers to a truth that was unknown to people living in Old Testament times, but is now revealed to humankind by God (Matthew 13:17; Colossians 1:26). In the parables, Jesus provided information to believers about some aspect of the kingdom of heaven that had never been revealed before.

One might legitimately ask why Jesus engineered His parabolic teaching so that *believers* could understand His teaching but *unbelievers* could not. The backdrop to this strategy is that the disciples, having responded favorably to Jesus' teaching and having placed their faith in Him, already knew much truth about the Messiah. Careful reflection on Jesus' parables would enlighten them even further.

However, hardened unbelievers who had willfully and persistently refused Jesus' previous teachings were prevented from understanding the parables. Jesus was apparently following an injunction He had provided earlier in the Sermon on the Mount: "Do not give dogs what is sacred; do not throw your pearls to pigs" (Matthew 7:6). (I will address this verse later in the book.) Yet there is grace even here, for it is possible that Jesus may have prevented unbelievers from understanding the parables because He did not want to add more responsibility to them by imparting new truth for which they would be held responsible at the time of final judgment.

One should not miss the fact that the parables of the *sower* (Matthew 13:3-9) and the *weeds* (13:24-30) show that Jesus wanted His parables to be clear to those who were receptive. Jesus Himself provided the interpretation of these parables for His disciples.[14] He did this not only so there would be no uncertainty as to their meaning, but also to guide believers in how to interpret the *other* parables. The fact that He did not interpret His subsequent parables shows that He fully expected believers to understand them.

Yet because these parables were taught in a first-century Jewish context, some help is needed in bridging the culture gap. That is one of the reasons I wrote this book. It is my hope and prayer that as you read this book, some of Jesus' most important teachings may come alive and become meaningful to you for the first time in your life.

Applying What We Learn

In this book my goal will be to examine over 150 puzzling sayings (some of them parables) of Jesus with a view to making them clearer to modern students of the Bible. I want you to keep in mind that Jesus' teachings—even His *hard* teachings—are liberating and life-changing ("the truth will set you free"—John 8:32). My advice, then, is that you not read this book merely to cram your head full of more facts about Jesus' teachings. *Let His words penetrate your heart as well.*

If you let Him, Christ will speak to you. With His words He will convict you and yet comfort you. He will liberate you and set you free. He will change you forever.

Lord Jesus, open our hearts.

ONE

JESUS' CLAIMS
ABOUT HIMSELF

▶ Does Jesus' reference to Himself as God's "only begotten Son" imply that He is less divine than the Father (John 3:16 NASB)?

The words "only begotten" do not mean that Christ was *created*, or that He was in some way brought into existence by the Father. Rather, the Greek word for "only begotten" means "unique" or "one of a kind." Jesus is *uniquely* God's Son.

As God's "Son," Jesus has the same nature as the Father (a *divine* nature)—every bit as much as my son, David, has *my* nature (a *human* nature).[1] Jesus is uniquely God's Son *by nature*, meaning that He has the very nature of God.

Though the term "son of" can sometimes refer to "offspring of" in certain biblical contexts, when used of Christ it carries the more important meaning "of the order of."[2] The phrase is often used this way in the Old Testament. For example, "sons of the prophets" meant "of the order of prophets" (1 Kings 20:35). "Sons of the singers" meant "of the order of singers" (Nehemiah 12:28 NASB). Likewise, the phrase "Son of God" means "of the order of God," and represents a claim to undiminished deity.

So the fact that Jesus is called God's "Son" does not mean He is somehow less divine than the Father is. Jesus is *fully* divine. This is why, whenever Jesus claimed to be the Son of God in the New Testament, His Jewish critics tried to stone

Him because they correctly understood that He was claiming to be God (see John 5:18; 19:7).

Like many other Christians, I believe that Christ's Sonship is an *eternal* Sonship. Evidence for Christ's eternal Sonship is found in the fact that He is represented as *already being* the Son of God before His human birth in Bethlehem (John 3:16,17; compare Proverbs 30:4). Hebrews 1:2 says that God created the universe *through* His "Son," implying that Christ was the Son of God prior to the creation. Moreover, Christ *as* the Son is explicitly said to have existed "before all things" (Colossians 1:17; compare with verses 13 and 14). As well, Jesus, speaking as the Son of God (John 8:54-56), asserted His eternal preexistence before Abraham (verse 58). Seen in this light, Christ's identity as the Son of God does not connote any kind of inferiority regarding His deity.

▶ If Jesus was the Son of God, why did He also call Himself the Son of Man (Matthew 20:18; 24:30)?

This may sound like a contradiction at first glance, but in fact there is no contradiction. To begin, even if the phrase "Son of Man" were solely a reference to Jesus' humanity, it does not constitute a denial of His deity. In becoming a human being, Jesus did not thereby cease to be God. The incarnation of Christ did not involve the *subtraction of deity* but the *addition of humanity*. Jesus clearly asserted His deity on many occasions (Matthew 16:16,17; John 8:58; 10:30). But besides being divine, He was also human in the incarnation (see Philippians 2:6-8). He had two natures (divine and human) conjoined in *one* person.[3]

Furthermore, Scripture itself indicates that Jesus was not denying He was God when He referred to Himself as the Son of Man. It is highly revealing that the term "Son of Man" is used of Christ in contexts where His deity is quite evident. For example, the Bible indicates that only God has the prerogative of forgiving sins (Isaiah 43:25; Mark 2:7). But Jesus as the "Son of Man" exercised this prerogative (Mark 2:10). Likewise, at the second coming Christ will return to earth as the "Son of Man" in clouds of glory to reign on earth (Matthew 26:63,64). In this passage Jesus is alluding to Daniel 7:13, where the Messiah is described as the "Ancient of Days," a phrase used to indicate His deity (see Daniel 7:9).[4] So Jesus as the Son of Man is the divine Messiah.

Finally, the phrase "Son of Man" surely includes the idea of Christ's role as humankind's Kinsman-Redeemer. In the Old Testament (Leviticus 25:25,26,48,49; Ruth 2:20), the next of kin (one related *by blood*) always functioned as the kinsman-redeemer of a family member who needed redemption from jail. In the incarnation, Jesus became related to us *by blood* so He could function as our Kinsman-Redeemer and rescue us from sin. Jesus as the "Son of Man" was the Kinsman-Redeemer for a lost humanity, fully divine and yet fully human.

▶ What did Jesus mean when He said that He and the Father "are one" (John 10:30)?

In John 10:30 Jesus said, "I and the Father are one." Some people have wrongly concluded that Jesus was claiming to be the Father in this verse. Others have wrongly concluded that the Father must have a physical body like Jesus does, since Jesus and the Father are said to be "one." Still others have claimed that Jesus was simply indicating that He and the Father are "one in purpose."

While it is positively true that Jesus and the Father are "one in purpose," that is most certainly *not* what Jesus is talking about in this verse. Keep in mind that when Jesus said He and the Father were "one," the Jewish leaders immediately picked up stones to put Him to death. It is clear that they understood Jesus to be claiming to be God. According to verse 33, the Jews said, "For a good work we do not stone You, but for blasphemy; and because You, being a man, *make Yourself out to be God*" (NASB, italics added). The penalty for blasphemy, according to Old Testament law, was death by stoning.

Notice that Jesus did not respond by saying, "Oh, no, you have it all wrong. I was not claiming to be God; I was merely claiming to be 'one in purpose' with God." Even the Jews claimed to have a unity of purpose with God. They would not have tried to stone Jesus for that claim. They understood Jesus as He *intended* to be understood—claiming to be deity.[5]

How does this relate to the doctrine of the Trinity? Jesus was one with the Father *in nature* while being distinct from Him *in person.* The triune Godhead has one *essence* (a divine essence or nature) but three distinct *persons* (Father, Son, and Holy Spirit).[6]

▶ What did Jesus mean when He said that the Father is "greater" than He (John 14:28)?

In John 14:28 Jesus said to His disciples, "If you loved me, you would be glad that I am going to the Father, for the Father is greater than I." Jesus in this verse is not speaking about His nature or His essential being, which is divine (Christ had earlier said "I and the Father are one" in this regard—John 10:30), but is rather speaking of His lowly position in the incarnation.[7] As the Athanasian Creed put it, Christ is "equal to the Father as touching his Godhood and inferior to the Father as touching his manhood."[8] In other words, Jesus is just as divine as the Father is, but in His humanity (in the incarnation) Jesus was "lesser" than the Father.

Keep in mind that the Father was seated upon the throne of highest majesty in heaven; the brightness of His glory was uneclipsed as He was surrounded by hosts of holy angels perpetually worshiping Him with uninterrupted praise. Far different was it with His incarnate Son—despised and rejected of men, surrounded by implacable enemies, and soon to be nailed to a criminal's cross.[9] It is from this lowly perspective of the incarnation that Jesus could say the Father is "greater" than He.

We might illustrate this with the President of the United States. The President is in a higher position than the rest of us. Therefore the President is "greater" than the rest of us.

However, the President is still just a human being, equal in nature to all other human beings.

Likewise, Jesus was fully equal with the Father in terms of nature (a *divine* nature). But the Father was "greater" than Jesus from the perspective of the incarnation, because Jesus had to condescend to great depths in becoming a human being. During the time of the incarnation, Jesus functioned in the world of humanity, and this of necessity involved Him being *positionally* lower than the Father.

▶ Did Jesus teach that only the Father (and not He Himself) should be worshiped (John 4:23)?

In John 4:23 Jesus said, "A time is coming and has now come when the true worshipers will worship the Father in spirit and truth." But in making this statement, He was not saying that He Himself should not be worshiped as well.

As mentioned earlier in this book, a fundamental principle of interpreting Scripture correctly is that "Scripture interprets Scripture." What I mean by this is that every single verse should be interpreted against the broader backdrop of what the entirety of Scripture teaches on a given subject.

The same Greek word used for worshiping the Father (*proskuneo*) is used of worshiping Christ throughout the New Testament. Jesus was worshiped by Thomas (John 20:28), angels (Hebrews 1:6), wise men (Matthew 2:11), a leper (Matthew 8:2), a ruler (Matthew 9:18), a blind man (John 9:38), an anonymous woman (Matthew 15:25), Mary Magdalene (Matthew 28:9), and the disciples (Matthew 28:17). In the book of Revelation, the worship that the Father receives (4:10) is exactly the same as the worship Jesus receives (5:11-14).

As a backdrop, it is significant that when the apostle Paul and Barnabas were in Lystra and miraculously healed a man by God's mighty power, those in the crowd shouted, "The gods have come down to us in human form!" (Acts 14:11). When Paul and Barnabas perceived that the people were preparing to worship them, "they tore their clothes and rushed out into the crowd, shouting: 'Men, why are you doing this? We too are only men, human like you'" (verses 14,15). As soon as they perceived what was happening, they immediately corrected the gross misconception that they were gods.

By contrast, Jesus *never* sought to correct His followers, or "set them straight," when they bowed down and worshiped Him. Indeed, Jesus considered such worship as perfectly appropriate. And of course we would not expect Jesus to try to correct people in worshiping Him if He truly was God in the flesh.

That Jesus is worshiped says a lot about His true identity, for it is the consistent testimony of Scripture that only God can be worshiped. Exodus 34:14 tells us, "Do not worship any other god, for the LORD, whose name is Jealous, is a jealous God" (see also Deuteronomy 6:13 and Matthew 4:10). In view of this, the fact that Jesus *was* worshiped on many occasions in the New Testament shows that He is God.

▶ If Jesus is really God, why did He say He could do nothing by Himself, but only what He sees His Father doing (John 5:19)?

In John 5:19 Jesus said, "I tell you the truth, the Son can do nothing by himself; he can do only what he sees his Father doing, because whatever the Father does the Son also does." At first glance Jesus may seem to be implying that He is not fully divine. However, understanding the biblical teaching on the Trinity helps to clear things up.

Jesus is fully equal to the Father in terms of His divine nature, but there is nevertheless a functional hierarchy that exists between the persons of the Trinity, with the Father in authority over the Son. To illustrate, my son, David, has my identical nature (fully human), but I am functionally in authority over him. Similarly, Jesus has the same nature as the Father (a *divine* nature), but the Father is functionally in authority over Him.

This verse thus indicates that Jesus does not act independent of the Father but in perfect harmony and submission to Him. We are told earlier in John's Gospel that the Father *sent*

Jesus into the world (John 3:16). We are now told in John 5:19 that the Father *directs* Him as well.

The Jewish backdrop is significant. Among the ancient Jews it was common wisdom that sons were to imitate their fathers.[10] Of course, Jewish sons had the same nature as their Jewish fathers (both were human). Similarly, though John 5:19 portrays Jesus as imitating the Father, Jesus nevertheless has the same nature as the Father (a divine nature). Bible commentator Albert Barnes explains it this way:

> When it is said that he can do nothing of himself, it is meant that such is the union subsisting between the Father and the Son that he can do nothing independently or separate from the Father.... In all things he must, from the necessity of his nature, act in accordance with the nature and will of God.... There is no separate action—no separate existence; but, alike in being and in action, there is the most perfect oneness between him and the Father.[11]

I think it is interesting to note that there is an implied claim to deity in this verse, for it plainly tells us that "whatever the Father does the Son also does" (John 5:19). The Father is God. And *who besides God can do what God does?* Since *Jesus* does what *only* God can do, Jesus Himself is quite obviously God (just as the Father is). Bible scholar Brooks Westcott thus declares that Jesus does what the Father does not in mere imitation "but in virtue of His sameness of nature."[12] Indeed, "the things that God does are the things that Jesus does; and the things that Jesus does are the things that God does."[13]

▶ If Jesus is really God, why did He say He could speak only what the Father taught Him (John 8:28)?

In John 8:28 Jesus said, "When you have lifted up the Son of Man, then you will know that I am the one I claim to be and that I do nothing on my own but speak just what the Father has taught me." The backdrop to properly understanding this verse is that other verses in Scripture make it clear that Jesus as God is *all-knowing* (Matthew 9:4; 11:27; 17:27; Luke 5:4; John 1:48; 2:24,25; 4:16-19; 6:64; 7:29; 8:55; 10:15; 17:25) and *all-powerful* (Mark 1:29-31; Luke 8:25; John 1:3; 11:1-44; Colossians 1:16; Hebrews 1:2). Hence, whatever is meant by John 8:28 cannot be taken to mean that He is devoid of these divine attributes.

Contextually, it helps us to go back to the very beginning of John's Gospel, where we are told that the whole reason Jesus became flesh (a human being) in the first place was to act as a *revealer* of God: "No one has ever seen God [the Father], but God the One and Only [Jesus Christ], who is at the Father's side, has made him known" (John 1:18). The perfect revelation of God *the Father* came in the person of God *the Son*.

In what ways was Jesus the perfect revealer of God? Theologian Robert Lightner explains it this way:

> Christ revealed the Person of God as He had never been made known before. He declared the Father to man (cf. John 1:18; 14:8,9; 1 Tim. 3:16). The glory of God was made known by Christ (John 1:14; 2 Cor. 4:6; Isa. 40:5). God's power was revealed by God's Son. He did this many times and in many different ways (John 3:2; 2 Cor. 1:24). The wisdom of God was made known in the Person of Christ (John 7:46; I Cor. 1:24). The life of God was also declared by Him (1 John 1:1-3). To be sure, God's boundless love was revealed and demonstrated by the Savior (John 3:16; Rom. 5:8; 1 John 3:16). The grace of God, the undeserved favor which He bestowed upon mankind, was also revealed by the Lord Jesus (Luke 2:40; John 1:17; 2 Thess. 1:12).[14]

As the divine revealer, then, what Jesus *did* and what He *said* were rooted in His relationship to the Father (John 8:28). Jesus never did anything *alone*—nothing in opposition to or in contradiction to the Father—but rather He did all things *in conjunction*—with the Father, with the same divine power, having the same divine will, being of the same divine nature, and fully equal to Him.[15]

John 8:28 most certainly does not point to any weakness in the Son or to deficiency of power to do anything by Himself. After all, Jesus by His *own* power created the entire universe (John 1:3), upholds the universe (Colossians 1:17), and raised Himself from the dead (John 2:19), among many other divine deeds.[16]

John 8:28 simply tells us that Jesus as the Son of God could never do anything contrary to the Father because they are of the same nature and therefore never act separately from each other. That Jesus does and says what the Father wills shows and proves their unity of nature and their perfect equality, since there was nothing in the Father's mind but what was also known to the divine Son.[17]

▶ Does the fact that Jesus called the Father the "only true God" mean that He Himself is not God (John 17:3)?

It might seem so at first glance, but interpreting this verse against the broader backdrop of all of Scripture puts things into proper perspective. To begin, recall that in this very same Gospel Jesus' deity is asserted time and time again:

- He is called God in John 1:1.
- He is portrayed as the divine Creator in John 1:3 (only God can be the Creator—see Isaiah 44:24).
- He is identified as the great "I AM" (Yahweh) in John 8:58 (compare with Exodus 3:14, where God said His name is "I AM").
- He is seen to have the same divine nature as the Father in John 10:30.
- He is recognized as God by doubting Thomas in John 20:28.
- His omnipresence (the quality of being *everywhere-present*) as God is evident in John 1:47-49.
- The fact that Jesus is all-knowing as God is clear from John 2:25, 16:30, and 21:17.

- The fact that Jesus is all-powerful as God is clear from John 1:3 and 11:1-44.

My point, then, is that however one interprets Jesus' statement in John 17:3, it should not be interpreted in such a way as to deny that Jesus Himself is God. In context the Father is called the only true God in this verse in opposition to the many *false* gods of the heathen (see 1 Thessalonians 1:9; 1 John 5:20,21; Revelation 3:7; 2 Chronicles 15:3; Isaiah 65:16), *but not to the exclusion of the Son.*[18] Recall that in 1 John 5:20 (written by the same John that wrote John's Gospel), we read of Jesus Christ, "He is the *true* God and eternal life" (italics added).[19]

Elsewhere in Scripture, Jesus, the Son of God, is called the "one Lord" (1 Corinthians 8:6), but this should not be taken to be true *only* of the Son to the exclusion of the Father. The fallacy we must be careful to avoid is the assumption that the use of a title for *one* person of the Trinity in *one* context automatically rules out its application to *another* person of the Trinity in *another* context. Instead of making such a faulty assumption, the proper policy would be to consult what all of Scripture has to say about the Father *and* Jesus Christ and then come to a correct and logical conclusion. From Scripture we know that the Father is called both God (1 Peter 1:2) and Lord (Matthew 11:25), and we know that Jesus Christ is called both God (John 20:28; Hebrews 1:8) and Lord (Romans 10:9). *Jesus and the Father are equally divine.*

We might also note that while Jesus called the Father the "only true God" in John 17:3, the Father in Hebrews 1:8 said of the Son, "Your throne, O God, will last forever and ever." The Son thus testified to the Father's deity; the Father testified to the Son's deity!

▶ Does the fact that Jesus said no one knows the day or hour of His return except the Father mean that He is less than God Almighty (Mark 13:32)?

No, I do not think so. But explaining this issue calls for a little theological background. Please follow the thinking as we dive into deep theological waters for a few moments.

Though a bit of a complex concept, the eternal Son of God was, prior to His incarnation, *one* in person and nature (wholly divine). In the incarnation (when He was born of Mary), He became *two* in nature (divine and human) while remaining *one* person. In the incarnation, the person of Christ is the partaker of the attributes of both natures, so that whatever may be affirmed of *either* nature—human or divine—may be affirmed of the *one* person of Jesus Christ.

Though Christ sometimes operated in the sphere of His humanity and in other cases in the sphere of His deity, in *all* cases what He did and what He was could be attributed to His one *person*. Thus, though Christ in His human nature knew hunger (Luke 4:2), weariness (John 4:6), and the need for sleep (Luke 8:23)—just as Christ in His divine nature was omniscient (*all-knowing*) (John 2:24), omnipresent (*everywhere-present*) (John 1:48), and omnipotent (*all-powerful*) (John 11:1-44)—all of this was experienced by the *one* person of Jesus Christ.

The Gospel accounts indicate clearly that Christ operated at different times under the *major* influence of one or the other of His two natures. Indeed, Christ operated in the human sphere to the extent that it was necessary for Him to accomplish His earthly purpose as determined in the eternal plan of salvation. At the same time, He operated in the divine sphere on numerous occasions in openly demonstrating that He was and is the divine Messiah (see Philippians 2:6-9).

Here is the important point: Both of Christ's natures come into play in many events recorded in the Gospels. For example, Christ's initial approach to the fig tree to pick and eat a fig to relieve His hunger reflected the natural limits of the *human* mind (Matthew 21:19a). (That is, in His humanity He *did not know* from a distance that there was no fruit on that particular tree.)[20] But then He immediately exercised His *divine* omnipotence by causing the tree to wither (verse 19b).

On another occasion, Jesus in His *divine* omniscience (all-knowingness) knew that His friend Lazarus had died and set off for Bethany (John 11:11). When Jesus arrived in Bethany, He asked (in his *humanness*, without exercising omniscience) where

Lazarus had been laid (verse 34). Theologian Robert Reymond notes that "as the God-man, [Jesus] is simultaneously omniscient as God (in company with the other persons of the Godhead) and ignorant of some things as man (in company with the other persons of the human race)."[21]

All this serves as a backdrop to a proper understanding of Jesus' comment in Mark 13:32, "But of that day or hour no one knows, not even the angels in heaven, nor the Son, but the Father alone" (NASB). *Jesus was here speaking from the vantage point of His humanity.* In His humanity, Jesus was not omniscient but was limited in understanding just as all human beings are. If Jesus had been speaking from the perspective of His divinity, He would not have said the same thing.

Scripture is abundantly clear in stating that in His divine nature Jesus is omniscient—just as omniscient as the Father is. The apostle John said that Jesus "did not need man's testimony about man, for he knew what was in a man" (John 2:25). Jesus' disciples said, "Now we can see that you know all things...." (John 16:30). After the resurrection, when Jesus asked Peter for the third time if Peter loved Him, Peter responded, "Lord, you know all things; you know that I love you" (John 21:17). Jesus knew just where the fish were in the water (Luke 5:4,6; John 21:6-11), and He knew which particular fish contained the coin (Matthew 17:27). He knows the Father as the Father knows Him (Matthew 11:27; John 7:29; 8:55; 10:15; 17:25), something that quite clearly requires the attribute of omniscience.

My friend and colleague Norman Geisler summarizes all this in the following chart:[22]

JESUS AS GOD	JESUS AS MAN
Unlimited in knowledge	Limited in knowledge
No growth in knowledge	Growth in knowledge
Knew time of His coming	Did not know time of His coming

▶ Does the fact that Jesus made reference to "my God" and "your God" in John 20:17 prove that He Himself is not God?

Following His resurrection from the dead, Jesus said to Mary, "I am returning to my Father and your Father, to my God and your God" (John 20:17). At first reading it might seem that Jesus is indicating He is not God. But that is not the intent of His words.

As noted above, before the incarnation, Christ—the second person of the Trinity—had only a divine nature. But in the incarnation He took on a human nature. It is thus *in His humanity* that Christ acknowledged the Father as "my God." Positionally speaking as a man, as a Jew, and as our high priest ("made like his brothers in every way"—Hebrews 2:17), Jesus could address the Father as "God." However, in His divine nature He could never refer to the Father as "my God," for Jesus was fully equal to the Father in every way regarding His divine nature.

There is another point that bears mentioning here: Why didn't Jesus just say, "I am ascending to *our* Father and *our* God"? The reason for this is that Jesus was always careful to distinguish His relationship with the Father from the relationship of human beings to the Father. Jesus was God's Son *by nature*, whereas Christians are God's "sons" *by adoption* into His eternal family. The Father was Jesus' God only from the vantage point of His humanity (Philippians 2:7), whereas the Father is our God because we are by nature finite creatures.[23]

▶ Did Jesus imply that He was not good in Mark 10:17,18? Is this an argument against His deity?

In Mark 10:17,18 we read, "As Jesus started on his way, a man ran up to him and fell on his knees before him. 'Good teacher,' he asked, 'what must I do to inherit eternal life?' 'Why do you call me good?' Jesus answered. 'No one is good—except God alone.'"

In this verse Jesus was most certainly *not* denying He was God to the young ruler. He was simply asking him to consider the implications of calling Him "good." Jesus was essentially saying to him, "Do you realize what you are saying when you call me good? Do you realize that this is something you should attribute only to God? Are you saying I am God?"[24]

Apparently the young man failed to realize the implications of what he was saying. Jesus thus forced him to draw this conclusion: "Either Jesus was good and God, or else He was bad and man. A good God or a bad man, but not merely a good man. Those are the real alternatives with regard to Christ. For no good man would claim to be God when he was not."[25]

Hence Jesus' response did not deny His own deity but was rather a veiled claim to it. The man who called him "good" needed to perceive this reality.

▶ Could Jesus have succumbed to temptation (Matthew 4:7)?

In Matthew 4:7 Jesus responded to the temptation of the Devil by saying, "Do not put the Lord your God to the test." Is it possible that Jesus *could have* given in to this and other temptations and sinned?

Some theologians believe that because Jesus became a man, He must have been susceptible to the possibility of sinning. This view is known among theologians as the "peccability of Christ."

Other theologians believe it would have been impossible for Jesus to sin by virtue of the fact that He was also God. This view is known as the "impeccability of Christ," and this is my personal view on the matter.

I believe that Christ as the God-man could not have sinned because:

1. In His divine nature, He is immutable (does not change);
2. In His divine nature, He is omniscient (all-knowing) and is hence fully aware of all the consequences of sin;
3. In His divine nature, He is omnipotent (all-powerful) in His ability to resist sin;

4. Hebrews 4:15 tells us that He was tempted, yet was without sin;

5. Christ had no sin nature, as all other human beings do, and was perfectly holy from birth (Luke 1:35);

6. There is an analogy between the written Word of God (the Bible) and the living Word of God (Christ). Just as the authorship of the Bible involved humans (Matthew, Mark, Luke, and John, for example) and God (the Holy Spirit) and is completely without error, so Christ is fully divine and fully human and is completely without (and unable to) sin.

Does this mean that Christ's temptations were unreal? No. I believe that Christ was genuinely tempted, but the temptations stood no chance of luring Him to sin. It is much like a canoe attempting to launch an attack against a U.S. battleship, banging against the hull of the ship with all its might. The attack is genuine, but it stands no chance of success.

I believe the reason Christ went through the temptation experience with the Devil (Matthew 4) was not to see whether He could be made to sin, but to prove that He could not be made to sin. In fact, some theologians have suggested that Christ was the aggressor in this encounter.* The Devil may have hoped to avoid the encounter altogether. After 40 days in the wilderness, at the height of Christ's weakness from a human standpoint, the Devil gave his very best shot in tempting Christ. The rest is history. The Devil was unsuccessful. Christ proved that He could not be made to sin.

▶ What is the significance of Jesus pronouncing the paralytic's sins forgiven before physically healing him (Mark 2:1-12)?

In Mark 2:1-12 we read that a paralytic was lowered through a roof by his friends in order to get close to Jesus in hopes of a healing. The first thing Jesus said to the paralytic was, "Son, your sins are forgiven" (Mark 2:5).

---

* Professor J. Dwight Pentecost at Dallas Theological Seminary holds to this viewpoint.

Upon first reading, such words may seem out of place. But further investigation indicates that Jesus was making an important statement. Jesus knew that all those present were aware that only God could pronounce someone's sins as being forgiven. (In Isaiah 43:25, for example, God said, "I, even I, am he who blots out your transgressions, for my own sake, and remembers your sins no more.") Hence, when Jesus said, "Your sins are forgiven," He was clearly placing Himself in the position of God.

The scribes that were present understood Jesus' words this way, for they reasoned, "Why does this man speak that way? He is blaspheming; who can forgive sins but God alone?" (Mark 2:7 NASB). Of course, Jesus' subsequent healing of the paralytic served to substantiate His claim to be God (Mark 2:10-12).

Pronouncing the man's sins forgiven before healing him was Jesus' way of indicating that the man's highest need was not physical healing but spiritual healing. The spiritual healing was the more important of the two. Once that was taken care of, Jesus proceeded to heal the man physically as well.

There is another point that bears mentioning. In the Old Testament healing is ultimately viewed as being conditioned upon God's forgiveness and is viewed as an outward demonstration of that forgiveness (see 2 Chronicles 7:14; Psalm 103:3; 147:3; Isaiah 19:22). It may be in view of this Old Testament backdrop that Jesus first proclaimed the man's sins forgiven.[26] Jesus helped the paralytic with his greatest problem first (the forgiveness of sin), and then moved on to help him with his secondary problem (physical healing, which, in Old Testament thought, was conditioned on the forgiveness of sin).

▶ What did Jesus mean when He referred to Himself as the "Alpha and Omega" (Revelation 1:8 and 22:13)?

The backdrop to understanding this is Isaiah 44:6, where God Almighty proclaimed, "I am the first and I am the last; apart from me there is no God." In Isaiah 48:12 God likewise affirmed, "I am he; I am the first and I am the last," and God said this right after His pronouncement that "I will not yield my glory to another" (verse 11b). Christ's use of this title in Revelation 22:13 was thus undoubtedly intended to be taken as a claim to be God Almighty. No other conclusion is sufficient.

Of course, to the modern ear, the claim to be the Alpha and the Omega may seem strange. But for the ancient Jew, Christ was describing Himself in a way they would have readily understood. Though the letters *Alpha* and *Omega* are the first and last letters of the *Greek* alphabet, John recorded the book of Revelation for Jewish readers who were also familiar with the *Hebrew* language and alphabet. And there lies the significance of Christ's claim. In Jewish thinking, a reference to the first and last letters of an alphabet (*aleph* and *tau* in Hebrew) was regarded as including all the intermediate letters, and came to represent totality or entirety.

It is with this idea in mind that the Jews in their ancient commentaries on the Old Testament said that Adam transgressed the whole law from *aleph* to *tau*. Abraham, by contrast, observed the whole law from *aleph* to *tau*. The Jews also believed that when God brings blessing upon Israel, He does so abundantly, from *aleph* to *tau*.

When used of God (or Christ), the first and last letters express eternality and omnipotence. Christ's claim to be the Alpha and the Omega is an affirmation that He is the all-powerful One of eternity past and eternity future (God Almighty).[27]

▶ What did Jesus mean when He said, "Before Abraham was born, I am!" (John 8:58)?

The backdrop to understanding this statement is Exodus 3:14, where God identified Himself to Moses as "I AM WHO I AM." This name of God indicates His eternal nature. It conveys eternal self-existence. God never came into being at a point in time, for He has always existed. He was never born; He will never die. He does not grow older, for He is beyond the realm of time. To know God is to know the Eternal One.

In John 8:58 Jesus was revealing His divine identity when He said, "Before Abraham was born, I AM." Since "I AM" echoes the words of God in Exodus 3:14, Jesus' use of these words constituted a claim to be eternal—to exist without ever having experienced a beginning.

All of this adds tremendous significance to Jesus' encounter with the Jews. Knowing how much they venerated Abraham, Jesus in John 8:58 deliberately contrasted the created origin of Abraham with His own eternal, uncreated nature. It was not just that Jesus was older than Abraham, but that His existence was of an entirely different kind from Abraham's. Abraham was created; Christ is eternal. Abraham had a beginning in time; Christ the eternal One is beyond time altogether. Jesus is therefore portrayed as timeless God in John 8:58.

Jesus' claim is all the more significant when we realize that He began His assertion of deity with the words "*I tell you the truth...before Abraham was born, I AM*" (italics added). In the King James Version, the phrase "I tell you the truth" is rendered "verily, verily." Jesus used such language only when He was making an emphatic statement. It represents the strongest possible oath and claim.[28] We might paraphrase it, "I assure you, most solemnly I tell you." Jesus did not want there to be any confusion over the fact that He was claiming to be eternal God. He was claiming in the strongest possible terms that He had independent continuous existence from before time.

When Jesus made this claim, the Jews immediately picked up stones with the intention of killing Jesus, for they recognized He was claiming to be God Almighty—the "I AM" of the Old Testament (Exodus 3:14). They were acting on the prescribed penalty for blasphemy in Old Testament law: *death by stoning*.

▶ What did Jesus mean when He said that Abraham rejoiced at seeing His day (John 8:56)?

During His three-year ministry Jesus often encountered hostile Jews who rejected what He said. On one such occasion, Jesus engaged in a dialogue with some Jews about Abraham.

The Jews felt that because they were the natural descendants of Abraham, they were in the privileged position before God. Jesus countered this claim by pointing out that true spiritual descendants of Abraham do what Abraham did—that is, they *believe and obey* God. They should respond by placing their faith in the One sent by God (that is, Jesus) rather than merely trusting in their Abrahamic lineage.

It is at this point that Jesus made an astonishing statement to the Jews: "Your father Abraham rejoiced at the thought of seeing my day; he saw it and was glad" (John 8:56). Jesus in this verse affirmed that He was truly the One to whom Abraham looked forward. And when Abraham thought of seeing Christ's "day," he was filled with gladness. Seeing Christ's day was no doubt the summit of Abraham's life.

Personally, I believe that Abraham actually encountered the *preincarnate* Christ in the form of the Angel of the Lord.* You might recall that this "Angel of the Lord" appeared to Abraham and made an astonishing promise:

> I will surely bless you and make your descendants as numerous as the stars in the sky and as the sand on the seashore. Your descendants will take possession of the cities of their enemies, and *through your offspring* [or *seed*] all nations on earth will be blessed, because you have obeyed me" (Genesis 22:17,18, italics added).

There are two very important things I need to briefly discuss here: the *identity* of the Angel of the Lord (or, more literally, the "Angel of Yahweh"), and the *promise* this divine angel made to Abraham.

As to the Angel's *identity*, I am convinced it was the preincarnate Christ. I say this for the following reasons:

1. The "Angel" is clearly identified as being Yahweh (God) and fully divine. Recall that in Exodus 3:6 the Angel of the Lord said to Moses, "I am the God of

---

* Christ existed *as God* prior to His birth as *a man* (the incarnation). Many theologians believe that prior to becoming a man, Christ made several "preincarnate" appearances to various Old Testament saints as the "Angel of the Lord."

your father, the God of Abraham, the God of Isaac and the God of Jacob."

2. The "Angel" of Yahweh—while fully God in Himself—is seen to be distinct from another person called Yahweh, implying trinitarian distinctions. For example, the Angel of Yahweh is portrayed as praying to Yahweh on behalf of the people of God, much like Jesus prayed to the Father in New Testament times (see Zechariah 1:12; Hebrews 7:25).

3. The Holy Spirit is invisible as a spirit, and Scripture tells us that the Father is also invisible (Colossians 1:15; 1 Timothy 1:17), and that no one has ever seen Him (1 Timothy 6:16). This would seem to rule out the Holy Spirit and the Father as appearing as the Angel of the Lord in the Old Testament.

4. Just as Jesus was sent by the Father in the New Testament (John 3:17), so the Angel of Yahweh was sent by Yahweh in the Old Testament (Judges 13:8,9).

5. The divine Angel and Christ engaged in amazingly similar ministries—such as *interceding* to the Father on behalf of God's people (Zechariah 1:12; Hebrews 7:25), *revealing truth* (Daniel 4:13,17,23; 8:16; 9:21; John 1:1,14,18), *commissioning individuals for service* (Exodus 3:7,8; Judges 6:11-23; 13:1-21; Matthew 4:18-20; 28:19,20; Acts 26:14-18), *delivering those enslaved* (Exodus 3; Galatians 1:4; 1 Thessalonians 1:10; 2 Timothy 4:18; Hebrews 2:14,15), *comforting the downcast* (Genesis 16:7-13; 1 Kings 19:4-8; Matthew 14:14; 15:32-39), *protecting God's servants* (Psalm 34:7; Daniel 3:15-20; 6:16-23; Matthew 8:24-26), and *acting as Judge* (1 Chronicles 21:1,14,15; John 5:22; Acts 10:42), among many other things.

In view of such factors, I think a strong case can be made that the various appearances of the Angel of the Lord in the Old Testament were in fact preincarnate appearances of the Lord Jesus Christ. (For more on this, see my book *Christ Before* *the Manger: The Life and Times of the Preincarnate Christ* [Grand Rapids: Baker Book House, 1992].) So when the Angel of the Lord appeared to Abraham in Genesis 22, it was probably Jesus Christ in His preincarnate state that appeared to him.*

Now consider the promise made to Abraham by this divine Angel: "I will surely bless you and make your descendants as numerous as the stars in the sky and as the sand on the seashore. Your descendants will take possession of the cities of their enemies, and *through your offspring* [or *seed*] all nations on earth will be blessed, because you have obeyed me" (Genesis 22:17,18, italics added).

This gets really fascinating, but it is also a little challenging. The reference to "offspring" or "seed" in this verse is a messianic prophecy that *through the future incarnate Christ* (to be born of Mary) all the nations of the earth would be blessed. We know from Galatians 3:8-16 that the "seed" promise to Abraham had *one individual* in view—namely, Jesus Christ.[29]

It is therefore truly revealing of Christ's majesty that it was the Angel of the Lord (the *preincarnate* Christ) who informed Abraham that through his *future* earthly offspring (the *incarnate* Christ, who was yet to be born of the virgin Mary) all the nations of the earth would be blessed. In other words, the preincarnate Christ said something like this to Abraham: "One day in the future, I will be born as a human being, and I will be *your* direct descendant." No wonder Jesus said to the Jews in John 8:56, "Your father Abraham rejoiced at the thought of seeing my day; he saw it and was glad."

▶ Did Jesus indicate that His resurrection body was a flesh-and-bones body (Luke 24:39)?

The resurrected Christ said to His fearful disciples, "See My hands and My feet, that it is I Myself; touch Me and see, for a spirit does not have flesh and bones as you see that I have"

---

* The Hebrew word for *angel* can simply mean "envoy," "ambassador," or "one sent on behalf of another." Christ as "Angel of the Lord" was sent on behalf of the Father to engage in specific tasks in Old Testament times.

(Luke 24:39 NASB). Notice three things here: 1) The resurrected Christ indicates in this verse that He is not a spirit; 2) He indicates that His resurrection body is made up of flesh and bones; and 3) His physical hands and feet represent physical proof of the materiality of His resurrection from the dead.

Further support for the physical resurrection of Christ can be found in Christ's words recorded in John 2:19-21: "Jesus answered them, 'Destroy this temple, and I will raise it again in three days.' The Jews replied, 'It has taken forty-six years to build this temple, and you are going to raise it in three days?' But the temple he had spoken of was his body." Jesus here said that He would be *bodily* raised from the dead.

The resurrected Christ also ate physical food on four different occasions. He did this as a means of proving He had a real physical body (Luke 24:30; 24:42,43; John 21:12,13; Acts 1:4). It would have been deception on His part to offer His ability to eat physical food as a proof of His bodily resurrection if He had not been resurrected in a physical body.

Finally, the physical body of the resurrected Christ was touched by different people, including Mary (John 20:17) and some women (Matthew 28:9). He challenged the disciples to physically touch Him so they could rest assure that His body was material in nature (Luke 24:39). He also invited doubting Thomas to touch Him to see that He truly was physically risen from the dead (John 20:27).

Two

THE MIRACLES
OF JESUS

▶ Why couldn't Jesus do miracles in His own hometown
(Mark 6:4,5)?

In Mark 6:4,5 Jesus affirmed that a prophet is without honor
in his hometown, and in view of that reality He could not perform any miracles in Nazareth except for healing a few sick
people. The people of Nazareth were apparently plagued by
unbelief and paid little attention to His claims.

At first glance one might get the impression that Jesus' miraculous power was utterly dependent upon people's faith in order for
it to work. That is not the meaning of this passage, however. It is
not that Jesus was incapable of performing a miracle in Nazareth.
Rather, Jesus "could not" do miracles there in the sense that He
would not do so in view of the pervasive unbelief in that city.

Miracles serve a far greater purpose, from the divine perspective, than just providing a raw display of power. Indeed,
Jesus' miraculous deeds are sometimes called "signs" in the New
Testament because they serve to *signify* His identity as the
Messiah. Since the people of Nazareth had already made up
their minds *against* Jesus, and had provided more than ample
evidence of their lack of faith in Him, Jesus chose not to engage
in miraculous acts there except for healing a few sick people. He
refused to bestow miraculous *deeds* on a city that had rejected
the miraculous *Messiah*. "Unbelief excluded the people of

Nazareth from the dynamic disclosure of God's grace that others had experienced."[1]

Because of Nazareth's rejection of the person and message of Jesus Christ, He went on to other cities that *did* respond to and receive Him. There is no evidence that Jesus ever again returned to Nazareth.

▶ Why did Jesus respond to John the Baptist's inquiry about His identity by pointing to His own miraculous acts (Luke 7:22)?

In Luke 7:20 we read that John the Baptist, now in prison, sent some messengers to Jesus to ask, "Are you the one who was to come, or should we expect someone else?" Jesus replied to them, "Go back and report to John what you have seen and heard: The blind receive sight, the lame walk, those who have leprosy are cured, the deaf hear, the dead are raised, and the good news is preached to the poor" (verse 22).

As a backdrop to understanding this passage, it was the common viewpoint among the Jews of that time that when the Messiah came, He would set up His glorious kingdom. There were very high messianic expectations in the first century, and even John himself probably expected the soon emergence of the kingdom that he had been preaching about.

But now something unexpected happened: *John was imprisoned.* Instead of the kingdom, which (it was commonly thought) would be characterized by such things as liberty and freedom, John now found himself locked up in jail and in danger of execution. So what was John to make of this development? John may have expected that Jesus would use more coercive powers as the Messiah/deliverer of Israel. He thus decided to send messengers to Jesus to ask, "Are you the one who was to come, or should we expect someone else?" (Luke 7:20).

Jesus' response is extremely significant. Instead of merely giving verbal assurance that He was the Messiah, He pointed to His miraculous acts, including giving sight to the blind, enabling the lame to walk, and opening deaf ears (Luke 7:22). Why did Jesus do this? Because these were the precise miracles prophesied to be performed by the Messiah when He came (see Isaiah 29:18-21; 35:5,6; 61:1,2). The miraculous deeds alone were more than enough proof that Jesus was the promised Messiah. The miracles were Jesus' divine credentials—His divine "ID card," so to speak.

There is another point that bears mentioning. Jesus' choice to avoid coming right out and saying "You can rest assured that I am the Messiah" may be because of the popular misconceptions of the Messiah among the masses (and perhaps even John himself). It may be that Jesus' intention in sending the messengers to report about His miracles was to indicate to John, "Yes, I am the Messiah—the *true* Messiah prophesied in the Old Testament who will deliver people from bondage to sin—but not the Messiah of popular misconception, the coercive political deliverer that so many people are expecting today."

▶ When Jesus said, "Someone touched me; I know that power has gone out from me" (Luke 8:46), did His intrinsic divine power cause a miracle without Him purposing it?

In this verse we read that a woman who had been subject to bleeding for 12 years touched Jesus' garment and was instantly healed. Jesus then said, "Someone touched me; I know that power has gone out from me" (Luke 8:46). At first glance it might seem that Jesus was unaware of the identity of the woman. It might also appear that divine healing energy, without Jesus even intending or purposing it, came out of His body and healed the woman. This is not the case, however.

Scripture portrays Jesus as always being in complete control of His divine miraculous power (see John 2:1-11; 4:50-52; 5:8,9; 11:40-44). People could not just walk up to Jesus, touch Him, and activate His miracle-working power *without His consent.* The reason the woman was healed when she touched Jesus' garment was that He *willed* her to be healed as a result of her *faith.*

The context indicates that Jesus wanted this woman to "go public" with her faith that had led to her healing. Her desire to approach Jesus in stealth is understandable since her hemorrhage rendered her ceremonially unclean (Leviticus 15:25-30). As well, anyone who came into contact with her was also rendered unclean, according to the Jews. But Jesus forced her to "go public," as it were, and acknowledge that it was she who touched Him.

Jesus wanted the woman to understand that it was actually her *faith* that led to her healing (Luke 8:48). Jesus' cloak had no mysterious magical properties, but her touching of that cloak was an *expression* of her faith, which subsequently moved Jesus to heal her with His divine power. The woman's faith did indeed "go public" when she fell at Jesus' feet (verse 47).

There may be another reason Jesus wanted the woman to "go public." She was probably known in the community for her infirmity and was thus widely known as being unclean. By drawing attention to her healing, Jesus was publicly revealing to all present that she was no longer unclean and was fully healed.[2] She would thus be accepted back into society without hindrance.

▶ Why did Jesus curse the fig tree and miraculously cause it to wither (Matthew 21:19)?

In Matthew 21 we find that Jesus was hungry and saw a fig tree by the side of the road. As He came close to it, He saw that it had no figs on it, so He cursed it and it withered (verse 19). It may appear that Jesus was just responding in anger to the tree, cursing it in tantrum-like behavior. But this is not the case. One must keep in mind the broader backdrop of Jesus' teaching methodology, which often involved parables and word pictures. Scholars agree that Jesus in the present case was performing a living parable—an *acted-out* parable—to teach His disciples an important truth. His cursing of the fig tree was a dramatic "visual aid."

What important truth does the parable illustrate? Scholars have different opinions. Some say Jesus was illustrating the principle of faith to the disciples. If the disciples had such faith, they too could do such things as withering fig trees and moving mountains (see Matthew 17:20). They would need such faith in the hard days to come.

Other scholars believe that since the fig tree had leaves on it (Matthew 21:19), from a distance it gave the *appearance* of being fruitful. But upon closer examination it became clear that there was no fruit on it at all. So perhaps Jesus' cursing of the fig tree was an acted-out parable that taught the disciples that God will judge those who give an outer appearance of fruitfulness but in fact are not fruitful at all (like the Pharisees).

Still other scholars suggest that the fig tree is representative of faithless Israel. Israel professed to be faithful to God and fruitful as a nation, but in fact it was *faithless* and *fruitless.* Indeed, Israel had rejected Jesus the Messiah and was thus ripe for judgment. Perhaps the withering of the fig tree foreshadowed the withering (or destruction) of Israel in A.D. 70, when Titus and his Roman warriors trampled on and destroyed Jerusalem, ending Israel as a political entity (see Luke 21:20).

And still other scholars see significance in the fact that the account of Jesus' cleansing of the temple in Mark's Gospel (Mark 11:15-19) is sandwiched between the two sections of Scripture dealing with the fig tree (verses 12-14 and 20-24). It is suggested that perhaps Jesus was teaching that at a distance the temple and its sacrificial activities looked fine. But on closer inspection it was found to be mere religion without substance, full of hypocrisy, bearing no spiritual fruit, ripe for judgment.

In my opinion the second option above—God judges those who *appear* fruitful but are not *truly* fruitful—has the most going for it.

▶ Why did Jesus say the dead child was not dead but just asleep (Luke 8:51,52; Mark 5:39)?

Jairus had come to fetch Jesus in hopes of Him healing his daughter, who was on her deathbed. By the time they arrived at Jairus' house, they were informed that indeed the young girl had died. People at the house were wailing and mourning for her.

Jesus then said, "Stop wailing. She is not dead but asleep" (Luke 8:52).

Why did Jesus say this? We know that the girl was physically dead because verse 55 tells us that after Jesus healed her, her "spirit returned." (Death involves the departure of the soul or spirit from the body.)

Actually, this situation is not too difficult to explain. Jesus was simply saying that the girl's *present condition* of death was only temporary. He used the term "sleep" to indicate that her condition was not permanent. He may have been saying that when *He* is involved in the picture, death really is as sleep, for it is temporary. As effortlessly as a parent awakens a child from sleep, so Jesus supernaturally awakened the young girl from her temporary state of death (compare with John 11:11-14). We might paraphrase Jesus' words this way: "The girl is not permanently dead but only temporarily so. She is, metaphorically speaking, just asleep, as it were, and soon to be supernaturally awakened in life."

▶ Were all the sicknesses Jesus healed caused by demonic spirits (Matthew 12:22)?

In Matthew 12:22 we read, "Then they brought him a demon-possessed man who was blind and mute, and Jesus healed him, so that he could both talk and see." It might seem from verses like this that perhaps all the sicknesses Jesus healed were caused by demonic spirits. But this is not the case.

On the one hand, it is true that Scripture portrays Satan and demons as inflicting physical diseases on people (such as *muteness*—Matthew 9:32,33; *blindness*—12:22; and *epilepsy*—17:14-18). They can also afflict people with mental disorders (Mark 5:4,5; 9:22; Luke 8:27-29; 9:37-42) and can cause people to be self-destructive (Mark 5:5; Luke 9:42).

However, though demons can cause physical illnesses, Scripture distinguishes natural illnesses from demon-caused illnesses (Matthew 4:24; Mark 1:32; Luke 7:21; 9:1; Acts 5:16). In the case of numerous healings, no mention is made of demons.

For example, no mention is made of demon affliction in the cases where Jesus healed the centurion's servant (Matthew 8:5-13), the woman with the hemorrhage of 12 years' duration (9:19,20), the two blind men (9:27-30), the man with the withered hand (12:9-14), and those who touched the fringe of Jesus' garment (14:35,36).

▶ What did Jesus mean when He said this wicked generation would only be given the sign of Jonah (Luke 11:29,30)?

Jesus stated that though this wicked generation asked for a sign, the only sign it would be given would be the sign of Jonah: "For as Jonah was a sign to the Ninevites, so also will the Son of Man be to this generation" (Luke 11:30). What was Jesus saying here?

As a backdrop, the Jewish Pharisees had witnessed firsthand that Jesus was acting and speaking from a position of authority. They wondered what His authority was for acting and speaking in the way He did. In the Old Testament Moses had performed miracles before Pharaoh as a sign that demonstrated that this authority came from God. Elijah too performed mighty miracles to prove that his authority came from God. *What about Jesus?* Could He provide a sign to show His authority came from God?

But the sinfulness of the Pharisees quickly becomes evident. For one thing, Jesus had *already* performed many mighty miracles that constituted signs that pointed to His true identity. Recall that one Pharisee (Nicodemus) said to Him, "Rabbi, we know you are a teacher who has come from God. For no one could perform the miraculous signs you are doing if God were not with him" (John 3:2). Most of the Pharisees, however, were hard-hearted, and in their spiritual blindness rejected Jesus Christ.

Jesus responded to the Pharisees' request for a sign as an indication of wickedness. The real issue in Jesus' mind was obedience to the Word of God and the One whom God had sent. The only "sign" to be given this generation would be the "sign of Jonah."

Though scholars have made a number of suggestions as to what the sign of Jonah is, the context would seem to point to the resurrection of Jesus Christ. Jonah had been in the great fish for three days (Jonah 1:17) before, as it were, "coming to life again" by being regurgitated out of its mouth. After his "reappearance," he spoke his message of repentance, and the Ninevites quickly responded. The sign to be given to *Jesus'* generation would be the reappearance of the Son of Man on the third day after His death. And, as one scholar put it, "Christ's return from death was as great a proof of His ministry as Jonah's rescue was of his."[3]

In what way was Jesus' resurrection a sign? Among other things, Romans 1:4 indicates that by the resurrection Jesus was declared to be the Son of God. As well, Jesus' resurrection guarantees the approaching judgment of all humankind (Acts 17:31). Therefore, repentance is in order, every bit as much as repentance was in order among the Ninevites of Jonah's day.

▶ What did Jesus mean when He said, "Whoever is not against us is for us" (Mark 9:39,40)?

In this passage the disciples had encountered an exorcist who did not do things the way they thought he should, so they forbade him to continue. "Do not stop him," Jesus chastened them. "No one who does a miracle in my name can in the next moment say anything bad about me, for whoever is not against us is for us" (Mark 9:39,40).

Why did Jesus say this? The situation in this verse indicates that though there are many who follow Jesus Christ, not all follow Him in exactly the same way. Although this man did not follow Jesus in the same way the disciples did, he nevertheless did stand against Satan and had obviously "crossed the line" so that He was *on Jesus' side.*

It is interesting that while Jesus said, "Whoever is not against us is for us" in Mark 9:39,40, He also said, "He who is not with me is against me" in Matthew 12:30. In both verses Jesus' point was that it is not possible to remain in the "neutral zone" when it comes to Him. Either you are on the *rejection* side of the line or else you have crossed the line *in allegiance* to Jesus. *There is no middle ground.* The exorcist had crossed the line in allegiance to Jesus.

Since this was the case, the disciples were instructed not to hinder him, even though his commitment to Jesus was expressed in a different way than that of the disciples. All of them were working for the kingdom of God, though in different ways.

▶ Why did Jesus tell the healed leper not to tell anyone but instead go to the priest to offer sacrifices (Mark 1:44)?

In Mark 1:44 Jesus instructed the healed leper, "See that you don't tell this to anyone. But go, show yourself to the priest and offer the sacrifices that Moses commanded for your cleansing, as a testimony to them." There are two issues we must deal with here: 1) Why did Jesus tell the man not to tell anyone? and 2) why did Jesus send him to the priest to offer sacrifices?

As to why Jesus instructed the man not to tell anyone, He very well may have said this because of the popular misunderstandings that were floating around during that time about the Messiah. There was a very high messianic expectation to the effect that when the Messiah came, He would deliver the Jews from Roman domination. The people were expecting a political Messiah/deliverer. So for news that He was the Messiah to circulate at this early juncture in His ministry would immediately excite people's preconceived imaginations about what this Messiah-figure was supposed to do. The Romans might very well subsequently mark Him as a rebel leader.[4]

Seeking to avoid an erroneous popular response to His words and deeds, Jesus told the leper to keep quiet. He did not want anyone prematurely speaking of His actual identity until He had had sufficient opportunity to make the character of His mission clear to the masses. As time passed on in the Gospel accounts, Christ's identity became increasingly clear to those who came into contact with Him.

As to why Jesus instructed the man to go to the priest to offer sacrifices, He probably had in mind the Old Testament ritual requirements. The backdrop is that among the Jews leprosy was viewed as one of the worst forms of uncleanness.[5] According to the Mosaic Law, anyone who had leprosy, or who was even *thought* to have it, was required to undergo a ritual of cleansing to be accepted back into society. If this man had remained in Galilee, walking around telling everyone how Christ had healed him, he would have been quickly categorized as "unclean" by all the Jews in the city, and his witness would have thus been nullified.

Scholars have noted that there may be yet another reason why Christ sent the cleansed leper to the priest. He was sent in order to be a *witness* or *testimony* to them (Luke 5:14). The fact is that there was no record of a cleansed leper in Jewish history since the curing of Miriam in Numbers 12:10-15. So a cleansed leper would be very big news among the Jews.

Once the cleansed man presented evidence to the priest that he had indeed been cleansed by Jesus, the priest would be forced to investigate the claim, and the evidence would then be presented to the Jewish Sanhedrin for a final declaration on the matter. Thus by sending the man to the priest, Christ was in essence sending evidence to the highest recognized authority among the Jews that the miracle-working Messiah was in their midst.

▶ Did Jesus promise that all who believe will be accompanied by miracles like healing other people, speaking in tongues, driving out demons, and not being harmed by snakes and deadly poison (Mark 16:17,18)?

In Mark 16:17,18 we read, "And these signs will accompany those who believe: In my name they will drive out demons; they will speak in new tongues; they will pick up snakes with their hands; and when they drink deadly poison, it will not hurt them at all; they will place their hands on sick people, and they will get well."

Certainly we find ample evidence for some of these activities in New Testament times. Indeed, in the New Testament we witness the casting out of demons (Acts 8:7; 16:18; 19:15,16), speaking in tongues (Acts 2:4-11; 10:46; 19:6; 1 Corinthians 12:10; 14:1-25), and even protection from a poisonous snake (Acts 28:3-5).

A few observations are in order, however. First, the construction of the verse in the original Greek of Mark 16:18 utilizes "conditional clauses." The verse carries this idea: "And *if* they be compelled to pick up snakes with their hands and *if* they should be compelled to drink deadly poison, it shall by no means harm them."[6] What this means is that if some pagan or non-Christian authority or persecutor forced a Christian to engage in such activities (a real possibility in the early church), God would supernaturally protect them.

Understood in context, this verse certainly gives no justification for Christians to voluntarily drink poison or handle snakes in church services. We see no such activity in the early church. Note that Paul's encounter with the snake at Malta was completely unintentional (Acts 28:3-5).

Further, it should be noted that Christians today are divided over whether such phenomena as speaking in tongues and the gift of healing occur today; charismatics say *yes*, cessationists say *no*. The cessationists argue that the gift of healing and tongues passed away in the first century after the Bible had been delivered and verified by miraculous phenomena. Charismatics say there is nothing in Scripture to sustain such a conclusion.

Whichever side one ends up on, it is very important for *both* sides to understand that Mark 16:17,18 is most certainly not teaching that if you do not experience such phenomena, you are not a true Christian. That is an unwarranted conclusion that violates the broader context of Scripture.

Let us consider the issue of tongues as an example. It is clear that even though all the Corinthian believers were "saved" and had been baptized in the Holy Spirit (1 Corinthians 12:13), they had not all spoken in tongues (14:5). It is the Holy Spirit who decides on what gifts each believer receives (12:11), and the Spirit certainly did not give all Christians the gift of tongues in the first century. Thus it should not be considered a definitive sign of whether one is a Christian or not.

A final note. Mark 16:9-20 is absent from the two oldest Greek manuscripts presently in our possession—Codex Alexandrinus and Codex Sinaiticus. As well, these verses are absent from the Old Latin manuscripts, the Sinaitic Syriac manuscript, about a hundred Armenian manuscripts, and the two oldest Georgian manuscripts. Further, Clement of Alexandria and Origen (early church fathers) show no knowledge of the existence of these verses. Eusebius and Jerome attest that the passage was absent from almost all the Greek copies of Mark known to them. Understandably, then, many scholars believe that Mark 16:9-20 does not belong in the Bible. Fortunately, these verses do not affect a single major doctrine of Christianity.

▶ What did Jesus mean when He said we would do greater miracles than He did (John 14:12)?

In John 14:12 Jesus said, "I tell you the truth, anyone who has faith in me will do what I have been doing. He will do even greater things than these, because I am going to the Father." Does this mean that you and I can do even more amazing miracles than Jesus performed while He was on earth? Surely that is not the intent of His words.

In this verse Jesus was simply saying that His many followers would do things greater *in extent* (all over the world) and greater *in effect* (multitudes being touched by the power of God). During His short lifetime on earth, Jesus was confined in His influence to a comparatively small region of Palestine. Following His departure, His followers were able to work in widely scattered places and influence much larger numbers of human beings.[7]

Jesus in this verse was thus referring to "greater works" in terms of the whole scope of the impact of God's people and the church on the entire world throughout all history. In other words, Jesus was speaking *quantitatively*, not *qualitatively*. The works are quantitatively greater because Christ's work is multiplied through all His followers.[8]

It is interesting to note the view of some scholars that even these works done by Christ's followers all over the world are not done *independent* of Christ. After all, it was *He* who sent the Holy Spirit to human beings following His resurrection and ascension into heaven (John 15:26), and it is the Holy Spirit who enables believers to do these mighty works (see Acts 1:8; Romans 15:19; 1 Corinthians 12:7-11). Jesus also answers the prayers of His followers (see John 14:13,14; 16:23-26).[9] Further, only those believers who are "plugged into" Him as the true Vine produce abundant fruit (John 15). As Christ Himself put it, "Apart from me you can do nothing" (John 15:5).

THREE

THE KINGDOM OF GOD

⟨ꙮ⟩

▶ If entering the kingdom of God hinges on receiving it like a little child, what precisely is involved in receiving it like a little child (Mark 10:15)?

In Mark 10:15 Jesus said, "I tell you the truth, anyone who will not receive the kingdom of God like a little child will never enter it." Jesus is not saying here that adults should behave childishly. Rather, He is pointing to the need to have the same type of faith that little children exhibit.

The most trusting people in the world are children. Children have not acquired the obstructions to faith that often come with advanced education and exposure to the philosophies of the world. Christ calls us to have the same kind of trust that little children naturally have.

It may also be that Jesus has in mind the natural helplessness of children. In contrast to the self-assured attitude of the Pharisees, perhaps Jesus was intimating that to enter the kingdom of God people must become as little children in humbly recognizing their *helplessness* in attaining the kingdom in their own strength. Entrance into the kingdom is a gift that comes only by believing in Jesus Christ.[1]

▶ Why did Jesus say that the least person in the kingdom of God is greater than John the Baptist (Luke 7:28; Matthew 11:11)?

In Luke 7:28 Jesus said, "I tell you, among those born of women there is no one greater than John; yet the one who is least in the kingdom of God is greater than he" (see also Matthew 11:11). Jesus was not saying here that John had virtually no part in God's kingdom, for surely He did. All Jesus was saying was that John belonged to the age of the old covenant—the dispensation of the Law.* As great as John was in the age of the old covenant, even the least person in the age of the *new* covenant is greater than John by virtue of the high position ("in Christ") that becomes ours since the time of Jesus' resurrection and the descent of the Holy Spirit.

The New Testament church is the very "bride of Christ" (Ephesians 5:25-32), while John the Baptist was only a "friend of the bridegroom" (John 3:29). New Testament believers are *participants* of the realities John prophesied; John was only a *forerunner* and *predictor* of such realities.

▶ Why did Jesus tell a man to "let the dead bury the dead" (Luke 9:60)?

In Luke 9:60 Jesus said to a man who was contemplating following Him, "Let the dead bury their own dead, but you go and proclaim the kingdom of God." While this may seem a strange comment for Jesus to make, the context of the verse helps us to understand what He was really saying. Jesus encountered a man to whom He had said, "Follow me" (Luke 9:59). This was an invitation not for a quick week of service but for a continuous and ongoing relationship of serving Jesus Christ in spreading the news about the kingdom of God. What could be a higher priority than this?

---

* The "old covenant" was a covenant of *law* that God established with the Israelites at Mount Sinai (Exodus 20:1-17; Galatians 4:24-26; 2 Corinthians 3:7,9). The "new covenant" was a covenant *of grace* that benefits all people (Jews and Gentiles) and was sealed by the sacrificial death of Christ on the cross (Hebrews 7:28).

But the man immediately gave an excuse: "Lord, first let me go and bury my father" (Luke 9:59). Certainly the burial of the dead—especially the burial of a father—is an important thing. Commentator Leon Morris notes that "the Jews considered proper burial as most important. The duty of burial took precedence over the study of the Law, the Temple service, the killing of the Passover sacrifice, [and] the observance of circumcision."[2] But the demands of the kingdom were even *more* important, in Jesus' view.

Jesus therefore said, "Let the dead bury their own dead, but you go and proclaim the kingdom of God" (Luke 9:60). Jesus' words were not intended to be cruel. His meaning might be paraphrased this way: *Let the spiritually dead bury the physically dead. You, however, have a higher priority, for I have now called you to the greater work of proclaiming the kingdom of God to other people.*[3]

The young man's family members were not believers and thus had not yet emerged from spiritual death to eternal life. They were still "dead in trespasses and sins" (Ephesians 2:1).[4] But they were certainly perfectly capable of burying their father when the time came for it.

The spiritually alive, by contrast, should be about the business of bringing spiritual life *to others* by proclaiming the kingdom of God. The proclamation of the kingdom of God is so vitally important—involving the eternal destiny of innumerable people—that it cannot wait. *The kingdom of God takes top priority.*

There is another observation that brings things into clearer perspective here. Some scholars have suggested that if the father had actually already died, the man would be *presently involved* in burying his father. The context may suggest that the father had *not yet* died. He may have been just an old man, but still alive. If this is correct, the man's son to whom Jesus was speaking was essentially saying that he wanted to wait to serve the kingdom until that future time—possibly years away—when his father died and was subsequently buried.

There is yet one further interpretive possibility, which relates to Jewish burial customs. In this scenario, the man's father had indeed died, but the final burial was not yet complete. Bible interpreter Craig Keener explains this view:

> The initial burial took place shortly after [the father's] decease, and would have already occurred by the time this man would be speaking with Jesus. But a year after the first burial, after the flesh had rotted off the bones, the son would return to rebury the bones in a special box in a slot in the tomb wall. Thus the son here could be asking for as much as a year's delay.[5]

Whichever of the above interpretive options is correct, Jesus is calling for a radical commitment. It is not so much that burying one's father is unimportant. It is that the kingdom of God is *so much more* important. This is why Jesus suggested to the man that he should let the spiritually dead bury the physically dead. Eternal souls are at stake. The kingdom comes first!

▶ Did Jesus indicate that anyone who has second thoughts about being a Christian is not worthy of the kingdom of God (Luke 9:62)?

In Luke 9:62 Jesus said, "No one who puts his hand to the plow and looks back is fit for service in the kingdom of God." In this passage we find a continuation of the situation dealt with in the previous section involving the man who wanted to bury his father before engaging in proclaiming the kingdom of God. The man said to Jesus, "I will follow you, Lord; but first let me go back and say good-by to my family" (verse 61). It is at this point that Jesus said, "No one who puts his hand to the plow and looks back is fit for service in the kingdom of God."

Admittedly, this is a strong statement. But Jesus is actually painting a picture that would have been well familiar to His first-century hearers. The plows used in that day were quite primitive, constituting a mere piece of wood with a handle at one end and a metal tip at the other end to break up soil. If a man engaged in handling the plow took his eyes off his work and looked backward, it would cause the furrow he was plowing to become crooked, which would be unacceptable. He could do more damage than good. Holding the metal tip in such a way that it produced the desired results while plowing required *constant attention.*

The point Jesus was making here was that anyone who wishes to engage in service to Him must give his whole heart to the matter and not be double-minded, with one foot in service to the kingdom and one foot in the affairs of this world. There should be no divided interests. If someone wants to serve both the world *and* Christ at the same time, that person is not fit for service in the kingdom of God. The one who would follow Jesus and engage in kingdom work needs a firm hand and a steady eye on the forward-moving plow.[6]

Jesus stressed this truth to those who would follow Him because in the days to come they would be subjected to harsh persecution by the religious leaders of Israel. Jesus was telling His followers to settle their priorities now, or they would never last the distance.

Scholars have been careful to point out that there is a distinction between *entrance* into the kingdom (which comes by faith in Christ) and *service* in the kingdom of God. As Bible expositor William Arndt put it:

> The text...does not speak of *membership* in the kingdom but of the position of a special worker in it. The saying loses its harshness when one considers that Jesus does not forbid the man to say farewell to the members of his family. He merely expresses a warning against the thought that He, the Lord and Master, would be satisfied with lukewarmness in His *service.*[7]

▶ Why did Jesus say the kingdom of heaven had been forcefully advancing, and forceful men lay hold of it (Matthew 11:12)?

In Matthew 11:12 Jesus said, "From the days of John the Baptist until now, the kingdom of heaven has been forcefully advancing, and forceful men lay hold of it" (see also Luke 16:16). Scholars are quite divided as to what this means. Some believe that Jesus is here indicating that since the ministry of John the Baptist began, there had been a continually rising opposition to them both. The kingdom of heaven had been assaulted, and violent men—particularly the religious leaders of Israel—*continued* to assault it. Yet the kingdom also continued to advance. Stanley Toussaint, one of my former professors at Dallas Theological Seminary, put it this way:

> The leaders were attempting to wrest the reins of the kingdom from the Messiah and make the kingdom conform to their pleasures. Their hypocrisy and their hatred of Jesus and John caused the kingdom to suffer violence.[8]

Other scholars believe that perhaps Jesus is referring to His own disciples. If this view is correct, the disciples are here portrayed as "forceful men"—that is, men full of vigor, courage, and power, committed to spreading the good news of the kingdom of God despite any persecution they might face.

Still other scholars suggest that because of the dynamic preaching of John the Baptist, there was a great popular uprising, a virtual storming of people into the kingdom of God. People rushed with great eagerness to get into the kingdom—an eagerness that might even be called a violent zeal.[9]

And still other scholars suggest that the forceful advancing of the kingdom of heaven may refer to the tremendous miracles that accompanied the spread of the kingdom of God through the ministry of Jesus Christ. In this interpretation, Christ's miracles in spreading the kingdom are viewed as literally pushing back the forces of darkness, and hence it has been forcefully advancing.[10]

My personal interpretation of this verse is that indeed the kingdom of heaven had been forcefully advancing through the miraculous ministry of Jesus Christ, pushing back not just the powers of darkness (demonic powers in the spiritual realm) but also the current religious powers (for example, the Pharisees in the human realm). But this forceful *advance* also brought forceful *attacks* by violent men.[11] Not only was Jesus being heavily persecuted, but John the Baptist was thrown into jail and would soon be executed. Many of Jesus' disciples, too, would find themselves martyred before it was all over.

▶ Was Jesus in favor of eunuchs for the sake of the kingdom of God (Matthew 19:12)?

In Matthew 19:12 Jesus said, "For some are eunuchs because they were born that way; others were made that way by men; and others have renounced marriage because of the kingdom of heaven. The one who can accept this should accept it."

It is interesting to note that in the early church a scholar by the name of Origen of Alexandria (A.D. 185-254) took Jesus' words quite literally and in his youth he (tragically) performed the appropriate operation on himself. In his later years he recognized his youthful folly and rejected the literal interpretation "according to the flesh and the letter."[12]

In context, this verse is found in a broader discourse in which Jesus taught about marriage and divorce (Matthew 19:3-12). Some Pharisees had questioned Jesus about the grounds for divorce (verse 3), and Jesus answered that marriage was intended by God to be a permanent relationship (verses 4-6). The Pharisees then asked Jesus why Moses commanded that a man get a certificate of divorce (verse 7). Jesus responded that God did not intend it to be this way, but He permitted divorce because of the hardness of men's hearts (verse 8). Jesus then stated that divorce and remarriage constituted adultery unless the divorce was brought about by immorality (verse 9).

The disciples responded to Jesus' strict words about divorce by commenting that perhaps it is better that a person does not even get married (Matthew 19:10). Jesus then taught that each person should accept the lot which has been given to him by God—including that of a eunuch (verses 11-12). It is here that Jesus said, "For some are eunuchs because they were born that way; others were made that way by men; and others have renounced marriage because of the kingdom of heaven. The one who can accept this should accept it."

Jesus here indicates that the "eunuch solution" is indeed possible for some people—but only *some*. Indeed, those who were born eunuchs (that is—without sexual desire, or perhaps born with a congenital physical deformity) could certainly adopt that solution. Others who became eunuchs as a result of surgery (such as house slaves or bondservants* could accept that solution. Others who had renounced marriage because of the kingdom of God could accept that solution. Jesus said that one who *can* accept this solution *should* accept it. But He certainly knew that most people could not accept such a solution.

One must keep in mind that marriage is elsewhere in Scripture called a gift from God (1 Corinthians 7:7). Indeed, God Himself instituted marriage after creating Adam and Eve (Genesis 2:18-24). So one should be careful not to read into Jesus' words the idea that married people are somehow outside of God's will.

Certainly an important lesson one should discern behind Jesus' words about marriage and divorce is this: *Be very careful in selecting a marriage partner.*

▶ What was Jesus teaching about the kingdom of heaven in the parable of the ten virgins (Matthew 25:1-13)?

In this parable, Jesus compared the kingdom of heaven to ten virgins who went out to meet the bridegroom (Matthew 25:1). Five of the virgins were foolish and five of them were wise. The foolish virgins did not take oil for their lamps (verse 3) while the wise virgins did (verse 4). All the virgins subsequently went to sleep while waiting for the bridegroom (verse 5).

When the bridegroom arrived they all began to trim their lamps, but the foolish virgins did not have any oil (Matthew 25:6-8). While the foolish virgins were away buying oil, the

---

* Sometimes permanent house slaves became eunuchs as a safeguard for the female occupants of the household.

door to the wedding feast was shut after the wise virgins had entered (verses 9,10). When the foolish virgins returned, they begged to get into the feast but were told that they were not known (verses 11,12).

The main point of the parable seems to be that only those who are watchful for the kingdom of God and alert for the coming of the Son of Man (that is, *believers*) will be able to enter it (Matthew 25:13). Contextually, this refers to true believers who are living during the future tribulation period, prior to the second coming of Christ.* His coming will be sudden, when it is not expected. Believers are those who *anticipate* Jesus' coming and seek to be prepared for it, living their lives accordingly. Jesus' return will terminate the opportunity for people to "prepare themselves" (*trust in Jesus*) to enter His kingdom. Only those who are previously prepared (*saved*, by trusting in Christ) will be permitted to enter. No unprepared (*unsaved*) person will be permitted to enter.

▶ What was Jesus teaching about the kingdom of God by comparing it to a growing seed (Mark 4:26-29)?

In Mark 4:26-29 Jesus said:

> This is what the kingdom of God is like. A man scatters seed on the ground. Night and day, whether he sleeps or gets up, the seed sprouts and grows, though he does not know how. All by itself the soil produces grain—first the stalk, then the head, and then the full kernel in the ear. As soon as the grain is ripe, he puts the sickle to it, because the harvest has come.

In this parable, Jesus taught that the fruit that results from sowing a seed (in this case, the "seed" of the Word of God) depends not on the one doing the sowing but on the life that is in the seed itself (God's supernatural Word). Because the 11

---

* These verses about the ten virgins are part of a larger discourse of Jesus called the "Olivet Discourse" in which He teaches about the prophetic future.

disciples would soon be commissioned to proclaim Christ's message to the ends of the earth (Matthew 28:19,20), they might
fall into the trap of feeling that the harvest of souls depended
entirely on their efforts. Christ thus wanted to make it clear in
this parable that any harvest produced would be the result of
sowing the seed and then allowing the life in that seed to man-
ifest itself by growth and fruit at the time of the harvest.

In other words, the Word of God, if faithfully "sown," would
supernaturally produce *its own* results. The disciples were simply
responsible for doing the sowing. The harvest was in God's
hands. The growth of God's kingdom is the result not of the disciples' efforts but rather God's supernatural power.[13]

▶ What was Jesus teaching about the kingdom of heaven by comparing it to a mustard seed (Matthew 13:31,32)?

In Matthew 13:31,32 Jesus said, "The kingdom of heaven is
like a mustard seed, which a man took and planted in his field.
Though it is the smallest of all your seeds, yet when it grows, it
is the largest of garden plants and becomes a tree, so that the
birds of the air come and perch in its branches."

In this parable, Jesus taught that the kingdom of heaven
would have an almost imperceptible beginning—hardly even
noticeable. But just as a small mustard seed* can produce a large
plant (it can grow up past 15 feet high), so the kingdom would
start small but grow to be very large.

As Alfred Edersheim put it, "the kingdom of heaven,
planted in the field of the world as the smallest seed, in the most
humble and uncompromising manner, would grow till it far out-
stripped all other similar plants, and gave shelter to all nations
under heaven.[14]

---

* The mustard seed was the smallest seed used by Palestinian farmers and gardeners. Gleason
Archer notes: "No one yet has proved that ancient Palestinians planted anything that bore a
smaller seed than that of the black mustard" (*Encyclopedia of Bible Difficulties*, p. 329).

▶ Since yeast is often representative of evil in Scripture, why does Jesus say the kingdom of heaven is like yeast (Matthew 13:33)?

In Matthew 13:33 Jesus said, "The kingdom of heaven is like yeast that a woman took and mixed into a large amount of flour until it worked all through the dough." Scholars have different opinions about what Jesus is saying here. Some argue that since yeast represents evil elsewhere in Scripture (Matthew 16:12; Mark 8:15; Luke 12:1; 1 Corinthians 5:6-8; Galatians 5:9), Jesus must be saying that evil will be present in some form within Christendom up until Christ comes again (see 1 Timothy 4:1-5). Perhaps it refers to those who *profess* faith without having *genuine* faith.

Other scholars believe it would be wrong to assume that simply because yeast represents evil in other verses of Scripture it *must* represent evil in the context of Matthew 13. Indeed, perhaps yeast is used in a good sense in this context so that it simply represents the dynamic growth of the kingdom of God as a result of the penetrating power of the gospel of Christ and the supernatural work of the Holy Spirit.

When leaven is introduced into baking flour, a process begins that is steady, continuous, and irreversible. Applied to the present parable, the gospel of Christ combined with the supernatural power of the Holy Spirit is engaged in a process that is steady, continuous, and irreversible—and hence the parable points to the continued growth of the kingdom of heaven.

Personally, I think the second interpretative option above—yeast illustrating the dynamic growth of the kingdom—makes the most sense.

▶ What was Jesus teaching about the kingdom of heaven when He compared it to a hidden treasure and a pearl (Matthew 13:44-46)?

In Matthew 13:44-46 Jesus said, "The kingdom of heaven is like treasure hidden in a field. When a man found it, he hid it again, and then in his joy went and sold all he had and bought that field. Again, the kingdom of heaven is like a merchant looking for fine pearls. When he found one of great value, he went away and sold everything he had and bought it."

In the parables of the treasure hidden in the field (Matthew 13:44) and the merchant looking for fine pearls (verses 45,46), Jesus was simply pointing to the incredible value of the kingdom of heaven. Those who truly see its importance will do anything within their power to possess it. They will allow nothing to stand in their way.

Certainly these parables should *not* be taken to mean that a person could *buy* his or her way into the kingdom of heaven by material wealth. Such a conclusion violates the intent of the parables. In context, the parables simply point to the incalculable value of the kingdom, and that one should be willing to give up everything to attain it.

▶ Does Jesus' parable of the net indicate that unbelievers are presently part of the kingdom of heaven (Matthew 13:47-50)?

In Matthew 13:47-50 Jesus said, "Once again, the kingdom of heaven is like a net that was let down into the lake and caught all kinds of fish. When it was full, the fishermen pulled it up on the shore. Then they sat down and collected the good fish in baskets, but threw the bad away. This is how it will be at the end of the age. The angels will come and separate the wicked from the righteous and throw them into the fiery furnace, where there will be weeping and gnashing of teeth."

Many scholars believe that Jesus in this passage was emphasizing that up until His second coming, when judgment will take place, there will be both genuine Christians and phony (professing) Christians that coexist within the kingdom. At the end of the age, there will be a separation of the righteous from the unrighteous. The righteous (that is, *true believers*) will be invited into Christ's kingdom, while the unrighteous (*professing believers who are really unbelievers*) will be excluded from His kingdom and sent to a place of suffering.

Fishermen can tell you that when you pull up a net, you find all kinds of fish—some of them good and worth keeping, but others that are utterly useless. Hence the fishermen separate the good from the bad, keeping the good and throwing away the bad. At the end of the age, Christ will separate the good from the bad, the true Christians from the professing Christians, the "righteous" from the "unrighteous."

▶ In what sense did Jesus' contemporaries "see the kingdom of God come with power" (Mark 9:1; Matthew 16:28)?

In Mark 9:1 Jesus said to His disciples and a crowd of people, "I tell you the truth, some who are standing here will not taste death before they see the kingdom of God come with power" (see also Matthew 16:28). Scholars have different viewpoints as to what this means. Many believe that when Jesus said this He had in mind the transfiguration, which happened precisely one week later. In fact, in Matthew's account the transfiguration (Matthew 17:1-13) immediately follows the prediction itself (16:28). It is suggested that the transfiguration served as a preview or foretaste of the kingdom in which the divine Messiah would appear in a state of glory.

Other scholars see this verse as a reference to the future Day of Pentecost. It is suggested that starting at Pentecost (Acts 2) and throughout the rest of the book of Acts, we witness manifestations of the power of God through the Holy Spirit and the growth of the kingdom of God as a result of the preaching of the apostles. It is argued *against* this view, however, that Jesus did not actually "come" on the Day of Pentecost. He merely *sent* the Holy Spirit (John 16:7; Acts 1:5-8).

I believe the first view listed above (the transfiguration) has the most going for it. But I need to provide a little biblical backdrop to establish my case. So let me provide some details on the transfiguration.

In the transfiguration, we find that Jesus "pulled back the veil" (so to speak) and allowed His intrinsic divine glory to shine forth in all its splendor. According to three of the Gospels, while Jesus was praying, "the appearance of his face changed" (Luke 9:29). "His face shone like the sun," and his clothing was also changed so that it "became as white as the light" (Matthew 17:2) and "as bright as a flash of lightning" (Luke 9:29). His clothing was "dazzling white" (Mark 9:3). If this transformation took place at night, as Luke's Gospel seems to suggest (see 9:32,37), the scene unfolding before the disciples must have been all the more fearsomely awesome (Mark 9:6), beyond the capacity of words to fully describe. They witnessed the sheer power and glory of God shining from the person of Jesus Christ.

Consider the details in Matthew's version:

> After six days Jesus took with him Peter, James and John the brother of James, and led them up a high mountain by themselves. There he was transfigured before them. His face shone like the sun, and his clothes became as white as the light. Just then there appeared before them Moses and Elijah, talking with Jesus.
>
> Peter said to Jesus, "Lord, it is good for us to be here. If you wish, I will put up three shelters—one for you, one for Moses and one for Elijah."
>
> While he was still speaking, a bright cloud enveloped them, and a voice from the cloud said, "This is my Son, whom I love; with him I am well pleased. Listen to him!"
>
> When the disciples heard this, they fell face-down to the ground, terrified. But Jesus came and touched them. "Get up," he said. "Don't be afraid." When they looked up, they saw no one except Jesus (Matthew 17:1-8).

The mention of the "high mountain" recalls other Old Testament theophanies (appearances of God) on the "mountain of God" or Mount Sinai (Exodus 24; 1 Kings 19), in which Moses and Elijah received visions of the glory of God. How interesting that these two Old Testament saints who had received visions of God's glory in Old Testament times now appear to Christ on a high mountain as Christ is transfigured.

The word "transfigured" (Matthew 17:2) is rich with meaning. The verb (which comes from the Greek *metamorphoo*) does not refer to a superficial change of outward appearance. Rather, it denotes a transformation of Christ's essential form, proceeding from within. We get the word metamorphosis from this Greek word. It means "to be changed into another form," not merely a change in outward appearance. For a brief time Jesus' human body was transformed (that is, glorified) and the disciples witnessed Him as He will be when He returns visibly in power and glory to establish His kingdom on earth (see Acts 15:14-18; 1 Corinthians 15:20-28; Revelation 1:13-16; 19:15; 20:4-6).

Bible scholar J. Dwight Pentecost offers some helpful insights on how Christ's human body acted as a veil to Christ's intrinsic glory, a veil that was briefly "pulled back" during the transfiguration:

> Christ was not transfigured by means of an external light focused on Him so that He reflected the glory of God. Rather, this was the outshining of the essential glory that belongs to Jesus Christ. . . . It was necessary that Christ's glory be veiled when He came into this world. Christ's glory was not surrendered at the time of the Incarnation but was veiled, lest the people whom He had come to redeem should be consumed by its brightness. . . . In revealing plans for the tabernacle to Moses, God instructed him to erect a curtain between the Holy of Holies, where God purposed to dwell, and His people. That veil was not so much designed to teach Israel that they were unworthy to enter the presence of God—which in truth it did—as much as to protect Israel from being consumed by the brightness of God's glory. The veil, then, was a gracious provision by a holy God to make it possible for Him to dwell in the midst of an unholy people. The writer to the Hebrews said that the body of Jesus Christ was to Him what the veil was in the tabernacle (Heb. 10:19-20).[15]

Hence, at the transfiguration, the One who had hidden His glory beneath the form of a servant (Philippians 2:6-8) burst forth in glory, and it was nothing less than His intrinsic glory. The power and the divinity and the glory within broke through the veil of Christ's flesh and shone out, until His very clothing kindled to the dazzling brightness of the light.

This *very same glory* will be revealed to the world when Jesus Christ comes to this earth again to set up His kingdom (see Matthew 24:30; 25:31). The glory that will lighten the whole world at the second coming was here revealed to the three disciples who witnessed the transfiguration.[16]

It is *this* that I think Jesus was referring to when He said, "I tell you the truth, some who are standing here will not taste death before they see the kingdom of God come with power" (Mark 9:1 NASB). Peter, James, and John witnessed the kingdom of God coming with power because they witnessed the King in a full display of His power and glory.

Recall that Jesus had earlier said, "The kingdom of heaven is in your midst" (Luke 17:21 NASB). The kingdom was in their "midst" precisely because the *King* was in the midst. That is the case on the mount of transfiguration. *The kingdom of God was present in power and glory because the King of power and glory was Himself present.*

FOUR

THE JEWS
AND JUDAISM

ᕬᎿᏙᏙᏅ

▶ What was Jesus teaching about Christianity and Judaism in His comments about new wine in old wineskins (Mark 2:21,22; Matthew 9:16,17)?

Jesus, speaking of Judaism, said, "No one sews a patch of unshrunk cloth on an old garment. If he does, the new piece will pull away from the old, making the tear worse. And no one pours new wine into old wineskins. If he does, the wine will burst the skins, and both the wine and the wineskins will be ruined. No, he pours new wine into new wineskins" (Mark 2:21,22; see also Matthew 9:16,17).

In ancient times a wineskin was made from the skin of goats or another animal and was used as a bag for holding and dispensing wine. Such wineskins stretched over time and eventually lost their elasticity. Wineskins that had already been stretched to capacity by the previous fermenting wine would burst if filled with *new* unfermented wine, which would cause further stretching to the point of breaking.[1]

Jesus in this analogy was illustrating the fact that the Jewish legalism of the Old Testament—taken to extremes by the Pharisees of Jesus' time—was inflexible and outdated. The "old wineskin" of Judaism could not contain the dynamic new faith of Christianity. The grace teachings of Christ could not be contained within the legalistic wineskin of Judaism.

What Jesus was offering to the masses was not something that could simply be superimposed onto Judaism, like trying to sew new cloth onto a tattered garment. Jesus was not offering to bring about a reformation of Judaism; what He was offering was something *entirely new*—Christianity. The *living* faith He spoke of could not be patched onto a *dead* religious system.[2]

▶ Was Jesus teaching that Christians are still under the Law of Moses (Matthew 5:17,18)?

In Matthew 5:17 Jesus said, "Do not think that I came to abolish the Law or the Prophets. I did not come to abolish, but to fulfill" (NASB). Some who claim to be Christians today have emphasized various aspects of keeping of the Law—including Sabbath observance, the annual feast days, and dietary regulations. Are we still under the Law?

We need to be careful here. On the one hand, it is true that during His lifetime Jesus always kept the Law of Moses Himself. He sanctioned offering sacrifices to the Jewish priests (Matthew 8:4), attended Jewish festivals (John 7:10), and ate the Passover lamb (Matthew 26:19). He occasionally violated the false pharisaical *traditions* that had grown up around the Law (see Matthew 5:43,44), even chiding the hypocritical Pharisees, "You nullify the word of God for the sake of your tradition" (Matthew 15:6). However, following the death, resurrection, and ascension of Christ, key verses in the New Testament indicate that the Law was fulfilled in Christ (2 Corinthians 3:7,13,14; Colossians 2:16,17).[3]

The question is, Has the entire Law been nullified, or only certain portions of it? At least some (if not all) of the references to the Law being done away with in the New Testament are speaking of Old Testament *ceremonies* and *types*. These ceremonial and typological aspects of the Old Testament Law of Moses were clearly done away with when Jesus, our Passover lamb (1 Corinthians 5:7), fulfilled the law's types and predictions about His first coming (see Hebrews chapters 7–10). Jesus Himself apparently disposed of the ceremonial law by declaring all meats clean (Mark 7:19). In this sense, believers are clearly not under the Law of Moses.

Nor are Christians under the commandment of Moses to worship on Saturday (Exodus 20:8-11). In view of the fact that Jesus' resurrection, His subsequent appearances, and the ascension all occurred on Sunday, Christians worship on that day instead (see Acts 20:7; 1 Corinthians 16:2). Sabbath worship, according to the apostle Paul, was only an Old Testament "shadow" of the real substance that was inaugurated by Christ (Colossians 2:16,17).

Even the Ten Commandments *as such* were originally given to the Jews in a theocratic* framework. New Testament believers are *not* a part of that theocracy but are rather beneficiaries of the new covenant, and *these* believers are instructed that what was "engraved on stones" (the Ten Commandments) has been "taken away in Christ" (2 Corinthians 3:7,13,14).

This does not mean, of course, that the moral principles embodied in the Ten Commandments—which reflect the very nature of an unchanging God—are not still binding on believers today. It is highly revealing that every one of these principles in the Ten Commandments is restated *in another context* in the New Testament (except for the command to rest and worship on Saturday).

Still, it is important to understand that the moral law is not and never was intended to be a means of salvation. Romans 3:20 asserts, "No one will be declared righteous in his sight by observing the law."

So why did God give us the Law? First, to show us what sin is. The law set up God's holy standards of conduct. The Law also shows us the consequences if we do not measure up to those high standards. God did this purposefully, for as we grow to see that we do not measure up to the holy standards of the Law, we are all forced to admit that we have a sin problem.

---

* A *theocracy* is a God-ruled nation. Israel was a theocracy.

Second, though this may initially sound very strange, another purpose of the Law is to provoke sin all the more in people. Scripture tells us that the Law was given to us so that "trespass [or sin] might increase" (Romans 5:20). (It is similar to the child who immediately decides to do the very thing his mom just told him not to do. Mom's "law," as it were, provoked sin.) You see, God wants us to become so overwhelmed with the sin problem that we cannot deny its reality and severity. He wants us all to see how desperately we need the Savior, Jesus Christ. The Law, by provoking sin to increase, effectively points us to our dire need for a Savior. And, as the apostle Paul said, "where sin increased, *grace increased all the more*" (Romans 5:20, italics added).

Still another very important function of the Law is that it is like a tutor that leads us to Christ (Galatians 3:24,25). Among the ancient Romans it was the job of a tutor to lead a child to school. Likewise, the Law is our tutor in leading us straight to Jesus Christ, the Savior. The Law does this by showing us our sin and then pointing to the marvelous grace of Christ.

Once we have "arrived" to Christ—trusting in Him as our Savior—the Law has done its job and it no longer holds sway over us. For believers, "Christ is the end of the law so that there may be righteousness for everyone who believes" (Romans 10:4).

▶ Did Jesus teach it was all right to break the Sabbath (Mark 2:27,28)?

Jesus said to His Jewish opponents, "The Sabbath was made for man, not man for the Sabbath. So the Son of Man is Lord even of the Sabbath" (Mark 2:27,28). The context of this passage is that Jesus and His disciples had been passing through a grainfield on a Sabbath day. The disciples were hungry, so they took a few heads of grain and ate them. In the Old Testament Law, it was allowed for a hungry man to pick grain along a pathway to satisfy his hunger. However, the Pharisees said the disciples violated the Law because they did this on the Sabbath (it was unlawful to do any type of "work" on the Sabbath). In Jewish reckoning, the disciples were guilty of performing two acts of "work" on this holy day: 1) plucking the ears of corn, and 2) rubbing them in preparation for eating them.[4]

Christ then launched into His defense. He first pointed out to His Pharisaic critics that they were ignorant of their own Old Testament Scriptures. If they knew their Scriptures, they would have realized that there was a time when David became hungry, entered the house of God, and ate some bread—bread which, according to Levitical Law, was to be eaten only by the priests (1 Samuel 21:1-6).

In this case, David had been engaged in the service of the Lord and needed the provision of bread. Similarly, the disciples, who were engaged in the service of the Lord Jesus, needed the provision of the grain. It seems clear from this scriptural precedent that the Law of the Sabbath could be broken for works of necessity. In such cases the Old Testament ritual Law regarding work on the Sabbath is eclipsed by the higher law of survival and sustenance.

Jesus then launched into His next line of argumentation, which related to the original purpose of the Sabbath: "The Sabbath was made for man, not man for the Sabbath" (Mark 2:27). Jesus' point was that man is more important to God than any institution, and the institution of the Sabbath was for the benefit of man. The Pharisees had twisted the teaching of the Sabbath into a legalistic burden, multiplying Sabbath requirements to such a degree that they became intolerable.[5] Jesus thus corrected the Pharisees by saying that the Sabbath was made for man and was intended to bring him spiritual, mental, and physical refreshment and restoration.[6] The Sabbath was not to be a joyless ritual, as the Pharisees had made it, but rather a time of rest in which one joyfully remembers the greatness and wonder of God.

There is one further point worthy of mention: Jesus in this verse referred to Himself as the "Lord of the Sabbath." This is exceedingly relevant, for it proved Jesus' qualification to interpret the Law of the Sabbath.[7] His words thus carry far more authority than those of the Jewish leaders who were questioning Him. As the Lord of the Sabbath, He sought to restore its true intent as a day designed to benefit and not deprive man of well-being and health.[8]

▶ Who is Jesus referring to in the phrase "the lost sheep of Israel" (Matthew 15:24)?

In Matthew 15:24, Jesus said, "I was sent only to the lost sheep of Israel." In this verse, the phrase "the lost sheep of Israel" refers to the Israelites to whom Jesus was preaching in Judah and Galilee who were in a lost condition in God's eyes.[9] But why did Jesus say He was sent to them?

In the outworking of God's plan of salvation, the good news of the kingdom of God was apparently to be preached *first* to the Jews—God's covenant people. Scripture indicates that Jesus came to offer the Jews the kingdom promised to them through King David many centuries earlier (2 Samuel 7:12-14; compare with Luke 1:32,33). In view of this, it would be inappropriate for Him to prematurely bring blessings on the Gentiles *prior* to bringing blessing to Israel.[10] But it was never intended that the Gentiles be excluded. After all, many centuries earlier the Abrahamic covenant had affirmed that "all peoples on earth" would be blessed through the Messiah (Genesis 12:3). God's offer was ultimately for all humankind, as is clear in Christ's "Great Commission" to share the Good News with *all people everywhere* (Matthew 28:19,20).

▶ Who are the "other sheep" mentioned in John 10:16?

In John 10:16 Jesus said, "I have other sheep that are not of this sheep pen. I must bring them also. They too will listen to my voice, and there shall be one flock and one shepherd."

The context indicates that the "other sheep" mentioned here are *Gentile* believers as opposed to *Jewish* believers. As noted above, the unsaved Jews in the Gospels were called "the *lost* sheep of Israel" (Matthew 10:6; 15:24), and those Jews who followed Christ were called *His* "sheep" (John 10).

Jesus often referred to His Jewish disciples as sheep in His flock. For example, when Jesus was giving the 12 disciples instructions for their future service, He said, "I am sending you out *like sheep* among wolves. Therefore be as shrewd as snakes and as innocent as doves" (Matthew 10:16, italics added). Later, Jesus told the disciples that His crucifixion would cause them to scatter: "You will all fall away on account of me, for it is written: 'I will strike the shepherd, and *the sheep of the flock* will be scattered'" (Matthew 26:31, italics added).

To repeat, then, the "other" sheep Jesus makes reference to were non-Jewish, Gentile believers. The Gentile believers, along with the Jewish believers, "shall be *one flock*" under *one shepherd*" (John 10:16). This is in perfect accord with Ephesians 2:11-22, where we are told that in Christ, Jews and Gentiles are reconciled in *one body*. Galatians 3:28 tells us that "there is neither Jew nor Greek [Gentile], slave nor free, male nor female, for you are all *one* in Christ Jesus" (italics added). Likewise, Colossians 3:11 speaks of a renewal in which "there is no Greek [Gentile] or Jew, circumcised or uncircumcised, barbarian, Scythian, slave or free, but Christ is all, and is in all."

▶ Why did Jesus first tell His disciples not to go among the Gentiles? Does He not love them too (Matthew 10:5,6)?

Jesus sent out the disciples with the following instructions: "Do not go among the Gentiles or enter any town of the Samaritans. Go rather to the lost sheep of Israel" (Matthew 10:5,6). As noted previously in this chapter, in the outworking of God's plan of salvation, the good news of the kingdom of God was apparently to be preached *first to the Jews*—God's *covenant* people (2 Samuel 7:12-14). But the Gentiles would certainly not be excluded. God's offer was ultimately for *all* humankind, as is clear in the Abrahamic covenant in Genesis 12:3 (where we are told that *all* the people of the earth would be blessed through Messiah), and Christ's "Great Commission" to share the Good News with *all* people everywhere (Matthew 28:19,20).

▶ **What did Jesus mean when He made reference to the "yeast of the Pharisees" (Mark 8:15)?**

While Christ and the disciples were en route to their destination of Bethsaida, Jesus warned them, "Be careful . . . watch out for the yeast of the Pharisees and that of Herod" (Mark 8:15). In both Jewish and Hellenistic circles, yeast was often a symbol of evil or corruption.[11] Among the Jews, yeast often represented an invisible, pervasive influence.[12]

In the present context, the "yeast" of the Pharisees was unbelief and the spirit of hypocrisy that their teaching encouraged. Even a tiny amount of yeast has the ability of fermenting a large piece of dough. Like yeast, Pharisaic unbelief and hypocrisy—once it was introduced and admitted into the heart of Jewish society—spread so pervasively that it rendered true spirituality impossible. The yeast of the Pharisees had infected the whole nation so that the spiritual state of the nation was abysmal.

▶ **Why did Jesus speak in such harsh, unloving terms about the Pharisees (Matthew 23:27-33)?**

In Matthew 23:33 Jesus said of the Pharisees, "You snakes! You brood of vipers! How will you escape being condemned to hell?" (Matthew 23:33). Such words do indeed seem harsh. But there is good reason for it.

In the broader context of Matthew 23:1-36 Jesus is seen pronouncing woes on the nation of Israel, lamenting the abysmal spiritual state of the people. In verses 1-12, Jesus charged the multitudes and the disciples to obey the Law but not to follow the example and the deeds of the Pharisees. Then in verses 13-36 Jesus pronounced specific woes against the religious leaders of the nation. He pronounced woe on them because:

- They kept others from entering the kingdom of heaven (verse 13).

- Their actions did not match their pious-sounding words (verse 14).
- They bound people up in mere religiosity (verse 15).
- They were more interested in material wealth than in true worship of the living God (verses 16-22).
- They were picky about the minute matters of the Law while allowing the major matters of the Law to go unaddressed (verses 23,24).
- They were ceremonially clean in an external sense but were totally filthy on the inside (verses 25,26).
- They gave the *appearance* of righteousness while being full of hypocrisy on the inside (verses 27,28).
- They self-righteously boasted that they would have stood with the martyred prophets while at the same time they themselves were trying to kill holy men (verses 29-36).

So, while Jesus' words to the Pharisees may seem harsh, the words are nevertheless appropriate. The snake that approached Eve no doubt had the external appearance of beauty (Genesis 3:1),* but inside it was full of nothing but evil. Similarly, Jesus said, the Pharisees may have a good appearance on the outside, like a snake, but inside they are utterly corrupt.

▶ What catastrophic event is Jesus referring to in Luke 23:28-31?

In Luke 23:28,29, Jesus—who was shortly to be crucified—turned to a group of woman who were following Him and said, "Daughters of Jerusalem, do not weep for me; weep for yourselves and for your children. For the time will come when you will say, 'Blessed are the barren women, the wombs that never bore and the breasts that never nursed!'"

Scholars agree that Jesus' words were pointing forward to the coming destruction of Jerusalem that would occur in A.D. 70 at the hands of Titus and his Roman warriors. The temple in

---

* Prior to the fall of mankind, in its uncursed state the snake or serpent was apparently a beautiful creature.

Jerusalem—the heart of Jewish worship—would be utterly destroyed. Barren women living during that time would be considered blessed, for it would be better for women not to have any children than for them to have children experience such suffering as would come in A.D. 70. Jesus thus sadly told these women to "mourn for yourselves."[13]

The Jewish historian Flavius Josephus documented that some Jewish mothers were reduced to eating their own children during the famine that followed Rome's siege against Jerusalem. This fact adds all the more soberness to Jesus' words about the blessing of being barren during that time.[14]

FIVE

SENSE AND NONSENSE ABOUT GOD

⚘

▶ Did Jesus teach that human beings are gods in John 10:34?

In John 10:34 Jesus said to some Jewish critics, "Is it not written in your Law, 'I have said you are gods'?" This verse does not teach that human beings are gods, but rather must be understood in light of Psalm 82, from which Jesus was quoting.

In Psalm 82 we find God's judgment against the evil Israelite judges. These judges were called "gods" (with a small "g") because they pronounced life and death judgments against people. But they became corrupt and unjust in their dealings.

In verse 6, Asaph, speaking of these unjust human judges, said, "I said, 'You are "gods"; you are all sons of the Most High.' But you will die like mere men; you will fall like every other ruler."

Asaph is clearly speaking in irony. He is saying in effect, "I have called you 'gods,' but in fact you will die like the men you really are." When Jesus alluded to this psalm in John 10, He was saying that what the Israelite judges were called in irony and in judgment *He is in reality*. His argument takes this form: "If even finite human judges can be called 'gods,' then how much more is it appropriate that I call myself the Son of God, since I am God's Son *by nature*."

▶ Does Jesus' teaching about being "born again" mean that God imparts His divine nature into believers' human spirits (John 3:3)?

Some cultists have argued that this is the case, but such a conclusion is a gross violation of the context of John 3, which views the new birth as a *spiritual* birth. The new birth does not involve a change in essence or nature (that is, becoming divine) but rather involves the regeneration of (or impartation of life to) a uniquely human spirit by God (2 Corinthians 5:17; Titus 3:5). It involves a spiritual *transformation* that removes a person from the kingdom of darkness and places him into the kingdom of God (Colossians 1:13). To belong to God's spiritual kingdom, one must be spiritually "born" into it.

It is critical to realize that while those who are "born again" become "new creatures" (2 Corinthians 5:17), they most certainly *remain* creatures. The distinction between Creator and creature is a thread that runs throughout the entire Bible, from Genesis to Revelation. Humans never become deity.

It is interesting to note that when Jesus told Nicodemus that one must become born again, He spoke as if Nicodemus should have understood what He meant. And indeed, current studies indicate that among the ancient Jews the idea of "born again" was not unheard of. Gentile converts to Judaism were viewed as newborn children, and hence "born again" came to be a metaphor referring to *conversion.* But it never occurred to Nicodemus that he (a devout Jew) would be in need of conversion to the true faith of Israel (that is, conversion by believing in Israel's *true* Messiah).[1]

So, to sum up, Jesus' point was not that human beings become divine in some way, but rather that people must be converted by being born *from above* or born spiritually. It is a *spiritual birth* that brings one into Christ's *spiritual kingdom.*

▶ What did Jesus mean when He said the kingdom of God is "within" us (Luke 17:21)?

In Luke 17:21 Jesus said, "The kingdom of God is within you." Because Jesus was talking directly to the Pharisees—the religious hypocrites of the day—He surely did not mean that the kingdom of God was actually *"within"* them. God's holy kingdom was not "within" these unholy men.

Other interpretations of the verse are much more plausible. Many scholars believe the phrase translated "within you" is better rendered from the Greek "in your midst." In this understanding, Jesus was simply saying that the kingdom of God is "in your midst" because Christ (*the King*) is "in your midst." The *kingdom* is present because the *King* is present.

Other interpreters believe the phrase is best translated "within your possession" or "within your reach." In this understanding Jesus was saying that all His hearers had to do was acknowledge that He was the promised King/Messiah and He would issue in the kingdom.[2] But the Pharisees to whom Jesus was talking rejected Him as the King/Messiah.

▶ If God is spirit, as Jesus said (John 4:24), then how can Jesus be God in view of the fact that He has a physical body?

One must keep in mind that the incarnate* Christ is both 100 percent God and 100 percent man. Let me expand on that theme.

Prior to the incarnation, Jesus (the second person of the Trinity) was *one person* with *one nature* (a divine nature). Prior to the incarnation Jesus had no physical body; He was spirit, since the very nature of God is spirit (John 4:24). At the incarnation, however, Jesus was still one person, but He took on an additional nature—a human nature, which included both human body and human spirit.

Though Jesus in the incarnation had both a human and a divine nature, He was still only one person, as indicated by His consistent use of "I," "me," and "mine" in reference to Himself. Jesus never used the words "us," "we," or "ours" in reference to

---

* "Incarnate" literally means *in the flesh*. The incarnation refers to the Son of God's coming into the world *as a human being*.

His human-divine person. The divine nature of Christ never carried on a verbal conversation with His human nature.

One of the most complex aspects of the relationship of Christ's two natures is that, while the attributes of one nature are never attributed to the other, the attributes of both natures are properly attributed to His one person. Thus Christ at the same moment in time had what seem to be contradictory qualities. He was finite and yet infinite, weak and yet omnipotent (all-powerful), increasing in knowledge and yet omniscient (all-knowing), limited to being in one place at one time and yet omnipresent, having a physical body and yet being spirit. In the incarnation, the person of Christ is the partaker of the attributes of *both* natures, so that whatever may be affirmed of either nature—human or divine—may be affirmed of the one person of Jesus Christ.

Though Christ sometimes operated in the sphere of His humanity and in other cases in the sphere of His deity, in all cases what He did and what He was could be attributed to His one person. Thus, though Christ in His human nature knew hunger (Luke 4:2), weariness (John 4:6), and the need for sleep (Luke 8:23), just as Christ in His divine nature was omniscient (John 2:24), omnipresent (John 1:48), and omnipotent (John 11), *all this was experienced by the one person of Jesus Christ.*

My point in all the above is that while Jesus did indeed have a physical body in His *human* nature, He was nevertheless spirit in His *divine* nature. *Both* are true of Christ. He is 100 percent God and 100 percent man, with all the attributes that go along with each nature. So the fact that Christ has a physical body does not in any way argue against the fact that He is fully God.

▶ Since Jesus said, "Anyone who has seen me has seen the Father," does this mean the Father has a physical body like Jesus does (John 14:9)?

No. Remember that God is by nature spirit (John 4:24; see also Psalm 139:7-12; Isaiah 31:3; Acts 7:48-50; 2 Corinthians 3:17,18). When Jesus said that "anyone who has seen me has seen the Father" in John 14:9, He simply meant that He is the perfect revelation of God. Jesus' mission, His words, and His works centered on the Father.

Recall that Jesus had earlier said that He became a man specifically to reveal the Father to humankind: "No one has ever seen God, but God the One and Only [Jesus], who is at the Father's side, has made him known" (John 1:18). That is why Jesus could say, "When [a person] looks at me, he sees the one who sent me" (John 12:45). And that is why Jesus could affirm, "Whoever accepts me accepts the one who sent me" (John 13:20).

What are some of the ways Jesus revealed the Father?

- God's awesome *power* was revealed in Jesus (John 3:2).
- God's incredible *wisdom* was revealed in Jesus (1 Corinthians 1:24).
- God's boundless *love* was revealed and demonstrated by Jesus (1 John 3:16).
- God's unfathomable *grace* was revealed in Jesus (2 Thessalonians 1:12).

It is against this backdrop that Jesus said, "Anyone who has seen me has seen the Father" (John 14:9). Jesus came as the ultimate revelation of the Father.

▶ Is it true, as feminist writers claim, that Jesus set forth a sexist concept of God by calling God "Father" (Matthew 6:9)?

Jesus did teach that we should refer to God as our "Father." For example, we are instructed by Him to pray, "Our Father in heaven . . ." (Matthew 6:9). However, this does not mean Jesus set forth a sexist concept of God.

To begin, it is highly revealing that while God is referred to in the Bible as "Father" (and never "Mother"), some of His actions are occasionally described in feminine terms. For example, Jesus likened God to a loving and saddened mother hen crying over the waywardness of her children (Matthew 23:37-39). God is also said to have "given birth" to Israel (Deuteronomy 32:18).

Of course, God is not a gender being as humans are. He is not of the male sex per se. The primary emphasis in God being called "Father" is that He is personal. Unlike the dead and impersonal idols of paganism, the true God is a personal being with whom we can relate. In fact, we can even call Him "Abba" (an Aramaic term that loosely means "daddy"). That is how intimate a relationship we can have with Him.

Regarding the issue of gender equality, it is undeniable that Jesus had a very high view of women. In a Jewish culture, where women were discouraged from studying the Law, Jesus taught women right alongside men as equals (Matthew 14:21; 15:38). And when He taught, He often used women's activities to illustrate the character of the kingdom of God, such as baking bread (Luke 13:20,21), grinding corn (Luke 17:35), and sweeping the house to find a lost coin (Luke 15:8-10).

Some Jewish rabbis taught that a man should not speak to a woman in a public place, but Jesus not only spoke to a woman (who, incidentally, was a Samaritan) but also drank from her cup in a public place (John 4:1-30). The first person He appeared to after resurrecting from the dead was Mary and not the male disciples (Luke 24:1-8). Clearly Jesus had a very high view of women.

Galatians 3:28 tells us that there is neither male nor female in Jesus Christ. First Peter 3:7 says men and women are fellow heirs of grace. Ephesians 5:21 speaks of mutual submission between man and wife. In John 7:53–8:11 Jesus would not permit the double standard of the woman being taken in adultery and letting the man go free. In Luke 10:38,39 Jesus let a woman sit at His feet, which was a place reserved for the male disciples. Verses such as these show that in God's eyes men and women are spiritually equal. Any claims of sexism in Jesus or Christianity are absolutely groundless.

▶ Did Jesus affirm the doctrine of the Trinity when He said we are to baptize people in the "name" of the Father, the Son, and the Holy Spirit (Matthew 28:19)?

Yes, I think so. In the New American Standard Bible, Matthew 28:19 reads: "Go therefore and make disciples of all the nations, baptizing them in the name of *the* Father and *the* Son and *the* Holy Spirit" (italics added). It is highly revealing that the word *name* is singular in the Greek, indicating that there is one God, but three distinct persons within the Godhead—the Father, the Son, and the Holy Spirit.[3] Theologian Robert Reymond draws our attention to the importance of this verse for the doctrine of the Trinity:

> Jesus does not say, 1) "into the names [plural] of the Father and of the Son and of the Holy Spirit," or what is its virtual equivalent, 2) "into the name of the Father, and into the name of the Son, and into the name of the Holy Spirit," as if we had to deal with three separate Beings. Nor does He say, 3) "into the name of the Father, Son, and Holy Spirit" (omitting the three recurring articles), as if "the Father, Son, and Holy Ghost" might be taken as merely three designations of a single person. What He does say is this: 4) "into the name [singular] of *the* Father, and of *the* Son, and of *the* Holy Spirit," first asserting the unity of the three by combining them all within the bounds of the single Name, and then throwing into emphasis the distinctness of each by introducing them in turn with the repeated article.[4]

God is one in *essence*, but three in *persons*. God has one *nature*, but three *centers of consciousness*. That is, there is only one *what* in God, but there are three *whos*. There is one *it*, but three "*I*"s.[5] This is a mystery, but not a contradiction. It would be contradictory for Jesus to say that God was only one person but was also three persons, or that God is only one nature but that He also had three natures. But to declare, as orthodox Christians do, that God is one essence eternally revealed in three distinct persons is not a contradiction.

There are many other verses in Scripture that support the doctrine of the Trinity. Consider the following.

Evidence for one God. The fact that there is only one true God is the consistent testimony of Scripture from Genesis to Revelation. It is like a thread that runs through every page of the Bible. God positively affirmed through Isaiah the prophet, "This is what the LORD says—Israel's King and Redeemer, the LORD Almighty: I am the first and I am the last; apart from me there is no God" (Isaiah 44:6). God also said, "I am God, and there is no other; I am God, and there is none like me" (46:9).

The oneness of God is also often emphasized in the New Testament. In 1 Corinthians 8:4, for example, the apostle Paul asserted that "an idol is nothing at all in the world and that there is no God but one." James 2:19 says, "You believe that there is one God. Good! Even the demons believe that—and shudder." These and a multitude of other verses (including John 5:44; 17:3; Romans 3:29,30; 16:27; Galatians 3:20; Ephesians 4:6; and 1 Timothy 2:5) make it absolutely clear that there is one and only one God.

Evidence for three persons who are called God. While Scripture is absolutely clear that there is only one God, in the unfolding of God's revelation to humankind it also becomes clear that there are three distinct persons who are called God in Scripture.

- *The Father is God:* Peter makes reference to the saints "who have been chosen according to the foreknowledge of God the Father" (1 Peter 1:2).
- *Jesus is God:* When Jesus made a postresurrection appearance to doubting Thomas, Thomas said, "My Lord and my God!" (John 20:28). As well, the Father said of the Son, "Your throne, O God, will last forever and ever, and righteousness will be the scepter of your kingdom" (Hebrews 1:8).
- *The Holy Spirit is God:* In Acts 5:3,4, we are told that lying to the Holy Spirit is equivalent to lying to God.

Moreover, each of the three persons on different occasions is seen to possess the attributes of deity.

- For example, all three are said to be *omnipresent*: the Father (Matthew 19:26), the Son (Matthew 28:18,19), and the Holy Spirit (Psalm 139:7).

- All three are *omniscient*: the Father (Romans 11:33), the Son (Matthew 9:4), and the Holy Spirit (1 Corinthians 2:10).

- All three are *omnipotent*: the Father (1 Peter 1:5), the Son (Matthew 28:18), and the Holy Spirit (Romans 15:19).

- Furthermore, *holiness* is ascribed to each person: the Father (Revelation 15:4), the Son (Acts 3:14), and the Holy Spirit (John 16:7-14).

- *Eternity* is ascribed to each person: the Father (Psalm 90:2), the Son (Micah 5:2; John 1:2; Revelation 1:8,17), and the Holy Spirit (Hebrews 9:14).

- And each of the three is individually described as the *truth*: the Father (John 7:28), the Son (Revelation 3:7), and the Holy Spirit (1 John 5:6).

So, based on all these lines of evidence, it seems clear that while there is only one God, there are three coequal and coeternal persons within the one godhead.

▶ Is Jesus saying in John 10:30 that He and the Father are the same person (that Jesus is the Father), thereby refuting the doctrine of the Trinity?

In John 10:30 Jesus affirmed, "I and the Father are one" (John 10:30). This verse does not mean that Jesus and the Father are one and the same person. We know this to be true because in the phrase "I and the Father are one," a first-person plural—"we are" (*esmen* in the Greek)—is used. The verse literally reads from the Greek, "I and the Father *we are* one." If Jesus had intended to say that He and the Father were one *person*, He certainly would not have used the first person plural, which clearly implies *two* persons. As well, the verses that immediately precede and follow John 10:30 distinguish Jesus from the Father (see John 10:25,29,36,38).

Moreover, the Greek word for "one" (*hen*) in this verse refers *not* to personal unity (that is, the idea that the Father and Son are one person) but to unity of essence or nature (that is, that the Father and Son have the same divine nature). This is evident in the fact that the form of the word in the Greek is neuter, not masculine.[6] Certainly the Jewish leaders to whom Jesus was speaking understood Him to be claiming to be God, for they immediately picked up stones to put Jesus to death for committing what they perceived to be blasphemy (John 10:33).

Finally, it is the uniform testimony of the rest of John's Gospel (not to mention the rest of the Bible) that the Father and Jesus are distinct persons (within the unity of the one God). For example, the Father *sent* the Son (John 3:16,17); the Father and Son *love* each other (3:35); the Father and Son *speak* to each other (11:41,42); and the Father *knows* the Son just as the Son *knows* the Father (7:29; 8:55; 10:15).

▶ **Does Jesus in John 14:6-11 indicate that He is God the Father, thereby refuting the doctrine of the Trinity?**

In this extended passage Jesus said, "If you had known Me, you would have known My Father also. . . . He who has seen Me has seen the Father. . . . Do you not believe that I am in the Father, and the Father is in Me? . . . Believe Me that I am in the Father, and the Father in Me. . . ." (John 14:7-11 NASB). These verses prove only that the Father and the Son are *one in being*, not that they are *one person*.

Notice that in John 14:6 Jesus very clearly distinguished Himself from the Father when He said, "No one comes *to* the Father, except *through* Me" (italics added). The words "to" and "through" would not make any sense if Jesus and the Father were one and the same person. They only make sense if the Father and Jesus are distinct persons, with Jesus being the Mediator between the Father and humankind.

Further, when Jesus said, "He who has seen Me has seen the Father" (John 14:9 NASB), He was not saying He *was* the Father. Rather, Jesus is the perfect revealer of the Father (see John

1:18). The reason Jesus is the perfect revealer of the Father is that Jesus and the Father (along with the Holy Spirit) are one indivisible divine being (John 10:30). This is in keeping with a proper definition of the Trinity: There is only one God, but within the unity of the Godhead there are three coequal and coeternal persons who are equal in substance (the divine nature) but distinct in subsistence (personhood). Jesus, the second person of the Trinity, is the perfect revelation of the Father, the first person of the Trinity.

Finally, it is the uniform testimony of John's Gospel that the Father and Jesus are distinct persons. Let me repeat: As noted previously, the Father *sent* the Son (John 3:16,17); the Father and Son *love* each other (3:35); the Father and Son *speak* to each other (11:41,42); and the Father *knows* the Son just as the Son *knows* the Father (7:29; 8:55; 10:15).

▶ Is Jesus implying He is the Father in John 14:18, thereby disproving the doctrine of the Trinity?

Some cultists have claimed that since Jesus Himself said He would not leave His disciples as "orphans" (John 14:18), then He must be their Father. This interpretation is incorrect for several reasons. First, it confuses *action* with *identity*. Christ *in action* functions as a divine parent-figure who guides, nurtures, protects, and leads His disciples. But this does not mean that Christ *in identity* is the Father (the first person of the Trinity).

Second, the apostle John speaks of the recipients of his first epistle as "my little children" (1 John 2:1 NASB), "little children" (verse 12 NASB), "children" (verse 18 NASB), and so forth, but this does not mean that John was claiming to be God the Father or even their physical father. Neither is Christ "the Father" simply because He watches after His disciples and does not leave them as orphans.

Third, as noted previously in the chapter, it is the uniform testimony of Scripture that the Father and Son are distinct persons within the unity of the one God (John 3:16,17; 7:29; 8:55; 10:15; 11:41,42).

Six

THE HOLY SPIRIT

∽∞∾

▶ Did Jesus consider the Holy Spirit a "force of God" or a person (John 14–16)?

In John chapters 14 through 16 (which records Jesus' "Upper Room Discourse"), Jesus told the disciples that He would send the Holy Spirit to them. The fact that Jesus referred to "the Holy Spirit" instead of using a personal name has led some to conclude that the Holy Spirit is a force of God instead of a person. This is not correct, however.

In John 14:16 (NASB) Jesus informed the disciples: "I will ask the Father, and He will give you *another Helper*, that He may be with you forever" (italics added). There are two words in the Greek language for the English word "another." One word (*heteros*) means "another of a different kind." The other word (*allos*) means "another of the same kind." It is this second word, *allos*, that is used in John 14:16. Jesus is saying that He will ask the Father to send another Helper of the *same kind as Himself*—that is, personal! Just as Jesus was a personal advocate-representative who helped the disciples for three years during His earthly ministry, so now the disciples would have another personal advocate-representative—the Holy Spirit—who would be with them throughout their lives.

The purpose of this personal advocate-representative is to *bear witness* (or testify) to others about Christ and His teachings

(John 15:26,27). This is something that only a person can do. Indeed, it is highly revealing that the disciples are told to "bear witness" after receiving the witness borne by the Holy Spirit. Clearly, the act of bearing witness is a *personal* act.[1]

John 16:13 also tells us that the Holy Spirit "will not speak on His own initiative, but whatever He hears, He will speak" (NASB). It would be truly ridiculous to interpret this as meaning that a "force" repeats what "it" hears.[2] It is just as ridiculous as saying, "The electricity in my home will repeat to you all that it hears me say."

We read elsewhere in Scripture that the Holy Spirit can carry on a conversation with other persons (Acts 8:29; 13:2), which is something a mere force cannot do. Moreover, the Holy Spirit has all the *qualities* of personality—including mind (1 Corinthians 2:10), emotions (Ephesians 4:30), and a will (1 Corinthians 12:11). Further, the Holy Spirit performs *actions* of personality (see John 14:26; 15:26; Romans 8:14; Acts 8:29). Clearly, personality is attributed to the Holy Spirit throughout Scripture.

It is highly revealing that in Scripture the Holy Spirit is seen using personal pronouns *of Himself.* An example of this is Acts 13:2 NASB: "While they were ministering to the Lord and fasting, the Holy Spirit said, 'Set apart for *Me* Barnabas and Saul for the work to which *I* have called them'" (italics added). Clearly the Holy Spirit considered Himself a person!

▶ Why did Jesus indicate that the Holy Spirit would not come to His followers unless He first went into heaven (John 16:7)?

In John 16:7 Jesus informed the disciples, "It is for your good that I am going away. Unless I go away, the Counselor will not come to you; but if I go, I will send him to you." Jesus did not give any reason for this statement. However, we find a clue in John 7:39: "Up to that time the Spirit had not been given, since Jesus had not yet been glorified."

The implication is that the cross, resurrection, and subsequent glorification of Christ were necessary prior to the sending of the Holy Spirit.* In God's plan of salvation, Calvary had to precede Pentecost. The atoning work of Christ was needed as a prelude to the work of the Holy Spirit. *Sin* had to be dealt with by Christ's work before *holiness* could be worked out in the life of the believer by the Holy Spirit. Bible commentator Albert Barnes offers us this insight:

> It was an evident arrangement in the great plan of redemption that each of the persons of the Trinity should perform a part. As it was not the work of the Spirit to make an atonement, so it was not the work of the Savior to apply it. And until the Lord Jesus had performed this great work, the way was not open for the Holy Spirit to descend to perform his part of the great plan; yet, when the Savior had completed *his* portion of the work and had left the earth, the Spirit would carry forward the same plan and apply it to men.... It was the office of the Spirit to carry forward the work only when the Savior had died and ascended.[3]

Certainly as one compares the state of the disciples at the end of Jesus' ministry (they were fearful and powerless) with their ministry as recorded in the book of Acts (they were bold and powerful witnesses), Jesus' comment that it would be "good" for the disciples that He went away and send the Holy Spirit takes on new significance.[4]

▶ Did Jesus indicate that the disciples received the Holy Spirit before the Day of Pentecost (John 20:21,22)?

Following His resurrection from the dead, Jesus appeared to His disciples and said to them, "'Peace be with you! As the Father has sent me, I am sending you.' And with that he

---

* This does not mean the Holy Spirit was completely inactive until after Christ's ascension. Prior to this time, particularly in Old Testament times, the Holy Spirit temporarily came upon people for specific acts of service (Genesis 41:38; Numbers 27:18; Daniel 4:8; 5:11-14). But the baptism and the *permanent* indwelling of the Spirit awaited Christ's ascension.

breathed on them and said, 'Receive the Holy Spirit'" (John 20:21,22).

Some scholars have suggested that this was a prophetic utterance that would ultimately be fulfilled 50 days later on the Day of Pentecost.[5] The word "receive" is interpreted to mean "you *will* receive." However, this viewpoint does not seem to do justice to the sense of immediacy that is communicated in Jesus's words.

I believe that in this passage we witness Jesus giving the disciples a *temporary* empowerment from the Holy Spirit so they could carry on their work of ministry until they would be *fully* empowered on the Day of Pentecost.[6] Since Christ had called them to a unique work, He gave them a unique empowerment for that work which was not the privilege of other people to receive.[7] "This reception of the Spirit was in anticipation of the Day of Pentecost and should be understood as a partial limited gift of knowledge, understanding, and empowerment until Pentecost, 50 days later."[8]

This is similar to how the Holy Spirit operated in Old Testament times. God would often bestow the Holy Spirit on specific individuals because they had been called by God to perform a specific task (see, for example, Numbers 27:18). God would temporarily empower them for the work to which they had been called. In like manner, the disciples are here temporarily empowered by the Holy Spirit to carry on their assigned task. Later, on the Day of Pentecost, the Holy Spirit would fall in fullness upon them—and that relationship with the Holy Spirit would be permanent.

▶ What is the sin against the Holy Spirit that Jesus spoke about (Matthew 12:31,32; Mark 3:28,29)?

In Matthew 12:31,32 Jesus said, "Every sin and blasphemy will be forgiven men, but the blasphemy against the Spirit will not be forgiven. Anyone who speaks a word against the Son of Man will be forgiven, but anyone who speaks against the Holy

Spirit will not be forgiven, either in this age or in the age to come."

The backdrop to this passage is that the Jews who had just witnessed a mighty miracle of Christ should have recognized that Jesus performed this miracle in the power of the Holy Spirit. After all, the Hebrew Scriptures, with which the Jews were well familiar, prophesied that when the Messiah came He would perform specific mighty miracles in the power of the Spirit—like giving sight to the blind, opening deaf ears, and enabling the lame to walk (see Isaiah 35:5,6). But these Jewish leaders claimed that Christ did these miracles in the power of the Devil, the *un*holy spirit. This was a sin against the Holy Spirit. This shows that these Jewish leaders had completely hardened themselves against the things of God.[9]

I believe that Matthew 12 describes a unique situation among the Jews, and that the actual committing of this sin requires the presence of the Messiah on earth doing His messianic miracles. In view of this, I do not think this sin can be duplicated exactly today as described in Matthew 12.

Bible expositors point out that "blaspheming the Spirit" involves opposing Jesus' messiahship so firmly and definitively that one resorts to accusations of sorcery to avoid the impact of the Holy Spirit's miraculous signs that confirm Christ's messianic identity.[10] This is truly a damning sin, for there is no provision for man's sin other than the work of the one true Messiah as attested by the Holy Spirit.

Moreover, inasmuch as it is the particular function of the Holy Spirit to bring conviction upon people and lead their hearts to repentance—making people open and receptive to salvation in Jesus Christ—the one who blasphemes the Holy Spirit effectively *separates* himself from the only One who can lead him or her on the path to salvation in Jesus Christ.[11]

Still, I think it is important to realize that a human being can repent of his or her personal sins (*whatever* they be) and turn to God as long as there is breath still left in his or her lungs. Until the moment of death, every human being has the opportunity to turn to God and receive the free gift of salvation

(Ephesians 2:8,9). And, as the *NIV Bible Commentary* puts it, "any who are troubled about this sin give evidence that they have not committed it."[12] In other words, the very act of being concerned about the possibility of having committed this sin Jesus speaks of is a clear giveaway that one's heart has not been hardened in sin, as the context of Matthew 12 indicates was true of the Jewish leaders who initially committed this sin.

▶ What does Jesus mean when He speaks of "streams of living water" flowing from within us (John 7:38)?

In John 7:38, while at the Feast of Tabernacles, Jesus said, "Whoever believes in me, as the Scripture has said, streams of living water will flow from within him" (see also John 4:14). What did Jesus mean by this?

A short look at Jewish history helps us to understand what is going on in this passage. Each day during the celebration of the Feast of Tabernacles, there would be a procession of priests from the temple to the Pool of Siloam. These priests would draw water that would then be poured out as a libation at the altar. This would be accompanied by a recitation of Isaiah 12:3: "With joy you will draw water from the wells of salvation." This offering served to memorialize God's provision for the thirsty Israelites during the wilderness sojourn. Ultimately, though, *this* water proved unsatisfying, for it was never enough to permanently satisfy one's thirst.[13]

It was on the last day of the Feast of Tabernacles—when many people would have been present—that Jesus said that those who believe *in Him* will experience "streams of living water" flowing from within them. In verse 39 this living water is identified as the Holy Spirit within the believer. Jesus was clearly contrasting a dead ritual of Judaism with living water that becomes the possession of all who believe in Him.

The Holy Spirit in the life of the believer would be a continual and blessed source of joy, comfort, and satisfaction, as well as a sense of the very presence of God. The one who comes to Jesus and places faith in Him will not only have his spiritual thirst satisfied but will receive such an abundant supply that veritable rivers will overflow from within him. What a contrast this is to the dead and oppressive religion that Judaism had become!

SEVEN

THE REALITY
OF HUMAN SIN

▶ Did Jesus teach that there are some people righteous enough
that they do not need a Savior (Mark 2:17)?

In Mark 2:17 Jesus said, "I have not come to call the righteous, but sinners." By the word "righteous" Jesus was not referring to those who were *actually* righteous in God's sight, but
rather to those who were righteous *in their own esteem*, such as
the scribes and Pharisees (see Luke 16:14,15). He came to minister to people who humbly acknowledged that they were sinners
and needed a Savior. Jesus had no ministry to the self-righteous
except to announce their condemnation before God.[1]

What a dichotomy we see here! The sinners who trusted in
and followed Jesus in faith were made righteous as a result of
Christ's work at the cross. By contrast, those who were self-
righteous (like the Pharisees) blindly sank deeper into sin and
were ever more condemned by God.

▶ Did Jesus teach that only those who are sinless (pure of heart)
will ultimately end up in heaven and see God (Matthew 5:8)?

In the well-known section of Scripture known as the
Beatitudes, Jesus said, "Blessed are the pure in heart, for they
will see God" (Matthew 5:8). As a backdrop to understanding
Jesus' statement, let us begin by noting that the term *blessed*
carries the meaning of "happy." The word refers to the inner

happiness and serenity of a true follower of Christ. The self-righteous Pharisees might exude an outer appearance of being blessed, but in truth only those who follow Christ are blessed. The Pharisees were corrupt through and through on the inside.

The word "heart" is often used in Scripture to refer to the center of one's being—including mind, emotions, and will. To be pure in heart, then, would involve being pure in mind and emotions and will—indeed, in *one's whole being*.

It is important to realize that purity is not measured according to the standards of mankind. The Pharisees thought they were pure because when they measured themselves against the external behavior of other people, they convinced themselves they were righteous. But they were using the wrong standard. Purity is measured by the character of God Himself, and it is here that human corruption comes into such clear focus.

Of course, one who has trusted in Christ has been *made* pure, because he or she has had the very righteousness of Christ imputed to him or her. These individuals are accounted as "pure of heart" before God (Romans 4:5; 5:1; Hebrews 10:14). God's declaration of righteousness is given to believers "freely by his grace" (Romans 3:24). The word *grace* literally means "unmerited favor." It is because of God's unmerited favor that believers can freely be declared righteous before God.

This does not mean that God's declaration of righteousness has no objective basis. God did not just subjectively decide to overlook man's sin or wink at his unrighteousness. Jesus died on the cross for us. He died in our stead. He paid for our sins. He ransomed us from death by His own death on the cross (Romans 4:25).

There has thus been a great exchange. As the great Reformer Martin Luther said, "Lord Jesus, you are my righteousness, I am your sin. You have taken upon yourself what is mine and given me what is yours. You have become what You were not so that I might become what I was not."[2]

Allow me to illustrate. If I look through a piece of red glass, everything appears red. If I look through a piece of blue glass, everything appears blue. If I look through a piece of yellow glass, everything appears yellow, and so on. Likewise, when we believe in Jesus as our Savior, God looks at us through the "lens" of Jesus. He sees us in all the white holiness of His Son. Our sins are imputed to the account of Christ, and Christ's righteousness is imputed to our account (Romans 5:18,19). Hence, because of what Christ has done for us, we can be counted as "pure in heart" and will indeed see God, for we will dwell in His very presence for all eternity.

How different it was for the self-righteous Pharisees! These pompous individuals counted themselves as righteous *in themselves*, not knowing how truly vile they really were before God. Because they were not pure in heart by God's standard, and because they rejected the only One who could make them righteous (Jesus Christ), they will *not* dwell in God's presence for all eternity.

▶ What chance of salvation do people have in view of Jesus' teaching that sin is not just external but is an internal reality (Matthew 5:28)?

In Matthew 5:28 Jesus said, "I tell you that anyone who looks at a woman lustfully has already committed adultery with her in his heart." It is clear from verses like this that none of us stands a chance of salvation—*if not for the saving work of Jesus Christ our Lord*. None of us is righteous enough in ourselves to warrant salvation. But because of what Jesus has accomplished at the cross, salvation becomes a reality for those who believe in Him (John 3:16).

Let us look at the backdrop of Matthew 5. In verse 27 Jesus said, "You have heard that it was said, 'Do not commit adultery.'" This statement points to the external act of adultery as sin. But then Jesus went to the root of the problem and said, "But I tell you that anyone who looks at a woman lustfully has already committed adultery with her in his heart" (verse 28).

Over the years the Pharisees had codified the law into 365 prohibitions ("Thou shalt not...") and 248 commandments ("Thou shalt..."). The Pharisees communicated the idea to their followers that so long as one externally followed these commandments, they were considered righteous before God. Christ challenged the Pharisees, however, and stressed that externally keeping these commands was not enough—not *nearly* enough.

In the case of adultery, for example, Jesus said it is not just the external act that brings condemnation to a person. (The Pharisees taught that only a physical sexual union is adultery.) Jesus emphasized that if one lusted after a woman in his or her heart, that too constitutes adultery and therefore brings condemnation. Adultery begins in the heart. The lustful desire is where sin emerges.

Sin, seen as something that begins in the heart, renders us all guilty before our holy God (see Jeremiah 17:9; see also Genesis 6:5; Ecclesiastes 9:3; Matthew 15:19,20). None of us can be righteous enough in ourselves to earn salvation. But because of what Jesus accomplished at the cross, those who believe in Him have their sins washed away, and will live with Him forever (Romans 4:24,25; Hebrews 10:14).

▶ Did Jesus advocate maiming our bodies in order to become saved (Matthew 5:29,30; 18:8,9; Mark 9:43-48)?

In Matthew 5:29 Jesus said, "If your right eye causes you to sin, gouge it out and throw it away. It is better for you to lose one part of your body than for your whole body to be thrown into hell" (see also Matthew 18:8,9 and Mark 9:43-48). I do not think Jesus is actually teaching self-mutilation, for even a blind man can lust, and a man with no hands can yearn to steal. (Remember, *sin begins in the heart*—Jeremiah 17:9.)

Rather, I think Jesus is purposefully using very strong and graphic language to stress how utterly dangerous sin is and how it can lead to eternal condemnation. Many scholars believe that Jesus is using a hyperbole in this verse. A hyperbole is a figure of speech that purposefully exaggerates to make a powerful point.

In the present case, the hyperbole is used to emphasize the need for drastic action in dealing with sin. To keep from offending God by sin, radical changes are often necessary. Disciples of Christ must take immediate and decisive action against anything that would serve to draw him or her away from allegiance to Christ. Christians are to make no provision for temptation; every occasion that may lead to sin is to be eliminated.

▶ What did Jesus write on the ground when the adulterous woman was brought before Him (John 8:3-8)?

Early in the morning, while Jesus was teaching in the temple, the religious leaders brought to Jesus a woman caught in the act of adultery (John 8:1-3). The religious leaders then persisted in asking Jesus whether they should carry out the Law of Moses and stone her to death (verses 4-7a). (They were looking for a way to trap Jesus theologically by asking Him questions. They wanted to discredit Him as a teacher.) Jesus answered that the man who had no sin should cast the first stone at the woman (verses 7b-9). Finding no one to accuse her, Jesus sent the woman away with the admonition not to sin again (verses 10,11).

The interesting point that has drawn so much speculation down through the centuries is that when the Jewish leaders first asked Jesus whether they should stone her to death, He bent down and "started to write on the ground with his finger" (John 8:6). The question is, *what* did He write on the ground? Why did He engage in this action?

It has been assumed by many people that Jesus bent down and wrote *in sand*. All the Hollywood motion pictures about Christ portray the incident this way. But the context indicates in John 8:2 that Jesus was *inside the temple* when this event occurred. The temple, of course, is made of stone. So when Jesus bent down to write on the "ground," He was actually writing on stone with His finger.

Some scholars have found significance in this fact. They note that when the Jewish leaders came before Jesus, they were condemning the woman based on the commandments in the

Law. We read in Exodus 31:18 that the Law was on "the tablets of stone inscribed by the finger of God" (see also Deuteronomy 9:10). Some have thus concluded that Jesus' action was subtly communicating that the Law actually had its origin in Him (as God), and yet His assessment of the matter was that the woman should go her way and sin no more, instead of being stoned to death.

Of course, we cannot be sure that this was Jesus' intended meaning. There are other scholars who have suggested that Jesus bent down to write down the sins of the Jewish accusers. Another suggested possibility is that Jesus wrote down the words of Exodus 23:1: "Do not help a wicked man by being a malicious witness."[3] Still others suggest that perhaps Jesus wrote the Old Testament law that required the conviction of both the man and the woman in such a sin (Leviticus 20:10; Deuteronomy 22:22). The Jewish leaders had brought only the woman before Christ.

All of this is mere conjecture. The fact is that we really have no clue in the text as to what Jesus wrote on the ground.

▶ What did Jesus mean when He said the blind man was born that way so the work of God might be displayed in his life (John 9:1-3)?

In John 9:2 the disciples asked Jesus, "Rabbi, who sinned, this man or his parents, that he was born blind?" Jesus answered, "Neither this man nor his parents sinned...but this happened so that the work of God might be displayed in his life" (verse 3).

As a backdrop to understanding this passage, the Jewish theologians of the time said that physical birth defects might be caused by either *prenatal sin* (that is, sin before birth *but not* before conception) or *parental sin* (see Exodus 20:5; Psalm 109:14; Isaiah 65:6,7). Theologian Norman Geisler notes that when a pregnant woman worshiped in a heathen temple, the Jews viewed the fetus as committing idolatry as well.[4] According to the Bible scholar Alfred Edersheim, in Jewish thought "certain special sins in the parents would result in specific diseases in their offspring, and one is mentioned as causing blindness in the children."[5]

Hence, when the disciples saw this blind man, their assumption was either that his parents had committed some horrendous sin or that perhaps when he was in the womb his mother had visited a pagan temple. But Jesus explained that none of this accounted for why the man was born blind. Indeed, the man was born blind so that the "work of God" might be displayed in his life (verse 3). Providing sight to the blind was one of the miracles predicted of the divine Messiah (see Isaiah 29:18; 35:5; 42:7). This miraculous event pointed to Jesus' true identity.

It is highly revealing that in John 9:5 Christ claimed to be the "light of the world." Now Christ purposed to *demonstrate* that He was the light of the world by bringing literal light to one who had been in darkness from birth. In so doing, this event brought great glory to God. "The healing was not only a sample of Jesus' ability to restore sight to a man who was congenitally blind; but it also represented, figuratively, and for the blind man, experientially the dawning of spiritual light."[6]

▶ Can Jesus' words in John 20:23 be taken to mean that Christians have the power to forgive the sins of others?

In John 20:23 Jesus said, "If you forgive anyone his sins, they are forgiven; if you do not forgive them, they are not forgiven." This verse is translated more literally from the Greek, "Those whose sins you forgive *have already been* forgiven; those whose sins you do not forgive *have not* been forgiven.[7] The verse carries the idea, *not* that we have the power to forgive sins in ourselves, but that we are proclaiming what heaven has *already* proclaimed.

There is no dispute that the disciples to whom Christ was speaking were given the power to *pronounce* the forgiveness and/or retaining of sins. But all this means is that they were given the authority to declare what God does in regard to salvation when a person either accepts or rejects Jesus Christ as Savior. Remember, *only God* can actually forgive sin (Mark 2:7; Luke 7:48,49). The disciples (and, by extension, all believers) only have the prerogative of *announcing to others* that if they trust in Christ, their sins will be forgiven; if they reject Christ as Savior, their sins will not be forgiven. We have the authority to make that declaration because God Himself has already declared it in heaven. As His representatives, we declare to others what He has already declared in heaven.[8]

That this view is correct is clear from the fact that in the book of Acts we never witness the apostles themselves forgiving other people's sins. Rather, we witness them *proclaiming* God's forgiveness of sin in their preaching.[9]

EIGHT

JESUS' REDEMPTIVE SUFFERINGS

ᏮᎥᎥᎥᎥᎥᎥᎻᎥ

▶ What "baptism" did Jesus have to undergo that He so dreaded (Luke 12:50)?

In Luke 12:50 Jesus said, "I have a baptism to undergo, and how distressed I am until it is completed!" Scholars agree that the baptism Jesus faced was His suffering and death on the cross for the sins of humanity. We find a similar reference in Mark 10:38, where Jesus asked the disciples, "Can you drink the cup I drink or be baptized with the baptism I am baptized with?" Again, Jesus was referring to His suffering and death on the cross.

Jesus acknowledged that He would be "distressed" until this baptism was completed (Luke 12:50). He was anxious to get it over with.[1] The shadow of the cross hung over Him. But the moment came soon enough.

When Jesus was upon the cross, having taken the sins of the world upon Himself, we read, "Knowing that *all was now completed*, and so that the Scripture would be fulfilled, Jesus said, 'I am thirsty'" (John 19:28, italics added). Then, after He received the drink, He said, "It is finished," at which time He surrendered His spirit (verse 30).

▶ Was Jesus forsaken by the disciples in the Garden of
   Gethsemane (Matthew 26:36-45)?

According to Matthew 26:36, Jesus and His disciples
entered Gethsemane to pray. Then Jesus took Peter, James, and
John with Him to another part of the Garden and asked them
to watch and pray while He went on alone (verses 37-39). Jesus
said to them, "My soul is overwhelmed with sorrow to the point
of death. Stay here and keep watch with me" (verse 38).

On this occasion Jesus apparently experienced distress such
as He had never experienced before in His short earthly life. In
His hour of greatest need, the Lord wanted those dearest to Him
to be there for Him in prayer.

After Jesus separated from Peter, James, and John, He asked
the Father that if possible the "cup" (His imminent death for
the sins of humanity) be taken away. At the moment Jesus asked
this of the Father, whom He loved, He was no doubt looking in
His mind's eye toward the separation from the Father that He
would experience when the sins of humanity would be poured
out on Him (Matthew 27:46). Though He asked for this cup of
wrath to be removed, however, He willingly submitted His will
to that of the Father (26:39).

Jesus soon returned to Peter, James, and John and found
them asleep. He reprimanded Peter after waking him. Just a
short time before Peter had vowed that he would never forsake
the Lord (see verses 33,35). And yet he fell asleep during the
hour of the Lord's greatest need. Jesus urged the three to continue praying and went off alone again.

The Lord soon returned a second time, only to find the disciples asleep again. This time He did not awaken them. In His
hour of greatest need Jesus ended up "going it alone." The sleep
of the disciples is in obvious contrast to the agony He endured
during this time. Despite their lack of standing with Him in
prayer, Jesus remained utterly faithful to His purpose of facing
the cross and dying for the sins of humankind.

▶ Why did Jesus on the cross ask the Father why He had forsaken Him (Mark 15:34; Matthew 27:46)?

After Jesus had been nailed to the cross, He cried out in a loud voice at the ninth hour (3 P.M. in the afternoon), saying, "*Eloi, Eloi, lama sabachthani?*"—which means, "My God, my God, why have you forsaken me?" (Mark 15:34; see also Matthew 27:46).

The word *forsaken* here carries the idea of "abandonment." Jesus' statement reflects the fact that His greatest suffering upon the cross was not physical but was rather spiritual.[2] He bore the guilt of the entire world on Himself. Christ "became" sin for us (2 Corinthians 5:21). And that moment brought an agony of the soul that was unparalleled. Christ had become the object of the Father's displeasure, for He became the sinner's substitute.[3]

The sense of abandonment that Jesus sensed was *judicial*, not *relational*. Jesus sensed a separation from the Father He had never known before, for in becoming sin the Father had to turn judicially from His beloved Son (Romans 3:25,26). As John F. Walvoord and Roy B. Zuck put it, "Bearing the curse of sin and God's judgment on sin (cf. Deuteronomy 21:22-23; 2 Corinthians 5:21; Galatians 3:13), He experienced the unfathomable horror of separation from God, who cannot look on sin (cf. Habakkuk 1:13).[4] Jesus the Savior experienced the utter bitterness of the desolation of the cross.[5]

Of course, all of this was part of the divine plan of salvation, to which Jesus voluntarily submitted. Such was the love of Christ for fallen humanity. He died and was forsaken by God so that His people might claim God as *their* God and never be forsaken by Him (Hebrews 13:5).[6] What a wondrous Savior we have!

Scholars have noted that the words Christ cried out from the cross are from Psalm 22—a psalm that begins with despair but ends in its closing verses with renewed trust in God.[7] It has been suggested that in quoting this psalm, Jesus was pointing to the reality that even though He now sensed judicial separation from the Father, He knew it was temporary and that His relationship with the Father would soon be restored.[8]

▶ Why did Jesus say "It is finished" at the moment of His death (John 19:30)?

Just as Jesus was dying on the cross, He uttered, "It is finished." He then bowed His head and gave up His spirit (John 19:30).

This proclamation from the Savior's lips is fraught with meaning. Surely the Lord was doing more than announcing the termination of His physical life. That fact was self-evident. What was not known by those who were carrying out the brutal business at Calvary was that somehow, despite the sin they were committing, God through Christ had completed the final sacrifice for sin. "The work long contemplated, long promised, long expected by prophets and saints, *is done*. The toils in the ministry, the persecutions and mockeries, and the pangs of the garden and the cross, *are ended*, and man is redeemed."[9]

It is highly significant that the phrase "It is finished" can also be translated "paid in full." The backdrop to this is that in ancient days, whenever someone was found guilty of a crime, the offender was put in jail and a "certificate of debt" was posted on the jail door (Colossians 2:14). This certificate listed all the crimes the offender was found guilty of. Upon release, after serving the prescribed time in jail, the offender was given the certificate of debt, and on it was stamped "Paid in Full." Christ took the certificate of debt of all our lives (including all our sins) and nailed it on the cross. And Jesus said "paid in full" upon the cross (John 19:30).

Hence Jesus' words do not constitute a moan of defeat nor a sigh of patient resignation. Rather, His words were a triumphant recognition that He had now fully accomplished what He came into the world to do. The work of redemption was completed at the cross. Nothing further needed to be done. He had paid in full the price of our redemption (2 Corinthians 5:21).

▶ When Jesus said to the Father, "Into your hands I commit my spirit" (Luke 23:46), was He talking about His human spirit?

In Luke 23:46 we read, "Jesus called out with a loud voice, 'Father, into your hands I commit my spirit.' When he had said this, he breathed his last."

The Greek word translated "spirit" in this verse is *pneuma*. According to biblical language experts, this word can have a wide range of meanings, including "wind," "breath," "life-spirit," "soul," "the spirit as a part of the human personality," "the spirit of God," and "the Holy Spirit."[10]

Many of the above meanings are disqualified by the context as possible contenders for Luke 23:46. It does not make any sense for Jesus to commend His "wind" or His "breath" to the Father. Nor does it fit the context for Jesus to commit "the spirit of God" or " the Holy Spirit" to the Father. In fact, the only meanings of *pneuma* that make any sense in context are "soul" and "spirit as a part of the human personality." It seems clear from a plain reading of the passage that Jesus committed His human soul or spirit to the Father. And since Christ was not raised from the dead until three days after His crucifixion, we must conclude that His human soul or spirit went directly to the Father's presence in heaven while His body lay in the tomb.[11]

▶ How are we to interpret Jesus' words about the bread and wine being His body and blood (Mark 14:22-24; see also I Corinthians 11:24,25)?

According to Mark 14:22-24, "While [the disciples] were eating, Jesus took bread, gave thanks and broke it, and gave it to his disciples, saying, 'Take it; this is my body.' Then he took the cup, gave thanks and offered it to them, and they all drank from it. 'This is my blood of the covenant, which is poured out for many,' he said to them."

There are four primary views as to what Jesus meant by this statement.

1. *The Roman Catholic view is called transubstantiation.*
   This view says that the elements (bread and wine)
   actually change into the body of Jesus Christ at the
   prayer of the priest. It is said to impart grace to the
   recipient. Jesus is viewed as literally present. There is
   no change in the appearance of the elements, but the
   elements nevertheless change.

   There are a number of serious problems with this
   view. First, note that Jesus was present with the disciples when He said that the bread and wine were His
   body and blood (Luke 22:17-19). Obviously He
   intended that His words be taken figuratively. Jesus
   often spoke in metaphors and figures of speech. He
   called Himself the *gate* (John 10:9) and the *true vine*
   (John 15:1). These are not literal. In the same way,
   when Jesus said the *bread* was His body, He was
   speaking metaphorically.

   Beyond this, one must keep in mind the scriptural
   teaching that drinking blood is forbidden (Genesis
   9:4; Leviticus 3:17; Acts 15:29). However the verse is
   understood, it should not be taken to mean that the
   elements actually become the flesh and blood of the
   Lord.

2. *The Lutheran view is called consubstantiation.* This view
   says that Christ is present *in*, *with*, and *under* the bread
   and wine. There is a real presence of Christ but no
   change in the elements. The mere partaking of the
   elements after the prayer of consecration is said to
   spiritually communicate Christ to the participant
   along with the elements.

3. *The reformed view* is that Christ is spiritually present at
   the Lord's Supper and it is a means of grace. There is
   said to be a dynamic presence of Jesus in the elements
   made effective in the believer as he partakes. The par-

taking of His presence is not a physical eating and drinking, but is said to be an inner communion with His person.

4. *The memorial view* (my view) is that there is no change in the elements, and that the ordinance is not intended to be a means of communicating grace to the participant. (The verse says *nothing* about communicating grace.) The bread and wine are symbols and reminders of Jesus in His death and resurrection (1 Corinthians 11:24,25). It also reminds us of the basic facts of the gospel (11:26), our anticipation of the second coming (11:26), and our oneness as the body of Christ (10:17).

▶ Was Jesus' blood sacrifice only for "many" people and not "all"?

In Matthew 26:28 Jesus said, "This is my blood of the covenant, which is poured out for *many* for the forgiveness of sins" (italics added). Some interpreters have concluded from this wording that Jesus did not die on the cross for all people, but only for the elect (those whom God has chosen for salvation). This is a rather complicated and extremely controversial question. To do the issue justice requires an extended answer. It relates to the debate of whether "limited atonement" or "unlimited atonement" is the correct theological teaching of Scripture. Theologians have been debating this issue for many centuries.

Limited atonement (a doctrine I personally disagree with) is the view that Christ's atoning death was *only* for the elect. Another way to say this is that Christ made no atoning provision for those who are not of the elect. Following are some of the key verses which advocates of limited atonement cite in favor of their position. I have italicized the relevant portions of each verse:

- Matthew 1:21: "She will give birth to a son, and you are to give him the name Jesus, because he will save *his people* from their sins."

- Matthew 20:28: "The Son of Man did not come to be served, but to serve, and to give his life as a ransom *for many*."
- Matthew 26:28: "This is my blood of the covenant, which is poured out *for many* for the forgiveness of sins."
- John 10:15: "I lay down my life for *the sheep*."
- Acts 20:28: "Keep watch over yourselves and all the flock of which the Holy Spirit has made you overseers. Be shepherds of the *church of God*, which he bought with his own blood."
- Ephesians 5:25: "Husbands, love your wives, just as Christ loved *the church* and gave himself up for her."
- Hebrews 9:28: "So Christ was sacrificed once to take away the sins of *many people*; and he will appear a second time, not to bear sin, but to bring salvation *to those* who are waiting for him."
- John 15:13: "Greater love has no one than this, that he lay down his life for his *friends*."

Upon first reading, verses such as these seem to support the idea that Christ died on the cross not for all people but only for a particular group of people—the "many," the "church of God," His "sheep," His "friends." Many Reformed theologians believe that the doctrine of *unlimited* atonement (the doctrine that Christ died for the sins of *all* people) is utterly disproved by such verses.

Proponents of limited atonement set forth a number of arguments that they believe conclusively prove the truth of the doctrine. Following are eight of the more notable arguments:

1. The Bible says Christ died for a specific group of people. Those for whom He suffered and died are variously called His "sheep" (John 10:11,15), His "church" (Acts 20:28; Ephesians 5:25-27), His "people" (Matthew 1:21), and the "elect" (Romans 8:32-35).

2. Since the elect were chosen before the foundation of the world (Ephesians 1), Christ could not honestly be said to have died *for all* human beings. It would have been a waste and a lack of foresight on the part of God to have Christ die for those whom He had not chosen to salvation.

3. Some advocates of limited atonement say Christ is defeated if He died for all people but not all people are saved.

4. Some advocates of limited atonement say that if Christ died for all people, then God would be unfair in sending people to hell for their own sins. It is argued that no law court allows payment to be exacted twice for the same crime, and God will not do that either. Christ paid for the sins of the elect; the lost pay for *their own* sins.

5. Since Christ did not pray for everyone in His high-priestly prayer in John 17, but only prayed for *His own*, Christ must not have died for everyone. It is argued that since the intercession is limited in extent, the atonement must be too.

6. Some advocates of limited atonement have charged that unlimited atonement tends toward universalism (the idea that all will be saved in the end). Hence, unlimited atonement cannot be the correct view.

7. In the Middle Ages, such scholars as Prosper of Aquitaine, Thomas Bradwardine, and John Staupitz taught limited atonement. It is claimed that even though John Calvin did not explicitly teach the doctrine, it seems implicit in some of his writings. Calvin's successors then made limited atonement explicit and included it in Reformed confessions of faith such as the Canons of Dort and the Westminster Confession of Faith.

8. Though terms such as "all," "world," and "whosoever" are used in Scripture in reference to those for whom Christ died (for example, John 3:16), these words are

to be understood in terms of the elect. In other words, "all" refers to "all *the elect*" or "all *classes of men*" (Jew and Gentile). Similarly, the word "world" is said to refer to the "world *of the elect*" or to people without distinction (Jews and Gentiles). The word "whosoever" is interpreted to mean "whosoever of the elect."

Based on arguments such as these, Reformed scholars believe that Christ died only for the elect. However, I believe the above logic is flawed. I believe the doctrine of *unlimited* atonement is the scriptural view, and there are numerous verses that support it. Following is a sampling, with relevant portions italicized:

- In Luke 19:10 we read, "For the Son of Man came to seek and to save *what was lost*." The "lost" in this verse refers to the collective whole of lost humanity, not just to the lost elect. This is the most natural understanding of this verse.
- In John 1:29 we read, "The next day John saw Jesus coming toward him and said, 'Look, the Lamb of God, who takes away the sin *of the world*.'" What is the "world" here? The world represents humanity in its fallen state, alienated from its Maker. Reformer John Calvin said of this verse, "When he says the sin *of the world*, he extends this favor indiscriminately to the whole human race."[12] Though Calvin is often cited in favor of limited atonement, here is a clear statement in which unlimited atonement is in view.
- In John 3:16 we read, "For God so loved *the world* that he gave his one and only Son, that *whoever* believes in him shall not perish but have eternal life." It is critical to observe that John 3:16 cannot be divorced from the context that is set in verses 14 and 15, in which Christ alludes to Numbers 21. In this passage Moses is seen setting up the brazen serpent in the camp of Israel, so that if "any man" looked to it, he experi-

enced physical deliverance. In verse 15 Christ applied the story spiritually when He said that "whosoever" believes on the uplifted Son of Man shall experience spiritual deliverance.

- In John 4:42 we read, "They said to the woman, 'We no longer believe just because of what you said; now we have heard for ourselves, and we know that this man really is the Savior *of the world*.'" It is quite certain that when the Samaritans called Jesus "the Savior of the world," they were not thinking of the world of the elect.

- First Timothy 4:10 says, "We have put our hope in the living God, who is the Savior *of all men*, and especially of those who believe." There is a clear distinction in this verse between "all men" and "those who believe." Apparently the Savior has done something for *all* human beings, though it is less in degree than what He has done for those who believe.[13] In other words, Christ has made a provision of salvation for all men, though it only becomes effective for those who exercise faith in Christ.

- Hebrews 2:9 says, "But we see Jesus, who was made a little lower than the angels, now crowned with glory and honor because he suffered death, so that by the grace of God he might taste death *for everyone*." The Greek word "everyone" (*pantos*) is better translated "each." Why use the word *pantos* (each) rather than *panton* (all)? Because the singular brings out more emphatically the applicability of Christ's death to each individual human being. Christ tasted death for every single person.

- Romans 5:6 says, "At just the right time, when we were still powerless, Christ died *for the ungodly*." It does not make much sense to read this as saying that Christ died for the ungodly among the elect. Rather the verse, read plainly, indicates that Christ died for *all* the ungodly of the earth.

- Romans 5:18 tells us, "Consequently, just as the result of one trespass was condemnation *for all men*, so also the result of one act of righteousness was justification that brings life *for all men*." Commenting on this verse, John Calvin said, "Though Christ suffered for the sins of the whole world, and is offered through God's benignity indiscriminately to all, yet all do not receive Him."[14] This sounds very much like Calvin was teaching unlimited atonement in this statement.

- First John 2:2 says, "He is the atoning sacrifice for our sins, and not only for ours but also for the sins *of the whole world*." A natural reading of this verse, without imposing theological presuppositions on it, supports unlimited atonement. In fact, a plain reading of this verse would seem to deal a knockout punch to the limited atonement position. It simply would not make sense to interpret this verse as saying, "He is the atoning sacrifice for our [*the elect*] sins, and not only for ours [*the elect*] but also for the sins of the whole world [*of the elect*]."

- Isaiah 53:6 says, "*We all*, like sheep, have gone astray, *each of us* has turned to his own way; and the LORD has laid on him the iniquity *of us all*." This verse does not make sense unless it is read to say that the same "all" that went astray is the "all" for whom the Lord died.

- In 2 Peter 2:1, we are told that Christ even paid the price of redemption for false teachers who deny Him: "But there were also false prophets among the people, just as there will be false teachers among you. They will secretly introduce destructive heresies, even denying the sovereign Lord who bought them— bringing swift destruction on themselves." Second Peter 2:1 seems to point out quite clearly that people for whom Christ died may be lost; there is a distinction between those for whom Christ died and those who are finally saved.

- John 3:17 says, "For God did not send his Son into *the world* to condemn *the world*, but to save *the world* through him." Commenting on this verse, John Calvin said that "God is unwilling that we should be overwhelmed with everlasting destruction, because He has appointed His Son to be the salvation *of the world*."[15] Calvin also stated, "The word *world* is again repeated, that no man may think himself wholly excluded, if he only keeps the road of faith."[16] Clearly, God has made the *provision* of salvation available to all human beings.

In keeping with the above verses, there are also many verses which indicate that the gospel is to be universally proclaimed to *all* human beings. Such a universal proclamation would make sense only if the doctrine of unlimited atonement were true. Consider the following:

- Matthew 24:14 says, "This gospel of the kingdom will be preached *in the whole world* as a testimony *to all nations*, and then the end will come."
- Matthew 28:19 says, "Therefore go and make disciples *of all nations*, baptizing them in the name of the Father and of the Son and of the Holy Spirit."
- In Acts 1:8 Jesus said, "But you will receive power when the Holy Spirit comes on you; and you will be my witnesses in Jerusalem, and in all Judea and Samaria, and *to the ends of the earth*."

In view of such passages it is legitimate to ask, "If Christ died only for the elect, how can an offer of salvation be made to all persons without some sort of insincerity, artificiality, or dishonesty being involved in the process?" Is it not improper to offer salvation to everyone if in fact Christ did not die to save everyone? The fact is that those who hold to limited atonement cannot say to any sinner with true conviction, "Christ died *for you*."

How do we put the "limited" and "unlimited" verses together so that, taken as a whole, all the verses are interpreted in a harmonious way without contradicting each other? I believe that seemingly restrictive references can be logically fit into an unlimited scenario much more easily than universal references made to fit into a limited atonement scenario.

The two sets of passages—one seemingly in support of limited atonement, the other in support of unlimited atonement—are not irreconcilable. While it is true that the benefits of Christ's death are referred to as belonging to God's "sheep," His "people," the "many" (Matthew 26:28), and the like, it would have to be shown that Christ died *only* for them in order for limited atonement to be true. No one denies that Christ died for God's "sheep" and His "people." It is only denied that Christ died *exclusively* for them.[17] Certainly if Christ died for the whole of humanity, there is no logical problem in saying that He died for a specific *part* of the whole.

NINE

THE SALVATION
OF HUMANKIND

൭ᗝ᠑

▶ Did Jesus teach that one must become perfect to be saved
(Matthew 5:48)?

In Matthew 5:48 Jesus said, "Be perfect, therefore, as your
heavenly Father is perfect." In this verse Jesus is not communicating the idea that human beings can actually attain sinless
perfection in this life. Such an idea is foreign not only to the
immediate context of Matthew's Gospel but to the broader context of all of Scripture.

To begin, 1 John 1:8 tells us, "If we claim to be without sin,
we deceive ourselves and the truth is not in us." Since this
epistle was written to Christians (1 John 2:12-14,19; 3:1; 5:13),
it seems clear that Christians in mortal life should never make
the claim to have attained perfection.

Further, the great saints of the Bible seemed to all recognize
their own intrinsic sinfulness (Isaiah 6:5; Daniel 9:4-19;
Ephesians 3:8). If anyone could have attained perfection, certainly Isaiah, Daniel, and the apostle Paul would have been
contenders. But none of them succeeded. Why? Because they
still had the sin nature in them that erupted in their lives from
time to time (Ephesians 2:3).

Jesus taught that people without exception are utterly
sinful. Indeed, He taught that human beings have a grave sin
problem that is altogether beyond their means to solve. He

taught that human beings are evil (Matthew 12:34) and are capable of great wickedness (Mark 7:20-23). Moreover, He said human beings are utterly lost (Luke 19:10), are sinners (Luke 15:10), are in need of repentance before a holy God (Mark 1:15), and need to be born again (John 3:3,5,7).

Jesus often spoke of sin in metaphors that illustrate the havoc sin can wreak in one's life. He described sin as blindness (Matthew 23:16-26), sickness (Matthew 9:12), being enslaved in bondage (John 8:34), and living in darkness (John 8:12; 12:35-46). Moreover, He taught that this is a universal condition and that all people are guilty before God (Luke 7:37-48).

Jesus also taught that both inner thoughts and external acts render a person guilty (Matthew 5:28). He taught that from within the human heart come evil thoughts, sexual immorality, theft, murder, adultery, greed, malice, deceit, lewdness, envy, slander, arrogance, and folly (Mark 7:21,22). Moreover, He affirmed that God is fully aware of every person's sins, both external acts and inner thoughts; nothing escapes His notice (Matthew 22:18; Luke 6:8; John 4:17-19).

In view of humanity's dire sin problem as defined by Scripture, Matthew 5:48 cannot be interpreted to mean that human beings can actually attain sinless perfection in this life. How then can we make sense of this verse?

Contextually, this verse is found in a section of Scripture dealing not with the issue of sin but with the *law of love*. The Jewish leaders of Jesus' day had taught that we should love those who are near and dear to us (Leviticus 19:18), but *hate* those who are enemies. Jesus refuted this idea, instructing us to love even our enemies. After all, Jesus said, God's love extends to all people (Matthew 5:45). And since God is our righteous standard, we should seek to be as He is in this regard. We are to be "perfect" (or complete) *in loving* as He is perfect. As we walk in dependence upon the Holy Spirit, God's kind of love is progressively reproduced in our lives (see Galatians 5:22,23).

▶ Was Jesus teaching salvation by works to the rich young ruler
    (Luke 18:18-23; Matthew 19:16-24; Mark 10:17-25)?

In Luke 18:18 a rich young ruler asked Jesus how to inherit eternal life. Jesus responded by telling him he must follow the commandments of God (verses 19,20). The ruler responded by saying he had kept the commandments (verse 21). So Jesus informed him he must do one thing more—sell all that he had and give it all to the poor (verse 22). At hearing this the man became very sad, for he was a man of great wealth.

At first glance it might seem that Jesus was teaching salvation by works to the rich young ruler. But this was not the case. Scripture is clear in stating that the Law does not save (Romans 3:28), but it does condemn (3:19). Jesus was demonstrating to the young man that he stood condemned before the Law. The fact that he was unwilling to give his money to the poor was a sure indication that he had not even kept the first great commandment: to love God more than anything else (cf. Matthew 22:36,37).[1]

Furthermore, as theologian Norman Geisler points out, the rich young ruler's question was confused.[2] A person cannot "do" anything to receive an inheritance of any kind, including eternal life. An "inheritance" by its very nature is a gift. Since eternal life is presented throughout Scripture as a gift (Romans 6:23; John 3:36; 5:24; 20:31; 1 John 5:13), one cannot "do" anything to earn it. The apostle Paul said, "Now when a man works, his wages are not credited to him as a gift, but as an obligation. However, to the man who does not work but trusts God who justifies the wicked, his faith is credited as righteousness" (Romans 4:4,5).

The only "work" by which a person can be saved is "faith." Recall that when Jesus was asked, "What can we do to accomplish the works of God?" Jesus answered, "The work of God is this: to *believe* in the one he has sent" (John 6:29, italics added).

▶ Was Jesus advocating salvation by works in John 5:28,29?

Jesus said in John 5:28,29 that the time is coming when people in their graves will hear His voice "and come out—those who have done good will rise to live, and those who have done evil will rise to be condemned." At first reading these verses may seem to indicate salvation by works. But this is not the case.

Elsewhere in John's Gospel, Jesus states clearly that salvation is based solely on trusting in Him as Savior. For example, in John 3:16-18 (NASB) Jesus affirmed: "For God so loved the world that He gave His only begotten Son, that whoever *believes in Him* should not perish but have eternal life. For God did not send His Son into the world to judge the world, but that the world should be saved through Him. He who *believes in Him* is not judged; he who does not *believe* is judged already, because he has not *believed in the name* of the only begotten Son of God" (italics added).

We must conclude that the good works of those who experience the "resurrection of life" (Christians) are those that occur *after* one trusts in Christ for salvation. Salvation is by *grace* and is laid hold of solely by *faith* (Ephesians 2:8,9). But authentic faith expresses itself in good works (verse 10). Indeed, the lives that people live form the test of the faith they profess.[3] Those who are saved give evidence of that salvation in the good works they perform, and it is *these* individuals who will be resurrected unto life by Jesus Christ. By the contrast, unbelievers give evidence of their lack of faith by their unceasing evil deeds, and these individuals will experience the resurrection of condemnation (see Revelation 20:12).

▶ Does Jesus teach that we must successfully and consistently obey God's will to be saved (Matthew 7:21-23)?

In Matthew 7:21-23 Jesus said, "Not everyone who says to me, 'Lord, Lord,' will enter the kingdom of heaven, but only he who does the will of my Father who is in heaven. Many will say to me on that day, 'Lord, Lord, did we not prophesy in your name, and in your name drive out demons and perform many miracles?' Then I will tell them plainly, 'I never knew you. Away from me, you evildoers!'"

In context Jesus was dealing with the Pharisees, whom He categorized as false prophets (Matthew 7:15). While these individuals claimed to be God's representatives with God's message, in fact they were not at all what they appeared to be. Instead, they were ferocious wolves who had come to destroy God's flock (see Matthew 23:4-36). They were full of hypocrisy and unrighteousness. Despite all their righteous claims, Christ in Matthew 7:21-23 indicated that mere lip service is not enough.

The lesson we learn here is that many people may make an outward profession of faith and even give an external appearance of being devout. But many individuals never come into a real relationship with Jesus Christ. They make an empty profession of faith. On the day of judgment Jesus will say to them, "I never knew you." Without a genuine relationship with Jesus, it does not matter how many good things one does. Salvation can never be earned by such activities.

Those who will be saved are those who do the will of the Father. And Jesus spoke of the will of the Father as "work" in John 6:29: "The work of God is this: *to believe in the one he has sent*" (italics added). This is most fundamentally the will of God for every person. This is the beginning point for a relationship with God. If that is missing, all else is meaningless in regard to the issue of salvation.

▶ In what way are we to take up our cross and follow Jesus (Mark 8:34)?

In Mark 8:34 Jesus called a crowd alongside His disciples and said to them, "If anyone would come after me, he must deny himself and take up his cross and follow me" (see also Luke 14:27). Jesus' statement would certainly have made sense to His first-century hearers, since the cross as a tool of execution was quite common. When a man had been condemned to die, and the time of execution had arrived, the man would be required by the Roman executioners to carry his own cross to the place of execution.[4] This is much as it was with Jesus when the time of His execution came: "Carrying his cross, he went out to the place of the Skull (which in Aramaic is called Golgotha)" (John 19:17).

As we "take up" our "cross" and follow Jesus, we are willingly submitting ourselves to suffering and even dying for His sake. Jesus is quite obviously calling for a total commitment. The idea is this: "If you really want to follow me, do not do so in word only, but put your life on the line and follow me on the path of the cross—a path that will involve sacrifice, suffering, and possibly even death."

Keep in mind that there is a distinction between becoming saved and following Christ as a disciple. Scripture is clear in stating that we become saved by placing faith in Jesus Christ. Close to 200 times in the New Testament, salvation is said to be by faith alone—with no works in sight. Here are some representative verses:

- In John 5:24 Jesus said, "I tell you the truth, whoever hears my word and believes him who sent me has eternal life and will not be condemned; he has crossed over from death to life."
- In John 11:25 Jesus said, "I am the resurrection and the life. He who believes in me will live, even though he dies."
- In John 12:46 Jesus said, "I have come into the world as a light, so that no one who believes in me should stay in darkness."

Clearly, salvation is by faith in Christ!

A life of discipleship, however, goes beyond the initial conversion experience and calls for a life sacrifice and commitment. The disciple is to "deny" himself. He must turn his back on selfish interests. He is no longer to live his life with *self* on the throne of his heart, but Christ must reign supreme. As Bible scholar William Lane puts it:

Jesus stipulated that those who wish to follow him must be prepared to shift the center of gravity in their lives from a concern for self to reckless abandon to the will of God. The central thought in self-denial is a disowning of any claim that may be urged by the self, a sustained willingness to say "No" to oneself in order to be able to say "Yes" to God. This involves a radical denunciation of all self-idolatry and of every attempt to establish one's own life in accordance with the dictates of the self.[5]

As noted above, the disciple is also to "take up his cross" and follow Jesus. Some scholars have noted that the very act of having to bear one's cross en route to the place of execution showed one's submission to the authority against which the person had *previously rebelled*. There is a lesson we learn here. Formerly we ourselves were of the world, and we certainly were not in submission to Jesus Christ (Ephesians 2:1-3). But the act of taking up our crosses and following Him involves openly showing our submission to the One against whom we had formerly rebelled.[6]

It is also interesting to note that, among the ancients, when a person had been sentenced to die and was carrying his cross to the place of execution, he would often pass by crowds of people who would mock and scorn him.[7] There is a parallel in the life of the Christian. As we take up our crosses to follow Jesus, there very well may be times when we are scorned for following Him (see Matthew 5:11; John 15:18-21).

There is one further observation that bears mentioning. When Jesus instructed those listening to take up their crosses and "follow" Him, the word *follow* in the Greek is what is called a "present imperative." This is highly significant. The present tense indicates continuous action. We are to *perpetually* and *unceasingly* follow Jesus, day in and day out. (It is not just a Sunday thing.) The imperative indicates that it is a command. It is not a mere option for the Christian. We are commanded to follow Jesus on a daily basis.

▶ Do we have to actually lose our lives to be saved (Matthew 16:24-26)?

Immediately after Jesus instructed His followers to take up their crosses and follow Him, He said, "Whoever wants to save his life will lose it, but whoever loses his life for me will find it. What good will it be for a man if he gains the whole world, yet forfeits his soul? Or what can a man give in exchange for his soul?" (Matthew 16:25,26; see also Mark 8:35).

The point Jesus was making in this verse is that following Him as a disciple involves a cost. There will be times of suffering and sacrifice in the life of a disciple who follows Christ. But in "losing" one's life—in saying no to "self," in denying a life of self-centeredness, in placing Christ on the throne of one's heart—one will in fact "find" life. Truly there is no one more spiritually alive and vibrant in his relationship to God than one who has completely "sold out" to Jesus Christ.

Again, we must draw a distinction between becoming saved and following Christ as a disciple. As noted earlier in this chapter, Scripture states clearly that we become saved solely by placing our faith in Jesus Christ (John 3:16; 5:24; 11:25; 12:46). But the life of discipleship goes beyond the initial conversion experience and calls for a continuous life of sacrifice and commitment. The disciple is to "deny" himself and turn his back on selfish interests. Christ must reign supreme.

▶ Did Jesus teach it is impossible for a rich person to be saved (Luke 6:24)?

In Luke 6:24 Jesus commented, "Woe to you who are rich, for you have already received your comfort." The backdrop to this verse is that the disciples had given up everything to follow Jesus. In contrast to these disciples were those people who were loaded with money and wealth, and hence did not sense the gravity of their true situation (that is, they were blind to their need of redemption in view of the sin problem). Their basic mindset was that personal wealth could solve most problems. Wealth predisposed them to think they had need of nothing.

They relied on riches, not on God.[8] As one theologian put it, "Those who enjoy the 'good life' may be more easily tempted to neglect the godly life."[9] For rich people, the world itself—with all its wealth and extravaganzas—is often their personal "heaven."

It is these blinded, self-exalted individuals that Jesus spoke of in Luke 6:24. It is these individuals—who have not trusted in Him but instead trust in their riches and the comfort that wealth brings—who will one day experience a reversal and find themselves engulfed in eternal punishment. They will realize too late that their comfort "in the now" caused them to be shortsighted about their eternal future.

While extreme wealth can blind one to the need for God, there are exceptions to this in the Bible, involving men like Abraham and Job. These individuals were materially rich but were nevertheless committed to God. So being rich does not in itself bar one from entrance to heaven. Jesus' warning was against the *love* of riches and making money a god.

▶ What does Jesus mean when He says we must be "born of water and the Spirit" (John 3:5)?

Jesus said we must be "born of water and the Spirit" (John 3:5). The context that helps us understand what He meant is set for us in verse 3, where He said, "No one can see the kingdom of God unless he is born again." Being "born again"—literally, "born from above"—refers to the spiritual birth of one who believes in Christ (Titus 3:5). Being "born again" places one into God's eternal family (1 Peter 1:23), and gives the believer a new capacity and desire to please the Father (2 Corinthians 5:17).

This is in keeping with what we read in John 3:6: "That which is born of the flesh is flesh, and that which is born of the Spirit is spirit" (NASB). The "flesh" includes not only what is *natural* but what is *sinful* in man—that is, man as he is born into this fallen world and lives his life apart from God's grace. Flesh can only reproduce itself as flesh, and this cannot pass muster with God (Romans 8:8). The law of reproduction is "after its kind" (see Genesis 1:11). Likewise, the "Spirit" produces spirit—a life born, nurtured, and matured by the Spirit of God.[10] This experience of fallen man receiving eternal life from God is open to all who believe in Christ.

In Nicodemus' case, we find a Pharisee who would have been trusting in his physical descent from Abraham for entrance into the Messiah's kingdom. The Jews believed that because they were physically related to Abraham, they were in a specially privileged position before God. Christ, however, denied such a possibility. As Bible scholar J. Dwight Pentecost points out, "Parents can transmit to their children only the nature which they themselves possess. Since each parent's nature, because of Adam's sin, is sinful, each parent transmits a sinful nature to the child. What is sinful cannot enter the kingdom of God (verse 5)."[11] The only way one can enter God's kingdom is to experience a spiritual rebirth, and this is precisely what Jesus was emphasizing to Nicodemus.

All this helps us to understand what Jesus meant by the phrase "born of water." Contextually, Jesus first spoke about being "born of water and the Spirit" in John 3:5, and then explained what He meant by this in verse 6. That is to say, "born of water" in verse 5 seems to be parallel to "born of the flesh" in verse 6, just as "born of . . . the Spirit" in verse 5 is parallel to "born of the Spirit" in verse 6. Jesus' message, then, is that just as one has had a fleshly birth (a physical birth, with the accompanying sin nature), so one must also have a spiritual birth to enter the kingdom of God. One must be born *from above* to become a part of God's forever family.

▶ Does Jesus in Mark 16:16 teach that a person must be baptized to be saved?

In Mark 16:16 Jesus said, "Whoever believes and is baptized will be saved, but whoever does not believe will be condemned." Admittedly, this is a difficult passage. However, a basic principle of Bible interpretation is that difficult passages are to be interpreted in the light of clear passages.

Notice the latter part of the verse: "Whoever believes and is baptized will be saved, but *whoever does not believe will be condemned*" (Mark 16:16). It is *unbelief*, according to Jesus, that brings damnation, not a lack of being baptized. When one rejects the gospel, refusing to believe it, that person is damned.

Now let us consider the broader context of Scripture.

1. When Jesus was crucified between two thieves, one of them placed his faith in Christ right there on the cross. And Jesus immediately said to him, "I tell you the truth, today you will be with me in paradise" (Luke 23:43). The thief became saved without being baptized.

2. In Acts 10 Cornelius exercised faith in Christ and became saved at the moment of faith. He was clearly saved *prior* to being baptized in water. After all, the moment Cornelius believed in Christ, the gift of the Holy Spirit was poured out on him (Acts 10:45).

3. In 1 Corinthians 1:17 the apostle Paul said, "For Christ did not send me to baptize, but to preach the gospel." Here a distinction is made between the gospel and being baptized. We are told elsewhere that it is the gospel that brings salvation (1 Corinthians 15:2). And baptism is not a part of that gospel.

All of this is not to say that baptism is unimportant. Baptism should be the first act of obedience to God following a person's conversion to Christ. But even though we should obey God and get baptized, we must not forget that our *faith in Christ* is what saves us (Acts 16:31; John 3:16), not baptism. Baptism is basically a public profession of faith. It says to the whole world, "I am a believer in Christ and have identified my life with Him."

▶ What did Jesus mean when He said, "Many are invited, but few are chosen" (Matthew 22:14)?

In Matthew 22:1-14 Jesus is seen teaching His followers the parable of the feast. He taught that the kingdom of heaven can be compared to a king who was giving a wedding feast for his son (verses 1,2). When the king invited the guests, they either were indifferent to the request or they mistreated and killed the slave who was delivering the invitation (verses 3-6). The king subsequently punished the murderers (verse 7).

Following this, the king commanded that his slaves go out and find anyone who was willing to come to the feast (Matthew 22:8-10). Of course, those who chose to come to the feast were expected to prepare properly for it, including putting on wedding clothes that would be supplied by the king's servants. When the king himself arrived at the feast, he found one man who was not properly attired in wedding clothes and commanded him to be cast into punishment (verses 11-13). It is at this point that Jesus said, "Many are invited, but few are chosen" (verse 14).

What does this parable teach us about the kingdom of heaven? It teaches that the King (Jesus) and His kingdom had been offered to the nation of Israel, but the Jews were virtually indifferent to the offer. The Jews even murdered those who delivered the message (the prophets).

The invitation was then broadened to include "any who would come"—including the Gentiles. It may be that the wedding garments that are offered to all who attend "the feast" metaphorically refer to the righteousness of Christ, which adorns all who trust in Him for salvation (see Romans 13:14). Individual responsibility is seen in the parable because people who come to the feast are responsible to *put on* the garments (that is, trust in Christ for salvation). All who reject Christ (refusing to put on the "garment" of the righteousness of Christ) are cast out into punishment. The invitation to salvation is sent out to many people, Jews and Gentiles, but comparatively few accept the invitation.

Theologians point out that the phrase "many are invited, but few are chosen" (Matthew 22:14) indicates that while God issues a general call to sinners inviting them to receive His salvation, there is also a specific call (or *election*) of some. At the same time, it is clear from the parable that human beings are responsible for their decision to receive or reject Christ, whether it is the result of indifference (verse 5), rebellion (verse 6), or self-righteousness (verse 12).[12]

▶ What did Jesus mean when He said that no one can come to Him unless the Father "draws him" (John 6:44)?

In John 6:44 Jesus said, "No one can come to me unless the Father who sent me draws him, and I will raise him up at the last day." In this verse Jesus seems to be teaching that human beings do not have the capacity to come to Christ strictly on their own initiative. The Father Himself sovereignly "draws" them to Jesus.

Some theologians have suggested that perhaps the term *draw* carries the idea of "entice," or "woo," or "seek to persuade." Seen in this light, the Father merely tries to *persuade* people to come to Christ.

Other theologians, however, have noted that whenever this particular word is used elsewhere in the New Testament it carries a much stronger meaning. For example, the word is used in the book of Acts where Paul and Silas were thrown into prison (Acts 16:19-24). They were not *wooed* into prison, but were *thrown* into prison rather forcefully. So it is suggested that the Father does more than "woo" us to Christ, He *compels* us to Christ. "This word is used here, evidently, to denote such an influence from God as to secure the result, or as to incline the mind to believe."[13]

Personally, I think this "drawing" ministry of the Father is a merciful act of grace. Think about it: Human beings are so deeply engulfed in sin and its horrendous effects (including pervasive unbelief and hardness of heart) that no one would end up coming to Christ of their own accord unless God the Father sovereignly drew him or her to Christ. We should be thankful for this ministry of the Father.

▶ What is the "food" that endures to eternal life (John 6:27)?

In John 6:27 Jesus said to a crowd, "Do not work for food that spoils, but for food that endures to eternal life, which the Son of Man will give you. On him God the Father has placed his seal of approval."

This "food" is defined for us as we continue to read chapter 6 in John's Gospel. In verse 35 Jesus affirmed, "I am the bread of life. He who comes to me will never go hungry, and he who believes in me will never be thirsty." So *Jesus Himself* is the food that endures to eternal life. By believing in Him a person partakes of this food and becomes the possessor of the gift of eternal life. As Bible scholar F. F. Bruce put it, "What we have in Jesus' strange language is a powerful metaphor stating that a share in the life of God, eternal life, is granted to those who in faith come to Jesus, appropriate him, enter into union with him."[14]

▶ Why did Jesus say we have no life in us if we do not eat His flesh and drink His blood (John 6:53)?

In John 6:53 Jesus said, "I tell you the truth, unless you eat the flesh of the Son of Man and drink his blood, you have no life in you." Some interpreters have assumed that Jesus is referring in some way to communion (the Lord's Supper) in this verse. Actually, though, this is just a continuation of what Jesus said in John 6:27 (discussed above): Jesus Himself is the "food" that endures to eternal life.

John 6:53 is simply saying that just as one must consume or partake of physical food to sustain physical life, so one must appropriate* Christ to have spiritual life. Food that is eaten and then digested is assimilated so that it becomes a part of the body. Likewise, people must appropriate Christ and become one with Him by faith to receive the gift of eternal life.[15]

The references to flesh and blood in this verse point us to the work of Christ on the cross. It was there that His *flesh* was

---

* By "appropriate" I mean we must spiritually "lay hold" of Christ by trusting in Him for salvation. *Faith* is the operative word when it comes to appropriating Christ.

nailed to the cross and His *blood* was shed to make man's salvation possible. By placing faith in the crucified Christ, we appropriate Him and His work of salvation.

▶ Did Jesus claim to be the only way of salvation (John 14:6)?

In John 14:6 Jesus said, "I am the way and the truth and the life. No one comes to the Father except through me." Jesus did indeed claim to be the only way of salvation. This claim was confirmed by those who followed Him. A bold Peter said in Acts 4:12, "Salvation is found in no one else, for there is no other name under heaven given to men by which we must be saved." The apostle Paul said, "For there is one God and *one mediator* between God and men, the man Christ Jesus" (1 Timothy 2:5, italics added). Moreover, Jesus sternly warned His followers about those who would try to set forth a different "Christ" (Matthew 24:4,5).

It is important to understand that Jesus is totally unique. He proved the veracity of all He said by rising from the dead (Acts 17:31). None of the other leaders of the different world religions did that. Jesus' resurrection proved that He was who He claimed to be—the divine Messiah (Romans 1:4).

I should also note that there is a practical problem with the current "politically correct" idea that all religions basically teach the same truth. The problem is that the leaders of the different world religions taught different (and *contradictory*) ideas about God. For example:

- *Jesus* taught that there is only one God and that He is triune in nature (Matthew 28:19).
- *Muhammad* taught that there is only one God, but that God cannot have a son.
- *Krishna* in the Bhagavad Gita (a Hindu scripture) indicated that he believed in a combination of polytheism (there are many gods) and pantheism (all is God).
- *Confucius* believed in many gods.
- *Zoroaster* taught that there is both a good god and a bad god.

- *Buddha* taught that the concept of God was essentially irrelevant.

Obviously, these religious leaders cannot be said to be teaching the same basic truth. If one is right, all the others are wrong. If Jesus was right (and *He is*), then all the others are wrong.

▶ If believing in Jesus is the only way of salvation (John 14:6), how can infants and young children who die, retarded people, and those who have never heard the gospel be saved?

Jesus emphatically stated, "I am the way and the truth and the life. No one comes to the Father except through me" (John 14:6). Many Christians have expressed concern about how Jesus' statement relates to infants and young children who die, retarded people, and those who have never heard the gospel. How can these individuals be saved?

This is a critically important issue and calls for an extended answer. I will first deal with those who lack the capacity to exercise cognitive faith in Christ, such as an infant or a young child (the same arguments would hold true for a retarded person).

I believe the Scriptures teach that every young child who dies is immediately ushered into God's glorious presence in heaven. I believe that at the moment of death, Jesus applies the benefits of His sacrificial death to that child, thereby saving him or her.

At the outset, though, we must recognize that the whole of Scripture points to the universal need of salvation, even among little children. All of us—including infants who cannot believe—are lost (Luke 19:10), perishing (John 3:16), condemned (John 3:18), and under God's wrath (John 3:36). In view of this, we cannot say that little children are in a sinless state. That is why it is necessary for Christ to apply the benefits of His sacrificial death to each child that dies.

In attaining a balanced perspective on this issue, one must keep in mind that God's primary purpose in saving human beings is to display His wondrous grace. One must ask, Would the "riches of God's grace" be displayed in "wisdom and understanding" (Ephesians 1:7,8) in sending little children to hell? I think not. It would be a cruel mockery for God to call upon little children to do—and to hold them *responsible* for doing—what they *could not* do. At that young age, children simply do not have the capacity to exercise saving faith in Christ.

I believe it is the uniform testimony of Scripture that those who are not capable of making a decision to receive Jesus Christ, and who have died, are now with Christ in heaven, resting in His tender arms, enjoying the sweetness of His love. There are many factors supporting this viewpoint.

It is highly revealing that in all the descriptions of hell in the Bible, we *never* read of infants or little children there. Only people capable of making decisions are seen there. Nor do we read of infants and little children standing before the Great White Throne judgment, which is the judgment of the wicked dead and the precursor to the lake of fire (Revelation 20:11-15). The complete silence of Scripture regarding the presence of infants in eternal torment militates against their being there.

Moreover, as we examine instances in which Christ encountered children during His earthly ministry, it appears that children have a special place in His kingdom. Jesus even said, "Unless you change and become like little children, you will never enter the kingdom of heaven" (Matthew 18:3). He also said, "Whoever welcomes a little child like this in my name welcomes me" (verse 5). I do not think there is any way someone could read Matthew 18 and conclude that it is within the realm of possibility that Jesus could damn such little ones to hell.

Certainly King David in the Old Testament believed he would again be with his young son who died (2 Samuel 12:22,23). David firmly believed in life after death. He had no doubt that he would spend eternity with his beloved little one.

Another consideration that points to the assurance of infant salvation relates to the basis of the judgment of the lost. We read in Revelation 20:11-13 that the lost are judged according to what they have done. The basis of the judgment of the wicked is clearly *deeds done while on earth*. Hence, infants and young children cannot possibly be the objects of this judgment because they are not responsible for their deeds. Such a judgment against infants would be a travesty of justice.

These and other scriptural factors make it clear that babies and young children go straight to heaven at the moment of death.

But what about those who have never heard the gospel? Since Jesus is "the only way" (John 14:6), are they saved or lost?

If the heathen are *not* really lost, then many teachings of Christ become absurd. For example, John 3:16—"For God so loved the world that he gave his one and only Son, that whoever believes in him shall not perish but have eternal life"— becomes meaningless.

If the heathen are not lost, Christ's postresurrection and preascension commands to His disciples are a mockery. In Luke 24:47 Christ commanded that "repentance and forgiveness of sins will be preached in his name to all nations." Similarly, in Matthew 28:19 He said, "Therefore go and make disciples of all nations, baptizing them in the name of the Father and of the Son and of the Holy Spirit." These verses might well be stricken from the Scriptures if human beings without Christ are not lost.

If the heathen are not really lost, then the Lord's words were meaningless when He said to His disciples, "As the Father has sent me, I am sending you" (John 20:21). Why did the Father send Him? Jesus Himself explained that "the Son of Man came to seek and to save what was lost" (Luke 19:10).

If the heathen do not need Christ and His salvation, then neither do we. Conversely, if we need Him, *so do they*. The Scriptures become a bundle of contradictions, the Savior becomes a false teacher, and the Christian message becomes "much ado about nothing" if the heathen are not lost.

Scripture makes it very plain: "Salvation is found in no one else, for there is no other name under heaven given to men by which we must be saved" (Acts 4:12). The Bible says, "There is one God and one mediator between God and men, the man Christ Jesus" (1 Timothy 2:5).

Other religions do not lead to God. The one sin for which God judged the people of Israel more severely than any other was that of participating in heathen religions. The Bible repeatedly implies and states that God hates, despises, and utterly rejects anything associated with heathen religions and practices. Those who follow such idolatry are not regarded as groping their way to God but rather as having turned their backs on Him, following the ways of darkness.

Now I must point out the scriptural teaching that God has given a certain amount of revelational "light" to every single person in the world. Everyone has some sense of God's law in his or her heart. As John Blanchard put it so well, everyone "has some conception of the difference between right and wrong; he approves of honesty; he responds to love and kindness; he resents it if someone steals his goods or tries to injure him. In other words, he has a conscience which passes judgment on his behavior and the behavior of others, something the Bible calls a law written on his heart."[16] Paul speaks of this law written on human hearts in Romans 2:15.

God has also given witness of Himself in the universe around us. As we behold the world and the universe, it is evident that there is Someone who made the world and the universe. Since the creation of the world, God's invisible qualities—His eternal power and divine nature—have been clearly seen and understood from that which He created (Romans 1:20).

We know from other Scripture verses that God is an invisible spirit (John 4:24). The physical eye cannot see Him. But His existence is nevertheless reflected in what He has made—the creation. The *creation*, which is visible, reveals the existence of the *Creator*, who is invisible.

Because all human beings can see the revelation of God in creation, all people—regardless of whether they have heard about Christ or have read the Bible—are held accountable before God. *All are without excuse.* Their rightful condemnation, as objects of God's wrath, is justified because their choice to ignore the revelation of God in creation is indefensible (see Psalm 19:1-6; Romans 1:20).

The Scriptures clearly indicate that those who respond to the limited light around them (such as God's witness of Himself in the universe) will receive further, more specific "light." This is illustrated in the life of Cornelius. This Gentile was obedient to the limited amount of "light" he had received—that is, he had been obedient to Old Testament revelation (Acts 10:2). But he did not have enough "light" to believe in Jesus Christ as the Savior. So God sent Peter to Cornelius' house to explain the gospel, after which time Cornelius believed in Jesus and was saved (verses 44-48).

In view of the above, we must not allow God's name to be impugned by those who imply that God is unfair if He judges those who have never heard the gospel. As we have seen, God has given a witness of Himself to *all* humanity. Moreover, God desires all to be saved (1 Timothy 2:4) and does not want anyone to perish (2 Peter 3:9). He surely takes no pleasure in the death of the unsaved (Ezekiel 18:23).

Let us remember that God is a *fair* Judge. "It is unthinkable that God would do wrong, that the Almighty would pervert justice" (Job 34:12). "Will not the Judge of all the earth do right?" (Genesis 18:25).

TEN

CAN SALVATION
BE LOST?

◊⟐⟐◊

▶ Do we lose our salvation if we fail to tell others about Jesus
(Matthew 10:32,33; Luke 12:8,9)?

In Matthew 10:32,33 Jesus said, "Whoever acknowledges
me before men, I will also acknowledge him before my Father in
heaven. But whoever disowns me before men, I will disown him
before my Father in heaven" (see also Luke 12:8,9).

The immediate context of this passage is Matthew 10:24-42,
where Jesus is portrayed as instructing His disciples about their
relationship to Him. He told them that He is the only One they
should truly be concerned about (verses 24-33). He stressed that
He must be more important to them than even their families or
their very lives (verses 34-39). They were also to be His ambas-
sadors and tell others about Him (verses 40-42).

The broader context of this passage relates to the fact that
the Pharisees had continuously *disowned* Jesus while the disciples followed Him and spoke about Him in every city they visited. Seen against this backdrop, Jesus' words take on great
significance. We might paraphrase His teaching this way:
"Whoever acknowledges me before men (*such as you disciples*), I
will also acknowledge him before my Father in heaven. But
whoever disowns me before men (*like these Pharisees do on every
occasion they get*), I will disown before my Father in heaven."

Those who acknowledge Jesus are those who recognize Him as being the true Messiah and thus trust in Him as the way of salvation. Those who do not acknowledge Jesus, by contrast, are those who reject Him as the Messiah and therefore place themselves beyond any possibility of salvation, since salvation is found only in Him (John 14:6).[1]

There is a significant lexical insight we get from the original Greek text of this verse. The word for "disown" ("whoever *disowns* me") is an aorist tense. This points to the fact that Jesus is not talking about a single instance of denial or disowning (as was the case with Peter, who actually denied Christ three times—Luke 22:34), but is rather referring to *life in its entirety*. The aorist tense views a person's life "globally"—*a lifetime*. Hence, the person who throughout His life denies or disowns Christ (as was typically the case with the Pharisees) will be disowned by Christ before the Father.[2]

▶ Do we lose our salvation if we fail to bear fruit as Christians (John 15:2)?

In John 15:2, Jesus (who is the "true Vine") teaches about the fruitfulness of those who follow Him: The Father "cuts off every branch in me that bears no fruit, while every branch that does bear fruit he prunes so that it will be even more fruitful." At first glance it might seem that Jesus is saying we will lose our salvation if we fail to bear fruit as Christians. But I do not think this is what He was communicating.

First, as a backdrop, it is important to understand Jesus' words in view of what the rest of Scripture says about security in salvation. Other Scriptures indicate that once a person exercises saving faith in Jesus Christ, he or she is forever in the family of God. God never expels anyone from His forever family.

For example, in 1 Corinthians 12:13 we are told that at the moment of salvation the Holy Spirit places us into the body of Christ. Once we are infused into the body of Christ, we are never excised from the body. In fact, Ephesians 1:13 and 4:30

indicate that at the moment of believing in Jesus Christ for salvation, we are permanently "sealed" by the Holy Spirit. At that point we are God's everlasting property. His seal guarantees that we will make it to heaven.

Moreover, we read in John 10:28-30 that it is the Father's purpose to keep us secure despite anything that might happen once we have trusted in Christ. Nothing can snatch us out of His hands. God's plans cannot be thwarted (Isaiah 14:24). Further, Romans 8:29-39 portrays an unbroken chain that spans from the predestination of believers to their glorification in heaven. This indicates the certainty of all believers reaching heaven.

Another fact we need to keep in mind is that Christ regularly prays for each Christian (Hebrews 7:25). With Jesus interceding for us, we are secure. (His prayers are always answered!)

Of course, the fact that a believer is secure in his salvation does not mean that he or she is free to sin. If the Christian sins and *remains* in that sin, Scripture says that God will discipline him or her just as a father disciplines his children (Hebrews 12:7-11).

In view of the above, what are we to make of John 15:2: "He cuts off every branch in me that bears no fruit, while every branch that does bear fruit he prunes so that it will be even more fruitful"? Scholars have most often interpreted the phrase "cut off" in one of four ways.

Some scholars see this as referring to literally lopping of the branch and throwing it away. Seen in this light, the phrase could refer to the physical death of fruitless Christians.[3] This would be the ultimate form of divine discipline for a believer engaged in persistent and unrepentant sin (see 1 John 5:16; 1 Corinthians 11:30).

Other interpreters see the "lopping off" as a metaphorical way of describing less drastic forms of God's discipline—that is, God disciplines the lives of believers so they are led to be more fruitful.[4] God works in the life of each believer in such a way as to "cut out" all that is bad so that he or she bears more spiritual fruit.

Still other interpreters say the "lopping off" involves the recognition that not all who claim to be followers of Jesus Christ are in fact *true* believers—a reality that soon evidences itself by a complete lack of spiritual fruit. In such a case, this branch is truly "dead," and can only be lopped off, much as Judas Iscariot was.[5]

And still others interpret the phrase "cut off" in the sense of "lift up."* In biblical times, gardeners would often lift vines off the ground, propping them up on sticks, so that they would bear more fruit.[6]

If this interpretation is correct, then the verse would not relate in any way to the possibility of losing one's salvation. But even if the verse carried the other meaning ("lopping off"), this would not demand a loss of salvation, but could simply refer to God's discipline of the Christian, or it could relate to *professing* Christians as opposed to genuine Christians.

▶ If we fail to "remain" in Jesus, do we lose our salvation (John 15:6)?

In His discussion of bearing fruit, using the vine-and-branch analogy, Jesus said, "If anyone does not remain in me, he is like a branch that is thrown away and withers; such branches are picked up, thrown into the fire and burned" (John 15:6).

This is admittedly a hard saying. But I do not think it refers to the loss of one's salvation, for this would contradict many key passages on eternal security, including John 3:16,36; 5:24; 10:28,29; and Romans 8:29-39 (see my earlier discussion in the previous section). Some scholars have interpreted this verse as referring to professing believers who soon evidence their lack of true faith by a complete absence of spiritual fruit.[7] Such individuals end up separate from Christ for all eternity—that is, they end up suffering in the eternal fire known as hell. "Like a

---

* The *Theological Dictionary of the New Testament* notes that the Greek word *airo* can carry the important meaning "to lift from the ground" (p.28). *Vine's Expository Dictionary of Biblical Words* agrees, noting that the word can mean "hoist up" (p. 700). The *Ryrie Study Bible* concedes that this is a viable interpretation (p. 1649).

dead branch, a person without Christ is spiritually dead and therefore will be punished in eternal fire (cf. Matthew 25:46)."[8]

Others interpret this verse as relating to the Christian who sins and *remains* in sin, thereby bringing about a loss of fellowship (*not* a loss of salvation) in his relationship with the Father until that believer repents. Professor Zane Hodges is an advocate of this view:

> The consequences that follow when a disciple fails to abide in Christ are fully comprehensible in terms of this kind of relationship. First, there is the loss of the relationship itself: "he is cast out as a branch." Next, there is the loss of the spiritual vitality associated with that relationship: "and is withered." Finally, there is chastening: "They gather them and throw them into the fire, and they are burned."[9]

Still others relate this "fire" and being "burned" to the future judgment of Christians that is described by the apostle Paul in 1 Corinthians 3:11-15:

> No one can lay any foundation other than the one already laid, which is Jesus Christ. If any man builds on this foundation using gold, silver, costly stones, wood, hay or straw, his work will be shown for what it is, because the Day will bring it to light. It will be revealed with fire, and the fire will test the quality of each man's work. If what he has built survives, he will receive his reward. If it is burned up, he will suffer loss; he himself will be saved, but only as one escaping through the flames.

If this interpretation is correct, then John 15:6 would refer to the fact that at the future judgment seat of Christ the believer's works will be judged, and those good works that result from abiding in Christ will withstand the fire, while those works done in the power of the flesh will pass away. Worthless works will be swept away like ashes in the wind. True fruit results only when one is vitally connected to Jesus Christ.[10]

▶ Can a Christian have his or her name blotted out of the Book of Life (Revelation 3:5)?

In Revelation 3:5 Jesus said, "He who overcomes will, like them, be dressed in white. I will never blot out his name from the book of life, but will acknowledge his name before my Father and his angels." One might initially conclude that Jesus is here saying that the Christian can have his name blotted out of the Book of Life. But I do not think this is the intent of His words.

The backdrop to my answer relates to the many *clear* passages of Scripture that point to the security of one's salvation (see my earlier discussion in this chapter). Notice that the same John who wrote the book of Revelation wrote elsewhere about the security of salvation of each individual believer (see John 5:24; 6:35-37,39; 10:28,29). Hence, however Revelation 3:5 is interpreted, I do not think it should be taken to mean a believer can lose his or her salvation.

Theologian John F. Walvoord points out that while this passage may seem to imply that a believer's name could be erased from the Book of Life, actually it only gives a positive affirmation that their names *will not* be erased.[11] Jesus' statement may thus be considered not a threat but indeed an *assurance* that saved people's names will always *be in* the Book of Life.

This seems to be the gist of what other verses communicate about the Book of Life. For example, in Luke 10:20 Jesus said to the disciples, "Do not rejoice that the spirits submit to you, but rejoice that your names *are written* in heaven." In Hebrews 12:23 we read of "the church of the firstborn, whose names *are written* in heaven."

▶ Are we in danger of the fire of hell for saying "You fool!" to someone (Matthew 5:22)?

In Matthew 5:22 Jesus sternly warned, "I tell you that anyone who is angry with his brother will be subject to judgment. Again, anyone who says to his brother, 'Raca,' is answerable to the Sanhedrin. But anyone who says, 'You fool!' will be in danger of the fire of hell."

In context, this verse is found in a broader discourse in which Jesus is teaching about the law against murder (Matthew 5:22-26). Jesus declared that not only is a murderer guilty before the court, but also guilty is anyone who gets angry and calls another person a fool (verse 22).

The Jewish backdrop is that the Pharisees taught that murder involved the *external* act of taking someone else's life. They were concerned only with the physical act of murder. They interpreted the law to mean that so long as one did not actually take another person's life, he was innocent of breaking God's law. But Jesus challenged the Pharisees' understanding by pointing out that it is not just the *external act* but the *internal attitude that leads up to the act* that brings guilt. Yes, murder is wrong, but so is the anger that leads up to that murder. Seen in this light, the Pharisees certainly fell under condemnation because their inner attitudes were brimming with sin.

Jesus taught that the person who says to another "raca" ("empty-head," "shallow-brains")[12] or "you fool" is demonstrating within his own heart the anger that can lead to murder, and this inner sinful attitude alone is sufficient to bring condemnation before God. The sin has already taken place in the heart before any kind of external act of murder has occurred. A person with this inner attitude is obviously a sinner and is on a path that leads to hell (and will actually end up in hell if he or she does not trust in Christ). Such words indicate a violation of the *spirit* of God's commandment against murder (Exodus 20:13).

In the next section of His discourse, Jesus talks about the law of reconciliation. The wrong inner attitudes must be made right. The anger must be dismissed and replaced with forgiveness (Matthew 5:23-26). Words of hurt ("you fool") must be replaced with words of forgiveness. This is the path Christ calls Christians to.

▶ Can we lose our salvation if we speak careless words (Matthew
  12:36,37)?

In Matthew 12:36,37 Jesus warned, "I tell you that men will
have to give account on the day of judgment for every careless
word they have spoken. For by your words you will be acquitted,
and by your words you will be condemned."

In context, the Pharisees had just earlier used careless words
in charging that the miracles performed by Christ were done
not in the power of the Holy Spirit, as He claimed, but by the
power of Satan—the unholy spirit (Matthew 12:22-24). Jesus
then answered this charge of the Pharisees with three essential
points: 1) It makes no sense for a demonic force to cast out
demons (verses 25-29); 2) a sin against the Holy Spirit will
never be forgiven (verses 30-32); 3) a person's internal attitude—which comes out in his or her words—will either justify
or condemn him (verses 33-37).

It is in this context that Jesus said, "I tell you that men will
have to give account on the day of judgment for every careless
word they have spoken. For by your words you will be acquitted,
and by your words you will be condemned." In context, then,
the "careless words" Jesus was referring to were actually *blasphe-
mous* words spoken by the Pharisees.

In regard to judgment, John Wesley, in one of his famous
sermons, once commented: "Every man shall give an account of
his own works, a full and true account of all that he ever did
while alive, whether it was good or evil."[13]

Such words are needed in times like these. It seems that few
people today govern their words and actions with a view to
being held accountable for them at a future judgment. Though
many people prefer to ignore any mention of the subject, the
fact remains that every human being—both Christian and non-
Christian—will face judgment.

Of course, the purpose of the believer's judgment is altogether different from that of the unbeliever's judgment. The
believer is judged not in regard to salvation (which is absolutely
secure) but in regard to receiving or losing rewards from God

(1 Corinthians 3:10-15; 2 Corinthians 5:10). The unbeliever, however, is judged as a precursor to his being cast into the lake of fire (Revelation 20:11-15).

One aspect of the judgment we will face, as Jesus Himself indicates, involves the words we have spoken. This is an important aspect of judgment, for tremendous damage can be done through the human tongue (see James 3:1-12; Ephesians 5:3,4; Colossians 3:17). And the words we speak are an indicator of what is going on inside our hearts. What we say to others can, in many ways, reveal our inner spiritual state.

Evangelist John Blanchard once commented that "if even our careless words are carefully recorded, how can we bear the thought that our calculated boastful claims, the cutting criticisms, the off-color jokes, and the unkind comments will also be taken into account. Even our whispered asides and words spoken in confidence or when we thought we were 'safe' will be heard again."[14] That is something to think about!

So Jesus' words must be taken seriously. As noted above, the Christian's salvation is secure, and the purpose of the Christian's judgment relates only to receiving or losing rewards. But the reality is that Christians who choose to speak careless words will one day answer for those words and *will most definitely experience a loss of rewards.*

The fact that all of us will one day be judged should have a profound effect on the way we live our lives. There is little else that could so motivate us to do good and deter us from evil than a strong conviction that the divine Judge is standing at the door and we are shortly to stand before Him. Indeed, as a great eighteenth-century saint put it, "No better motive can be found to guarantee a steady pursuit of solid virtue and a uniform walk in justice, mercy, and truth."[15]

▶ What did Jesus mean when He said, "Blessed is the man who does not fall away on account of me" (Luke 7:23)?

In Luke 7:23 Jesus said, "Blessed is the man who does not fall away on account of me." In context, John the Baptist had sent messengers to Jesus to clarify that He was truly the promised Messiah (Luke 7:18-20). Jesus replied by pointing out that His miraculous deeds were signs that pointed to the reality that He indeed was the promised Messiah (verses 21,22).

It is in this context that Jesus said, "Blessed is the man who does not fall away on account of me" (verse 23). The point Jesus was making is this: By virtue of the fact that Christ fulfilled all the messianic prophesies of the Old Testament—such as bringing sight to the blind, hearing to the deaf, and the ability to walk for the lame—Jesus clearly was the promised Messiah. But *He was not the political-deliverer Messiah expected by the general populace.* Hence Jesus said, "Blessed is the man who does not fall away on account of me"—that is, blessed is the man who recognizes me as the promised Messiah and does not fall away from believing in me simply because I do not fulfill his personal preconceived expectations of what the Messiah would do. Blessed is the man who maintains faith in me as the Messiah even though I am not quite what he expected in terms of being a political deliverer."

ELEVEN

TREATING
OTHERS KINDLY

▶ How is it possible to truly love our enemies and pray for those who persecute us (Matthew 5:44)?

In Matthew 5:44 Jesus said, "Love your enemies and pray for those who persecute you." The backdrop to understanding Jesus' statement is that the Jewish leaders of His day taught that we should love those near and dear to us (Leviticus 19:18), but hate our enemies. The Pharisees had it in their minds that the very act of hating their enemies constituted a form of God's judgment against them. Jesus refuted this idea, instructing His followers to love even their enemies. After all, God the Father loves *all* people, and we as Christians are to take on the family likeness, imitating God in our love for all people (see Matthew 5:48).

Certainly Jesus put into practice what He preached. While on the cross, He prayed for His executioners, "Father, forgive them, for they do not know what they are doing" (Luke 23:34). Likewise, when Stephen was being stoned to death, he prayed, "Lord, do not hold this sin against them" (Acts 7:60).

In our own strength, loving our enemies is an impossibility. But as we walk in the power of the Holy Spirit, living in dependence on Him and His mighty power, such love becomes a reality in our lives (see Galatians 5:22,23; Colossians 3:12-15). This is a *supernatural* kind of love.

▶ Does Jesus teach that we should "turn the other cheek" in every circumstance in the course of daily living (Luke 6:29,30)?

In Luke 6:29 Jesus said, "If someone strikes you on one cheek, turn to him the other also." I do not think Jesus was teaching to "turn the other cheek" in *all* circumstances. Even Christ did not literally turn the other cheek when smitten by a member of the Sanhedrin (see John 18:19-23).

The backdrop to Jesus' teaching in Luke 6:29,30 is that the Jews considered it an insult to be hit in the face, much in the same way that we would interpret someone spitting in our face. The principle taught in the Sermon on the Mount would seem to be that Christians should not retaliate when insulted or slandered (see Romans 12:17-21). Such insults do not threaten a Christian's personal safety.

The question of rendering insult for insult, however, is a far cry from defending oneself against a mugger or a rapist or someone criminally attacking you or a loved one in some way. There are other verses in Scripture where, instead of turning the other cheek, defending oneself is clearly God's will in a matter, such as when the disciples are admonished by Christ to purchase a sword (Luke 22:36-38; John 15:13; see also Hebrews 11:30-40). (For more on this, see the question on self-defense in Chapter 12.)

▶ What did Jesus mean when He said we must become "the very last" and "the servant of all" (Mark 9:35)?

Jesus called the 12 disciples to Himself and said to them, "If anyone wants to be first, he must be the very last, and the servant of all" (Mark 9:35). In context, the disciples were in the midst of discussing who among them was the greatest (Mark 9:33,34). Using a child as an illustration, Jesus taught them that true greatness involved being a servant (verses 35-37). It is here that Jesus said, "If anyone wants to be first, he must be the very last, and the servant of all."

The basic meaning is clear: Instead of seeking to be "number one," focusing only on what gratifies self, placing the ego on the throne of the heart, we are to place the interests of others ahead of our own and become the servant of other people. We must attend to the needs of other people. *That* is how to attain greatness in the kingdom of heaven. Greatness in God's eyes involves not exalted status (like the Pharisees often sought) but lowly service.

▶ Why did Jesus tell the disciples that they should wash one another's feet (John 13:14)?

In John 13:14 Jesus said to the disciples, "Now that I, your Lord and Teacher, have washed your feet, you also should wash one another's feet." Why did He say this?

In context, Jesus in John 13:1-17 was teaching about humility and servanthood, and He does so through a living parable—an *acted-out* parable. Normally when one entered someone's house in New Testament days, it would be the job of the servant of that household to wash that person's feet, not the job of the master of the household. By washing the disciple's feet, Jesus placed Himself in the role of a servant. And even as the Son of God was a servant, so the disciples were to be servants to each other.

This was a tremendous lesson in humility and servanthood for the disciples. Instead of trying to exalt themselves over others (the normal human tendency), they were to become each other's servants. This is right in line with Jesus' teaching elsewhere that he who is greatest in the kingdom of heaven is the one who becomes the servant of all (Matthew 20:26).

Was Jesus teaching that foot-washing should become an ordinance in the church—like baptism and the Lord's Supper?* No. There is no indication in the text that this was to be so. Jesus was simply giving a much-needed lesson in servanthood to the disciples.

---

* Though not common, some churches have practiced three or more ordinances, including baptism, the Lord's Supper, and foot-washing.

▶ Will the Lord refuse to forgive us if we do not forgive others
  when they sin against us (Matthew 6:14,15; Mark 11:25)?

In Matthew 6:14,15 Jesus said, "For if you forgive men when
they sin against you, your heavenly Father will also forgive you.
But if you do not forgive men their sins, your Father will not forgive your sins." This verse must be interpreted against the
broader backdrop of the whole of Scripture. There are a number
of key passages in Scripture that indicate the absoluteness of the
forgiveness God bestows on us in terms of our eternal salvation.
For example, in Hebrews 10:17 God said, "Their sins and law-
less acts I will remember no more." In Psalm 103:11,12 we are
told, "For as high as the heavens are above the earth, so great is
his love for those who fear him; as far as the east is from the
west, so far has he removed our transgressions from us."

This last verse is particularly significant. There is a definite
point that is north and another that is south—the North and
South Poles. But there are no such points for east and west. It
does not matter how far you go to the east; you will never arrive
where east begins because by definition east is the opposite of
west. The two never meet. They never will meet and never
could meet because they are defined as opposites. To remove our
sins "as far as the east is from the west" is by definition to put
them where no one can ever find them. *That* is the forgiveness
God has granted us in terms of our eternal salvation (see
Colossians 2:14).

This being the case, how are we to interpret Matthew
6:14,15, where Jesus said, "If you forgive men when they sin
against you, your heavenly Father will also forgive you. But if
you do not forgive men their sins, your Father will not forgive
your sins"?

Theologians often answer this by pointing out that there is
one sense of forgiveness that relates to our *eternal salvation* and
another sense that relates to our daily *fellowship with God*. It is
suggested that in Matthew 6:14,15 the latter sense is in view.
Bible scholar Donald Burdick explains it this way:

Christ does not here address himself to the unsaved but to his disciples, those who have already entered into a saving relationship with himself. The forgiveness of which he speaks is not the initial forensic act of forgiveness that abolishes the guilt of sin. It is rather the forgiveness of a father that restores fellowship.[1]

The meaning of our passage would be this: If we do not forgive others in the body of Christ, then our fellowship with God is broken because our fellowship with Him hinges on our forgiveness of others. God still views us as saved in terms of our eternal destiny, but from a temporal perspective our fellowship with God is broken until the time we forgive others and repent.[2]

▶ What did Jesus mean when He said we should forgive up to 77 times (Matthew 18:21,22)?

Peter came to Jesus and asked, "Lord, how many times shall I forgive my brother when he sins against me? Up to seven times?" Jesus answered, "I tell you, not seven times, but seventy-seven times" (Matthew 18:21,22). The backdrop to this is that the Pharisees taught that righteousness demanded that a person be forgiven *two* times. The Jewish rabbis taught that if one wanted to be magnanimous one should forgive up to *three* times. So when Peter asked Jesus about forgiving someone *seven* times, he no doubt thought he was being quite generous.

But Jesus went far beyond what Peter had in mind by saying we should forgive 77 times—or, in other words, there should be no limitations on our forgiveness. (To the Jewish mindset, "77 times" meant *times without number*.) This should especially be the case because of how much God has forgiven us of our sins (see Matthew 18:23-35).

▶ Will the Lord treat us harshly if we refuse to forgive others (Matthew 18:32-35)?

In Matthew 18:23-34 Jesus told a parable about forgiveness in answer to Peter's question: "How many times shall I forgive my brother when he sins against me?" (verse 21). Jesus spoke of a king who commanded a servant to be sold along with his family to pay for the debt that he was owed (10,000 talents, which would amount to several million dollars in our present economy). But then the king forgave the servant and canceled the debt when the servant begged him to (verses 23-27).

The forgiven servant then found another servant who owed him a small amount of money (100 denarii, or about 16 dollars in today's economy) and would not forgive him, but rather threw him into prison (Matthew 18:28-30). When the other servants witnessed what happened, they reported it to the master (verse 31). The master then ordered the wicked slave to be tortured until he repaid all that was owed to him (verses 32-34).

It is in this context that Jesus said, "This is how my heavenly Father will treat each of you unless you forgive your brother from your heart" (Matthew 18:35). Jesus is making a very *important*—and very *serious*—point to Peter. Peter needed to realize that as a human being he was completely incapable of paying the debt he owed to God. (Peter, like all of us, was *morally* indebted to God because of sin.) Peter was represented by the man who had an insurmountable debt. But God had freely forgiven Peter all of His indebtedness. The story thus communicates the truth that Peter was obligated to forgive others who may have wronged him because their wrongs were a *mere pittance* in comparison with the wrong Peter had done to God and for which he had received forgiveness. To not forgive others in such circumstances invites God's discipline and judgment.

▶ Does our status before God hinge on our attitude toward others (Luke 6:37)?

In Luke 6:37 Jesus said, "Do not judge, and you will not be judged. Do not condemn, and you will not be condemned. Forgive, and you will be forgiven." Again, it is the Pharisaic backdrop that helps us to understand Christ's words. The Pharisees had a habit of setting themselves up as the judges of all human beings. They measured other people against themselves—and, of course, they considered themselves to be the very epitome of righteousness. The Pharisees not only judged a person's external behavior, but they also self-righteously claimed to know the motives behind each person's behavior. It is in view of this that Jesus said, "Do not judge, and you will not be judged. Do not condemn, and you will not be condemned. Forgive, and you will be forgiven." The Pharisees judged, they condemned, and they did not truly forgive.

Jesus' statement was thus aimed at the inner attitude of the Pharisees. He was saying His followers should avoid the self-righteous and hypocritical judgment that was characteristic of the Pharisees. They should avoid the kind of judgment that seeks only to criticize and find fault with one's neighbor.[3]

Jesus was *not* saying, however, that Christians should avoid making proper judgments about various issues. The apostle Paul said, "The spiritual man makes judgments about all things" (1 Corinthians 2:15). Christians are to judge between right and wrong, between true and false prophets, and between true and false doctrine (see 1 Corinthians 5:9; 2 Corinthians 11:14; Philippians 3:2; 1 John 4:1; 1 Thessalonians 5:21).

▶ Why did Jesus say we should not let our left hand know what our right hand is doing when we give to others (Matthew 6:3,4)?

While giving instructions on giving, Jesus said, "But when you give to the needy, do not let your left hand know what your right hand is doing, so that your giving may be in secret. Then your Father, who sees what is done in secret, will reward you" (Matthew 6:3,4).

As He often did, Jesus was aiming His comments primarily at the Pharisees. The Pharisees used opportunities of giving as a way of openly demonstrating their piety before people. They made a real show of it. They constantly tried to impress others with their liberality. The Pharisees were so well known for doing this that beggars soon caught on and would position themselves at the entrance of the temple so they might be the recipients of the giving of the Pharisees. (These beggars didn't care that the

Pharisees were merely showing off, so long as they ended up on the receiving end of their giving.)

In God's eyes the Pharisees were not really giving at all. Rather, they were essentially trying to buy respect and honor among the people. They wanted the praise of men. They "paid" for it, and they often got it. But that is *all* they got.

Christ, in dire contrast to the attitude of the Pharisees, said we should give quietly and with no fanfare to impress people. We should give in such a way that our left hand does not know what our right hand is doing—that is, it should be done *privately* and *in secret*. The one who gives with a righteous motive will receive a rich reward from the Father. Even if the giving takes place in secret, the Father sees it and will reward it accordingly.

▶ What lesson is Jesus teaching about giving in Luke 6:38?

In Luke 6:38 Jesus said, "Give, and it will be given to you. A good measure, pressed down, shaken together and running over, will be poured into your lap. For with the measure you use, it will be measured to you."

Jesus used imagery in this verse that His first-century hearers would have been well familiar with. The imagery is that of a large container of grain that is virtually filled to the brim and overflowing the edge. In the same way that grain overflows the container, so we should overflow in our generosity to others.

Jesus' point is that there is *reciprocity* in the affairs of life: "With the measure you use, it will be measured to you." Jesus' meaning is that we *get back* what we *put into* life. Or, as one scholar put it, "human generosity will be rewarded by divine superabundance."[4]

Of course, this does not mean, as some have tried to argue, that God will make one financially rich if one gives money to a particular ministry. This verse is not a get-rich formula. It simply communicates the idea that we are to be liberal in our giving to others. God smiles on such giving and pours out blessing as a result. But remember—God Himself determines *what form* that blessing will take.

TWELVE

LIVING
ETHICALLY

⊙〰〰〰⊙

▶ Since Jesus turned water into wine, was He thereby teaching it is all right to drink (John 2:9)?

Drunkenness, of course, is forbidden by God throughout Scripture. It is simply not an option for the Christian. In Ephesians 5:18 the apostle Paul explicitly instructed, "Do not get drunk on wine, which leads to debauchery. Instead, be filled with the Spirit."

Drinking wine *in moderation*, however, does seem to be permissible in Scripture (see John 2:9; 1 Timothy 3:3,8). I should note, though, that in biblical times wine was typically diluted by a ratio of 20 parts water to one part wine. Twenty-to-one water is essentially wine-flavored water. Sometimes in the ancient world, the mixture would be one part water and one part wine, and this was considered strong wine. Anyone who drank wine unmixed was looked upon by the Greeks as a Scythian, a barbarian.

Every Christian adult must decide for himself whether or not to drink. A question we must all ask ourselves is, While drinking may be *permissible*, is it *beneficial* for me to do so? The following verses speak to this issue:

- "'Everything is permissible for me'—but not everything is beneficial. 'Everything is permissible for me'—but I will not be mastered by anything" (1 Corinthians 6:12).

- "It is better not to eat meat or drink wine or to do anything else that will cause your brother to fall" (Romans 14:21).

- "So whether you eat or drink or whatever you do, do it all for the glory of God" (1 Corinthians 10:31).

- "Each of you should look not only to your own interests, but also to the interests of others" (Philippians 2:4).

▶ Did Jesus advocate the use of a sword for self-defense purposes (Luke 22:36-38)?

Jesus is well-known for His continued emphasis on love, forgiveness, and "turning the other cheek." It is therefore surprising to find Jesus advising the disciples to buy a sword in Luke 22:36: "But now if you have a purse, take it, and also a bag; and if you don't have a sword, sell your cloak and buy one." Did Jesus in this verse advocate the use of a sword for self-defense purposes?

This is an issue over which Christians have vehemently disagreed for many centuries. Following is a summary of the two basic views of how Christians have interpreted Jesus on this issue.

View 1: Christian pacifists believe it is always wrong to injure other humans, no matter what the circumstances. And the same principles supporting pacifism carry over to nonresistance—the belief that any form of self-defense is wrong. This view is usually based on the exemplary life and teachings of Jesus Christ.

According to Christian pacifist John Yoder, Jesus rejected the existing political state of affairs and taught a form of radical nonviolence. Central to Christ's teaching, Yoder says, is His biblical mandate to "turn the other cheek" when encountering violence (Matthew 5:38-48).

In Yoder's view, the way to victorious living is to refrain from the game of sociopolitical control. Jesus exposed the futility of the violence engrafted in the present world system by resisting its inclinations even to the point of death. Hence Christians are to refuse the world's violent methods and follow their Savior to the cross (Matthew 26:47-52).[1] When Jesus told the disciples to buy a sword (Luke 22:36), it is suggested that He was only speaking figuratively.[2]

View 2: It is true that Jesus said to turn the other cheek in Matthew 5:38-42. As noted in a previous chapter, however, many scholars do not believe that pacifism (or nonresistance) is the essential point of His teaching in this passage. These scholars do not believe Jesus was teaching to "turn the other cheek" in all circumstances. Even Christ did not literally turn the other cheek when smitten by a member of the Sanhedrin (see John 18:19-23).

As previously pointed out, the backdrop to this teaching is that the Jews considered it an insult to be hit in the face, much in the same way that we would interpret someone spitting in our face. Bible scholar R. C. Sproul comments:

> What's interesting in the expression is that Jesus specifically mentions the right side of the face [Matthew 5:39].... If I hit you on your right cheek, the most normal way would be if I did it with the back of my right hand.... To the best of our knowledge of the Hebrew language, that expression is a Jewish idiom that describes an insult, similar to the way challenges to duels in the days of King Arthur were made by a backhand slap to the right cheek of your opponent.[3]

The principle taught in the Sermon on the Mount in Matthew 5:38-42 would seem to be that Christians should not retaliate when insulted or slandered (see also Romans 12:17-21). Such insults do not threaten a Christian's personal safety. The question of rendering insult for insult, however, is a far cry from defending oneself against a mugger or a rapist.

In terms of following Christ's example, we must remember that His personal nonresistance at the cross was intertwined with His unique calling. He did not evade His arrest because it was God's will for Him to fulfill His prophetic role as the redemptive Lamb of God (Matthew 26:52-56). During His ministry, however, He refused to be arrested because God's timing for His death had not yet come (John 8:59). Thus Christ's unique nonresistance during the Passion does not mandate against self-protection.

It is noteworthy that the Bible records many accounts of fighting and warfare. The providence of God in war is exemplified by His name *YHWH Sabaoth* ("The LORD of hosts"). God is portrayed as the omnipotent Warrior-Leader of the Israelites. God, the LORD of hosts, raised up warriors among the Israelites called the *shophetim* (savior-deliverers). Samson, Deborah, Gideon, and others were anointed by the Spirit of God to conduct war. The New Testament commends Old Testament warriors for their military acts of faith (Hebrews 11:30-40). Moreover, it is significant that although given the opportunity to do so, none of the New Testament saints—nor even Jesus—are ever seen informing a military convert that he needed to resign from his line of work (Matthew 8:5-13; Luke 3:14).

Prior to His crucifixion, Jesus revealed to His disciples the future hostility they would face and encouraged them to sell their outer garments in order to buy a sword (Luke 22:36-38; cf. 2 Corinthians 11:26,27). Here the "sword" (Greek *maxairan*) is a "dagger or short sword [that] belonged to the Jewish traveler's equipment as protection against robbers and wild animals."[4] A plain reading of the passage indicates that Jesus approved of self-defense.

Self-defense may actually result in one of the greatest examples of human love. Christ Himself said, "Greater love has no one than this, that he lay down his life for his friends" (John 15:13). When protecting one's family or neighbor, a Christian is unselfishly risking his or her life for the sake of others.

Theologians J. P. Moreland and Norman Geisler say that—

> . . . to permit murder when one could have pre-
> vented it is morally wrong. To allow a rape when one
> could have hindered it is an evil. To watch an act of
> cruelty to children without trying to intervene is
> morally inexcusable. In brief, not resisting evil is an
> evil of omission, and an evil of omission can be just
> as evil as an evil of commission. Any man who
> refuses to protect his wife and children against a vio-
> lent intruder fails them morally.[5]

▶ **Did Jesus speak approvingly of dishonesty in Luke 16:1-8?**

We read in Luke 16:1-8 that Jesus told His disciples:

> There was a rich man whose manager was
> accused of wasting his possessions. So he called him
> in and asked him, "What is this I hear about you?
> Give an account of your management, because you
> cannot be manager any longer."
>
> The manager said to himself, "What shall I do
> now? My master is taking away my job. I'm not
> strong enough to dig, and I'm ashamed to beg—I
> know what I'll do so that, when I lose my job here,
> people will welcome me into their houses."
>
> So he called in each one of his master's debtors. He
> asked the first, "How much do you owe my master?"
>
> "Eight hundred gallons of olive oil," he replied.
>
> The manager told him, "Take your bill, sit down
> quickly, and make it four hundred."
>
> Then he asked the second, "And how much do
> you owe?"
>
> "A thousand bushels of wheat," he replied.
>
> He told him, "Take your bill and make it eight
> hundred."
>
> The master commended the dishonest manager
> because he had acted shrewdly. For the people of this
> world are more shrewd in dealing with their own
> kind than are the people of the light.

At first glance it might seem that Christ in this passage is approving of dishonesty, but that is not the case. Jesus commended the manager* not for his dishonesty but for taking shrewd, resolute action in the midst of a crisis. Let us consider the details.

It is true that the dishonest manager worked things for his own benefit while cheating his master. And by giving a financial break to the debtors, charging them far less than what they actually owed, they would be obligated to him after he lost his job. He was making friends with them *now* so they would hire him *later*. As the manager put it in verse 4, "When I lose my job here, people will welcome me into their houses." The manager was planning for the future, and in so doing he was acting shrewdly.

When the rich man heard what the manager had done, he commended him because he had handled himself shrewdly. Now the manager had *not* been honest, and *that* part is not commended by the rich man. But the manager did act shrewdly in planning ahead, and it is for this *alone* that the manager was commended. As Bible scholar T. W. Manson put it, there is a world of difference between the statements "I applaud the dishonest steward because he acted cleverly" and "I applaud the clever steward because he acted dishonestly."[6]

It is important not to read more into this parable than is intended. It would be a complete violation of the text to conclude that Jesus was teaching His disciples to handle themselves dishonestly. His only point from the parable was that, like the shrewd manager, they should use material things in such a way as to bring about future spiritual benefit.[7] Bible scholar Robert H. Stein advises us:

> In interpreting any analogy, the interpreter should content himself with the basic point of comparison being made. If the details are not pressed in

---

* Not just a household servant, but apparently an estate manager who was in charge of all the economic affairs of the master.

the parable of the unjust steward, the problem that the parable causes will disappear. What is the point of comparison Jesus is making in the parable? What does he commend? It is not the dishonesty of the steward but his shrewdness: his cleverness and skill for self-preservation.[8]

▶ Does Jesus imply that God could lead us into temptation (Matthew 6:13)?

In the "Lord's Prayer" Jesus taught His followers to pray, "Lead us not into temptation, but deliver us from the evil one" (Matthew 6:13). At first glance it might appear that Jesus is here implying that God *could* lead us into temptation. But I do not think that is the intent of His words.

To begin, we must keep in mind what James 1:13 tells us: "When tempted, no one should say, 'God is tempting me.' For God cannot be tempted by evil, nor does he tempt anyone." Quite clearly, God is not the source of our temptations. James 1:14 teaches that we are tempted when, by our own "evil desire," we are "dragged away and enticed." In other words, our temptations are rooted in our own sinful nature.

It is with this backdrop in mind that scholars suggest two possible explanations of Jesus' words in the Lord's Prayer. Some believe that all Jesus was saying is that we should ask God to so order our lives and guide our steps that we are not brought into situations in which we will find ourselves tempted to do evil. We should ask God to keep our spiritual "radar screens" active so we can be constantly aware of things around us with a view to steering ourselves *away* from tempting circumstances.

Other scholars believe Jesus may be instructing us to pray, "Let us not *succumb* to temptation."[9] Seen in this light, this part of the Lord's Prayer would request of God that whenever temptations are encountered in the course of daily living, God will deliver us. This would be right in line with 1 Corinthians 10:13: "No temptation has seized you except what is common to man. And God is faithful; he will not let you be tempted beyond what you can bear. But when you are tempted, he will also provide a way out so that you can stand up under it."

▶ Did Jesus advocate hating one's mother, father, spouse, and children for His sake (Luke 14:26)?

In Luke 14:26 Jesus said, "If anyone comes to me and does not hate his father and mother, his wife and children, his brothers and sisters—yes, even his own life—he cannot be my disciple." It may initially appear in this verse that Jesus is saying that we should have the emotion of hate for our families for His sake. But I do not think that is what He intended with His words.

The beginning point for properly understanding this statement is that in Jesus' ethic there is no room for truly hating anyone. We are to love even our enemies (Luke 6:27). As well, the fifth commandment instructs us, "Honor your father and your mother" (Exodus 20:12), a commandment repeated in the New Testament (Ephesians 6:1-3; Colossians 3:20).[10] The *Bible Knowledge Commentary* notes: "Literally hating one's family would have been a violation of the Law. Since Jesus on several occasions admonished others to fulfill the Law, He must not have meant that one should literally hate his family."[11]

Jesus in this verse is apparently using a vivid hyperbole (an exaggeration or extravagant statement used as a figure of speech). In understanding Jesus' point, one must keep in mind that in the Hebrew mindset, to "hate" means to "love less" (see Genesis 29:31-33; Deuteronomy 21:15). Jesus is communicating that our supreme love must be for Him alone. Everything else (and everyone else) must take second place.

This is in keeping with what Jesus said in Matthew 10:37: "Anyone who loves his father or mother more than me is not worthy of me; anyone who loves his son or daughter more than me is not worthy of me." Measuring our supreme love for Christ against other lesser loves may make these lesser loves *seem* like hate by comparison.

Other Bible scholars have suggested that while the terms "love" and "hate" are manifestations of emotion in the Western mindset, the ancient Jews used these terms to refer more to a decision of the will. To "love" often carried the idea of *choosing to submit*, whereas "hate" often carried the idea of *choosing not to submit*. "When Christ demanded that one hate those to whom he is bound by the closest of blood ties, He was not speaking in the area of emotions but in the area of the will. A disciple must make a choice and submit to the authority of Christ rather than to the authority of the family headship."[12]

Whichever interpretation is correct above, this passage clearly communicates that one's loyalty to Jesus Christ must come before loyalty to family. Jesus takes first priority.

▶ Why did Jesus tell His followers not to take oaths (Matthew 5:33-37)?

In Matthew 5:33-37 Jesus taught:

> Again, you have heard that it was said to the people long ago, "Do not break your oath, but keep the oaths you have made to the Lord." But I tell you, Do not swear at all: either by heaven, for it is God's throne; or by the earth, for it is his footstool; or by Jerusalem, for it is the city of the Great King. And do not swear by your head, for you cannot make even one hair white or black. Simply let your "Yes" be "Yes," and your "No," "No"; anything beyond this comes from the evil one.

Why was Jesus against taking oaths?

As a backdrop, we should note that there are legitimate oaths mentioned throughout both the Old Testament (Leviticus 5:1; 19:12; Numbers 30:2-15; Deuteronomy 23:21-23; Exodus 20:7) and the New Testament (Acts 2:30; Hebrews 6:16-18; 7:20-22).[13] Even the apostle Paul said, "I call God as my witness . . ." (2 Corinthians 1:23), just as he also said, "I assure you before God that what I am writing to you is no lie"

(Galatians 1:20). On another occasion Paul said, "God can testify how I long for all of you with with the affection of Christ Jesus" (Philippians 1:8).[14] Clearly, there are some cases in which oaths can be made. What, then, should we make of Jesus' words?

The problem Jesus was dealing with in Matthew 5:33-37 is rooted in Pharisaism. The Pharisees promoted the use of oaths to affirm that one was telling the truth, and the oath always involved some type of curse that one placed on oneself if one's word was not true or the promise was not fulfilled. It got to the point that one assumed someone was *not* telling the truth if an oath was not attached to the statement.

Jesus was against *this* use of oaths. He was telling His followers that their character, their reputation for honesty, and the words they speak should be so consistently true, undefiled, and without duplicity that no one would ever think it necessary to put them under an oath, for no one would suspect them of deception.[15] By constantly adding oaths to our verbal statements, we are implying to others that our usual speech is untrustworthy.[16] It should not be that way. As F.F. Bruce put it, "The followers of Jesus should be known as men and women of their word. If they are known to have a scrupulous regard for truth, then what they say will be accepted without the support of any oath."[17]

Christ thus told His followers that when they were communicating with others they should let their yes be yes and their no be no. *Yes* cannot mean no, and *no* cannot mean yes. We should be as good as our word and have no duplicity! This is not to say there are not occasions in which an oath may be appropriate under certain circumstances. But our manner of speaking should be such that an oath is never required for people to know we are telling the truth.

▶ What did Jesus teach on the issue of adultery and divorce (Mark 10:11,12; Luke 16:18)?

In Mark 10:11,12 Jesus, speaking about divorce, said, "Anyone who divorces his wife and marries another woman commits adultery against her. And if she divorces her husband and marries another man, she commits adultery" (see also Luke 16:18). How are we to interpret Jesus' words on adultery and divorce?

The issue of divorce is very difficult. Scripture is clear in stating that God Himself created the institution of marriage, and He intended it to be permanent (Genesis 2:18-25; Matthew 19:4-6). Divorce was never a part of God's original plan. In fact, God hates divorce (Malachi 2:16). The marriage relationship was intended to be dissolved only when one of the marriage partners died (Romans 7:1-4; 1 Corinthians 7:8,9; 1 Timothy 5:14).

When sin entered the world, this affected God's ideal in marriage and many other things. Scripture tells us that even though divorce was not God's ideal, He nevertheless allowed it because of man's sinfulness (Matthew 19:7,8; see also Deuteronomy 24:1-4).

From a biblical perspective, divorce seems to be allowed only under two circumstances: 1) Jesus said it is allowed if one of the marriage partners is unfaithful (Matthew 19:9); 2) the apostle Paul said it is allowed if the unbelieving partner deserts the believing partner (1 Corinthians 7:15,16). Divorce for any other reason is a violation of God's ideal.

Even when a person clearly has biblical permission to divorce, God's desire is that the person if possible forgive the offending spouse and be reconciled to him or her. This follows from God's command to forgive others of their wrongs toward us (Ephesians 4:32; Colossians 3:13).

Of course, God forgives us of all our sins, including the sin of divorce (Colossians 2:13). However, simply because God forgives us does not remove the painful consequences of our actions on ourselves or on others. There is a heavy price to pay for violating God's ideal.

According to the popular rabbi Hillel (who lived in New Testament times), the husband could be granted a "bill of divorcement" for nearly any infraction on the part of the wife.

Even burning a meal was considered grounds for divorce. Divorce was rather easy in those days.

A key point that Jesus makes in Mark 10:11,12, however, is that even though one could easily obtain a bill of divorcement, such a *man-made* document did not in any way release the marriage partners from *God's* law of marriage and its moral obligations. One might look acceptable before his or her peers with a bill of divorcement in hand, but before God be guilty of adultery if that person should remarry following the divorce. One should therefore not consider divorce the "easy out" the Pharisees portrayed it to be.

THIRTEEN

PRAYER AND FAITH

▶ Did Jesus teach that God is resistant to answering our prayers (Luke 11:7-9)?

Luke 11:5-10 records Jesus' parable about prayer in which a person knocked on a friend's door at midnight in need of three loaves of bread. The one inside answered, "Don't bother me. The door is already locked, and my children are with me in bed. I can't get up and give you anything" (verse 7). (This was likely a one-room house, which means that if he got up in the night, he would probably wake the children.)[1] The parable concludes by pointing out that even though friendship was not enough to cause the person in the house to get up and provide bread, the *boldness* expressed in knocking on the door at midnight and the *persistence* in doing so (verse 8) was enough to yield the result of bread.

Since this is a parable about prayer, it may seem at first reading that Jesus is implying that God is resistant to answering our prayers. But that is not the intent of His words.

The whole of Scripture affirms that the Father readily responds to the needs of His children every bit as much as an earthly father responds to the needs of his children (Matthew 7:9-11). The heavenly Father is *not* resistant to answering our prayers. In fact, not only does the parable not teach that God is resistant to prayer, but it gives us an assurance that God *does* answer prayer. The primary purpose of the parable was to teach Christ's followers to be *persistent* in prayer. As expositor Leon Morris puts it, "It is not that God is unwilling and must be pressed into answering. The whole context makes it clear that He is eager to give. But if we do not want what we are asking for enough to be persistent, we do not want it very much."[2] The point, then, is that we need to be persistent in prayer *precisely because* God longs to give good gifts to us.[3]

We see this persistence stressed in verses 9 and 10, which follow the parable. Here Jesus said, "So I say to you: Ask and it will be given to you; seek and you will find; knock and the door will be opened to you. For everyone who asks receives; he who seeks finds; and to him who knocks, the door will be opened." In these verses the words "ask," "seek," and "knock" are in the present tense, which indicates continuous activity. We are to *keep on* asking, *keep on* seeking, and *keep on* knocking.[4] If we do so, we will obtain our desired result, assuming that our request is in keeping with God's will for our lives.

▶ Did Jesus teach that we should recite only short prayers (Matthew 6:7)?

In Jesus' instructions about prayer, He taught His followers, "When you pray, do not keep on babbling like pagans, for they think they will be heard because of their many words" (Matthew 6:7). These words of Jesus were aimed straight at the Pharisees. These individuals always made a public show of their prayers. They would typically pray in a public place—perhaps on a street corner—to impress people with their piety. They would pray *conspicuously*. They very much enjoyed being seen as they prayed.

The Pharisees also made their prayers excessively long, a practice picked up from the pagans, who engaged in endless repetition and incantation. An example of such endless babbling is found in 1 Kings 18:26: "They called on the name of Baal *from morning till noon.* 'O Baal, answer us!' they shouted" (italics added). The belief was that endless repetition of specific requests endeared the petitioner to God, and hence God would be obligated to answer. Prayer was used by the Pharisees as a lengthy formula or technique to manipulate God into action.

So the point of Jesus' instruction is not that we should necessarily utter short prayers before God (although short prayers are just fine if that is all you have time for or if that meets your particular need at the moment). The point of Jesus' instruction is that we should not engage in endless babbling, repeating the same request over and over again within the confines of a single prayer, as if that would force God's hand to answer. God answers prayer not because He can be moved to do so by endless babbling but rather because He desires to do so as your heavenly Father.

In support of the fact that Jesus is not forbidding long prayers is the fact that Jesus Himself is portrayed as praying at length (Luke 6:12). He also repeated Himself in prayer on occasion (Matthew 26:44). He further instructed His disciples that "they should always pray and not give up" (Luke 18:1).[5] Jesus' point was not that one should avoid long prayers, but that one should avoid the Pharisaic misconception that prayers are effective *simply because* they are long.

▶ Does Jesus teach that God shows favoritism in terms of whose prayers He answers (Matthew 15:22-28)?

In Matthew 15:22-28 we read:

> A Canaanite woman from that vicinity came to him, crying out, "Lord, Son of David, have mercy on me! My daughter is suffering terribly from demon-possession."
>
> Jesus did not answer a word. So his disciples came to him and urged him, "Send her away, for she keeps crying out after us."
>
> He answered, "I was sent only to the lost sheep of Israel."
>
> The woman came and knelt before him. "Lord, help me!" she said.

He replied, "It is not right to take the children's bread and toss it to their dogs."

"Yes, Lord," she said, "but even the dogs eat the crumbs that fall from their masters' table."

Then Jesus answered, "Woman, you have great faith! Your request is granted." And her daughter was healed from that very hour.

In this passage Jesus makes reference to the Gentiles as "dogs." Is He here showing favoritism in terms of whose prayers God answers?

Let us look at the context. In this passage we read about a Gentile woman who came to present her need to Jesus. Notice that she addressed Jesus by two messianic titles—"Lord" and "Son of David." She was begging from the One she knew to be Israel's Messiah.

It may seem odd at first glance that Jesus ignored her request (Matthew 15:23). But all becomes clear in the verses that follow. Jesus informed her, "I was sent only to the lost sheep of Israel" (verse 24). What Jesus means here is that He had come specifically to offer the nation of Israel the kingdom that had been promised in the Davidic Covenant many centuries earlier (2 Samuel 7:12-14). It would not be appropriate for Him to pour out blessings on a Gentile woman before such blessings were bestowed on Israel.[6]

But the woman continued in her plea. Jesus responded, "It is not right to take the children's bread and toss it to their dogs" (Matthew 15:26). It is well-known that the Jews of Jesus' day looked upon all Gentiles as being dogs. It is also well-known that the Jews considered themselves to be God's children.

The picture Jesus was painting was that of a family sitting around a table at dinnertime. In the analogy, it is the Jews who are the children seated at the table, eating the food provided by the head of the household. The Gentile woman recognized herself in the story as the household dog. The choicest morsels of food were for the "children" at the table, but as a "dog" the

Gentile woman saw herself as eligible for the crumbs that might fall from the table.[7]

It seems clear that the woman was not seeking to interfere with God's blessing of Israel but rather was hoping that a little bit of the overflow of such blessing might be extended to her in her time of need.[8] It took great faith for her to say this to Jesus. And because of this faith, Jesus granted her request. How ironic that the Gentile woman's faith was in great contrast to the lack of faith of Israel's hypocritical leaders!

I must confess that after studying this passage for some time, I began to wonder whether Jesus might have been exhibiting a sense of humor in His comments to the woman. Surely since Jesus is the Creator of all humanity (John 1:3; Colossians 1:16; Hebrews 1:2), He does not actually look upon *any* person as being a "dog." Could it be, then, that Jesus had a twinkle in His eye when He alluded to current Jewish sentiments and said to the woman, "It is not right to take the children's bread and toss it to their dogs." In my study I was glad to discover that such a preeminent scholar as F. F. Bruce concluded that indeed this was probably the case.[9]

▶ Did Jesus teach we can obtain anything we want if we ask for it in the name of Jesus (John 16:24)?

In John 16:24 Jesus said, "Until now you have asked for nothing in My name; ask and you will receive, that your joy may be made full" (NASB). These words should not be taken in isolation from what Jesus and the apostles taught elsewhere about prayer. In John 15:7, for example, Jesus said, "If you abide in Me, and My words abide in you, ask whatever you wish, and it shall be done for you" (NASB). Here *abiding* is a clear condition for receiving answers to prayer.

We are also told that "whatever we ask we receive from Him, *because we keep His commandments and do the things that are pleasing in His sight*" (1 John 3:22 NASB, italics added). Moreover, we are told, "This is the confidence which we have before Him, that, if we ask anything *according to His will*, He hears us. And if we know that He hears us in whatever we ask, we know that we have the requests which we have asked from Him" (1 John 5:14,15 NASB, italics added).

Finally, we are told that if we ask for something with *wrong motives* we will not receive what we asked for (James 4:3). These are important qualifications to keep in mind when seeking to understand what Jesus meant in John 16:24. Yes, we will receive whatever we pray for in Jesus' name so long as we abide in Christ, obey His commandments, and ask with the right motive, and so long as the thing we ask for is in keeping with God's will for our lives.

▶ Did Jesus promise to give us literally anything we ask for in faith (Mark 11:22-24)?

In Mark 11:23,24 Jesus said, "I tell you the truth, if anyone says to this mountain, 'Go, throw yourself into the sea,' and does not doubt in his heart but believes that what he says will happen, it will be done for him. Therefore I tell you, whatever you ask for in prayer, believe that you have received it, and it will be yours."

The fact is that there are limitations on what God will give us, indicated by the broader context of Scripture. As Bible scholar David O'Brien put it, Jesus in this passage "wasn't promising a heavenly Visa card with an unlimited line of credit, or a free shopping spree in heaven's treasure house."[10]

It is important to understand that God cannot literally give us *anything whatsoever*. Some things are quite impossible for God to give. For example, as Norman Geisler notes, God cannot grant a request of a creature to become God. Neither can He answer a request to approve of our sinful acts. God will not give us a stone if we ask for bread, nor will He give us a serpent if we ask for fish (Matthew 7:9,10).[11]

When the rest of Scripture is taken into consideration, there are many conditions placed on God's promise to answer prayer in addition to faith. We must abide in Him and let His Word abide in us (John 15:7). We cannot ask amiss out of our own selfishness (James 4:3). Furthermore, we must ask according to His will (1 John 5:14). This last condition—the will of God—is especially important.[12]

We might illustrate this with the issue of healing. It is clear from Scripture that God does not promise to heal *everyone* for whom we pray in faith, but rather that healing is subject to the will of God. Paul was not healed, though he prayed earnestly and faithfully (2 Corinthians 12:8,9). Despite the apostle Paul's divine ability to heal others (Acts 28:9), later he apparently could not heal either Epaphroditus (Philippians 2:25,26) or Trophimus (2 Timothy 4:20). It clearly was not unbelief that brought Job's sickness on him (Job 1:1). All our prayer requests should be conditioned by "if it be your will." Sometimes God says no because He has a greater purpose in mind for our lives.

▶ Does Scripture teach that Christians can receive a hundredfold return on the money they tithe in faith (Mark 10:29,30)?

In Mark 10:29,30 Jesus said to His followers, "I tell you the truth . . . no one who has left home or brothers or sisters or mother or father or children or fields for me and the gospel will fail to receive a hundred times as much in this present age (homes, brothers, sisters, mothers, children and fields—and with them, persecutions) and in the age to come, eternal life."

Contextually, this passage has nothing to do with money or riches. It is speaking specifically of those who forsake home and loved ones for the sake of Jesus and the gospel. *These* individuals will receive a "hundredfold return" in the sense that they become a part of a community of believers. It is in this new community that they find a multiplication of relationships, many of which are ultimately closer and more spiritually meaningful than blood relationships (Mark 3:31-35; Acts 2:41-47; 1 Timothy 5:1,2).

FOURTEEN

THE PROPHETIC FUTURE AND THE AFTERLIFE

ᏮᎢᎢᏞᎤ

▶ Why did Jesus say, "I am coming soon," when it has now been almost 2000 years since He said it (Revelation 22:12; 22:20)?

In the book of Revelation Jesus made several references to His second coming, saying, "Behold, I am coming soon!" (Revelation 22:7,12,20; see also 3:11). It has now been almost 2000 years since Jesus said this, which hardly seems "soon." Scholars have thus offered two primary suggestions as to what He might have meant.

Some scholars suggest that from the human perspective it may not seem soon, but from the divine perspective it is. According to the New Testament, we have been living in the "last days" since the incarnation of Christ (James 5:3; Hebrews 1:2). Moreover, we read in James 5:9 that "the Judge is standing at the door." Romans 13:12 exhorts us that "the night is nearly over; the day is almost here." Hebrews 10:25 admonishes, "Let us not give up meeting together, as some are in the habit of doing, but let us encourage one another—and all the more *as you see the Day approaching*" (italics added). And 1 Peter 4:7 warns, "The end of all things is near. Therefore be clear-minded and self-controlled so that you can pray." In view of such verses, it would seem that Christ is coming "soon" *from the divine perspective*.

Other scholars suggest that perhaps Jesus meant He is coming soon from the perspective of the events described in the book of Revelation. In other words, from the vantage point of those living during the time of the tribulation period itself—a seven-year period of trials that culminates in the Second Coming (see Revelation 4–19)—Christ is coming soon.[1]

▶ What did Jesus mean when He said, "This generation will certainly not pass away until all these things have happened" (Matthew 24:34)?

Evangelical Christians have generally held to one of two interpretations of Matthew 24:34. One is that Christ is simply saying that those people who witness the signs stated earlier in Matthew 24 (all of which deal with the future tribulation period) will see the coming of Jesus Christ within that very generation. In other words, the generation alive when such events as the abomination of desolation (verse 15), the great tribulation (verse 21), and the sign of the Son of Man in heaven (verse 30) begin to come to pass will *still* be alive when these prophetic judgments are completed. Since the tribulation is a period of seven years (Daniel 9:27; Revelation 11:2), then Jesus would be saying that the generation alive at the beginning of the tribulation will still be alive at the end of it, at which time the second coming of Christ will occur.[2]

Other evangelicals say the word *generation* in this verse is to be taken in its secondary meaning of "race," "kindred," "family," "stock," or "breed." Jesus' statement could mean that the Jewish race would not pass away until all things are fulfilled. Since many divine promises were made to Israel—including the eternal inheritance of the land of Palestine (Genesis 12, 15, 17) and the Davidic kingdom (2 Samuel 7)—then Jesus could be referring to God's preservation of the nation of Israel in order to fulfill His promises to the nation. Indeed, Paul speaks of a future of the nation of Israel when the Jews will be reinstated in God's covenantal promises (Romans 11:11-27).

▶ Was Jesus referring to the rapture or judgment in
Luke 17:34-37?

In Luke 17:34-47 Jesus, speaking of the time of the second
coming, said, "'I tell you, on that night two people will be in
one bed; one will be taken and the other left. Two women will
be grinding grain together; one will be taken and the other left.'
'Where, Lord?' they asked. He replied, 'Where there is a dead
body, there the vultures will gather.'"

Certainly there have been many Christians through the
years who have interpreted this passage as referring to the rapture. Several points militate against this interpretation, however. To begin, if you believe that the rapture happens *prior* to
the time of the tribulation (as I do—see 1 Thessalonians 1:10;
5:9), then Luke 17:34-37 could not be referring to the rapture,
since the events in Luke 17 happen *after* the tribulation, at the
time of the second coming of Christ.

Beyond this, the immediate context of Luke 17 seems to
argue against the possibility that the rapture is in view. I admit
that it initially *sounds* like the rapture (one being "taken" and
one being "left")—but once you get to verse 37 the rapture
interpretation seems to go up in smoke. The disciples asked
Jesus *where* these individuals would be taken. Jesus replied,
"Where there is a dead body, there the vultures will gather."
Jesus' answer clearly points to judgment.

In the Old Testament God is portrayed as leaving His enemies as food for vultures (Ezekiel 32:4–6; 39:17–20), which the
Jewish people considered a horrible fate (Deuteronomy 28:26;
1 Samuel 17:44; Psalm 79:2).[3] This is the fate of those in Luke
17. "Much as a dead body causes vultures to 'gather' on it, so
dead people are consigned to judgment if they are not ready for
the kingdom (cf. Matt. 24:28; Rev. 19:17-19)."[4]

Those who are left behind will be Christians who enter into
Christ's millennial kingdom—a period of 1000 years during
which Christ will rule on the earth (Revelation 20:1-6; see also
Matthew 25:31-46).

▶ Why are believers living in the tribulation period instructed to "be always on the watch" (Luke 21:36)?

In Luke 21:36 Jesus warned, "Be always on the watch, and pray that you may be able to escape all that is about to happen, and that you may be able to stand before the Son of Man." What precisely is Jesus saying these tribulation Christians are to pray to escape?

Contextually, this verse is part of a larger discourse that Jesus gave about the end times in verses 5-38. In this broad context Jesus discussed certain things that will precede His second coming, such as the rise in false Christs (verse 8), an increase in wars (verse 9), an increase in earthquakes and famines (verse 11), persecution (verse 12), the desolation of the Jewish temple that will exist during the tribulation period (verse 20), and catastrophic changes in the environment (verses 25,26). Clearly this will not be an easy time to be living on planet Earth.

Then, in verses 34 and 35, Jesus warned about how the hearts of people living during this time will be weighed down with dissipation, drunkenness, and the anxieties of life—anxieties no doubt related to the horrific events described in the preceding verses. With these anxieties in mind, Jesus warned these tribulation Christians in verse 36 to "watch" and be ready. His words might be paraphrased this way:

> These horrific events will take many people by surprise and will lead to great anxiety in their hearts. They will try to numb this anxiety by getting drunk. You, however, should not be taken by surprise, for I have warned you in advance that these things will happen. Therefore watch and be ready. Do not succumb to debilitating anxiety or drunkenness. Instead, keep your eyes focused on the fact that I am indeed coming again. Pray that you may escape being sidetracked like so many others during this time who will be paralyzed by fear. Do not have "double vision," with one eye on me and the other eye on the anxieties of the tribulation; maintain "single vision"

and keep your focus on me. Then, when I do come, you will be ready.

I personally believe Jesus' words here are intended for those people who *become* Christians during the tribulation period. I believe that the rapture of the church will take place *before* the tribulation begins (1 Thessalonians 4:13-17; see also 1:10; 5:9), thus removing the church from planet Earth. But following the rapture, there will be many people that convert to Christ during the tribulation (Matthew 24:14; see also Revelation 7:1-17). It is these individuals that Christ warns to keep watch as the time draws near for the Second Coming.

▶ Will there be no Christians on earth at the second coming of Christ (Luke 18:8)?

In Luke 18:8 Jesus asked the disciples, "When the Son of Man comes, will he find faith on the earth?" Most scholars believe that Jesus did not doubt that there would be Christians on earth when He returned again. After all, in Matthew 25:31-46 Jesus said He would separate His "sheep" (Christians) from the goats (unbelievers) following His second coming. Nevertheless, Jesus indicated in Luke 18:8 that the primary characteristic of people on earth at the time of His return would be unbelief.[5]

It is likely that Jesus strategically asked the question about finding faith on earth to spur His own disciples on to faithfulness. Among ancient Jewish writers, there were predictions that in the end times many would fall away from the faith (compare with 2 Thessalonians 2:3,4).[6] But Jesus did not want this to happen to His followers. Hence, He asked the question to motivate them. Jesus continued urging them on to faithfulness throughout the rest of this Gospel (see, for example, Luke 21:8-19,34-36; 22:31,32,40,46).

▶ What future feast is Jesus referring to in Matthew 8:10-12?

In Matthew 8:10-12 Jesus responded to the faith of the Gentile centurion who asked Him to heal his servant: "I tell you the truth, I have not found anyone in Israel with such great faith. I say to you that many will come from the east and the west, and will take their places at the feast with Abraham, Isaac and Jacob in the kingdom of heaven. But the subjects of the kingdom will be thrown outside, into the darkness, where there will be weeping and gnashing of teeth."

The backdrop to Jesus' statement is that participating in God's future kingdom was often pictured as eating at a banquet (see Isaiah 25:6; Matthew 22:1-14). Many Jews thought they would enter God's kingdom and be at this "banquet" solely because of their blood-relationship to Abraham. However, Jesus indicated in Matthew 8:11,12 that many who thought they would be at this banquet because of ties to Abraham would in fact be denied entrance altogether, while many who do not even have such blood ties (like the Gentile centurion) would be granted entrance.

Interestingly, according to Jewish thought, people were seated at banquets according to rank. So, in Matthew 8:11,12 Jesus was saying that even many Gentiles will be at this banquet and take a place of honor with the great patriarchs—Abraham, Isaac, and Jacob.[7] By contrast, the Jews who refused to believe in Jesus would be barred entrance.

▶ In what sense do the meek "inherit" the earth (Matthew 5:5)?

In the beatitudes, Jesus said, "Blessed are the meek, for they will inherit the earth" (Matthew 5:5). Scholars have noted that Jesus likely based this beatitude on Psalm 37:11, where we read, "But the meek will inherit the land and enjoy great peace." What is Psalm 37:11 referring to?

The Hebrew word for land (*eres*) is used in the context of Psalm 37 of the Promised Land. The central issue addressed in this psalm seems to be: Who will inherit the land (verses 9,11,22,29)—that is, who will live on to enjoy the blessings of the Lord in the Promised Land? *Will it be the wicked*, who plot (verse 12), scheme (verses 7,32), default on debts (verse 21), use raw power to gain advantage (verse 14), and thereby seem to flourish (verses 7,16,35)? *Or will it be the righteous*, who trust in the Lord (verses 3,5,7,34) and are humble (verse 11), blameless (verses 18,37), generous (verses 21,26), upright (verse 37), and peaceable (verse 37), and from whose mouth is heard the moral wisdom that reflects meditation on God's Law (verses 30,31)? The answer is obvious.

If it is the humble Old Testament believer who inherits the Promised Land and experiences its blessedness in Psalm 37:11, then what is Jesus saying in Matthew 5:5: "Blessed are the meek, for they will inherit the earth"? Bible expositors suggest that Jesus may be saying that those who meekly follow Him will one day inherit the *new* earth, which is a part of the new heavens and the new earth.[8]

In Isaiah 65:17 God spoke prophetically, "Behold, I will create new heavens and a new earth. The former things will not be remembered, nor will they come to mind." In the book of Revelation we read, "Then I saw a new heaven and a new earth, for the first heaven and the first earth had passed away, and there was no longer any sea. . . . He who was seated on the throne said, 'I am making everything new!'" (Revelation 21:1,5).

The Greek word used to designate the newness of the cosmos is not *neos* but *kainos*. *Neos* means new in time or new in origin. But *kainos* means new in nature or new in quality. Hence the phrase "new heavens and a new earth" refers not to a cosmos that is totally other than the present cosmos. Rather, the new cosmos will stand in continuity with the present cosmos, but it will be *utterly renewed and renovated.*[9]

In keeping with this, Matthew 19:28 (NASB) speaks of "the regeneration." Acts 3:21 speaks of the "restoration of all things." Bible expositor Walter Scott comments that "our planet will be put in the crucible, altered, changed, and made new, to abide forever."[10]

The new earth, being a renewed and an eternal earth, will be adapted to the vast moral and physical changes which the eternal state necessitates. Everything will be new in the eternal state. Everything will be according to God's own glorious nature. The new heavens and the new earth will be brought into blessed conformity with all that God is—in a state of fixed bliss and absolute perfection.

It seems clear that there will be geological changes in the new earth, for there will be no more sea (Revelation 21:1). At present about three-quarters of the earth's surface is covered with water and is therefore uninhabitable. In the new earth, an immensely increased land surface will exist as a result of the disappearance of the oceans. Glorified humanity will inhabit a glorified earth recreated and adapted to eternal conditions.

An amazing thing to ponder is that in the next life heaven and earth will no longer be separate realms, as they are now, but will be merged. Believers will thus continue to be in heaven even while they are on the new earth.[11] The new earth will be utterly sinless, and hence bathed and suffused in the light and splendor of God, unobscured by evil of any kind or tarnished by evildoers of any description. It is this earth that meek followers of the Lord Jesus will one day inherit.

▶ What did Jesus mean by "paradise" in the afterlife (Luke 23:43)?

In Luke 23:43 Jesus told the thief on the cross, "I tell you the truth, today you will be with me in paradise." The paradise Jesus spoke of here is the same "paradise" addressed elsewhere in regard to the afterlife. The word "paradise" literally means "garden of pleasure" or "garden of delight." Revelation 2:7 makes reference to heaven as the "paradise of God." The apostle Paul in 2 Corinthians 12:4 said he "was caught up to paradise" and "heard inexpressible things, things that man is not permitted to tell."

Apparently this paradise of God is so resplendently glorious, so ineffable, so wondrous, that Paul was forbidden to say anything about it to those still in the earthly realm. But what Paul saw instilled in him an eternal perspective that enabled him to face the trials that lay ahead of him (Romans 8:18; 2 Corinthians 4:17).

Paradise is a place of incredible bliss and serene rest in the very presence of God (2 Corinthians 12:2). Paul's assessment was this: "No eye has seen, no ear has heard, no mind has con-ceived what God has prepared for those who love him" (1 Corinthians 2:9). Paradise is the seat and dwelling place of the divine Majesty. It is where the glorified Christ dwells. It is the residence of the holy angels. And at the moment of death, Christians enter this blessed dwelling place.

▶ Is Jesus' description of Lazarus and the rich man in Abraham's bosom just a story, or is its picture of the afterlife (involving conscious existence) true (Luke 16:19-31)?

Some scholars have suggested that the parable of the rich man and Lazarus was just a story.[12] But other scholars have noted that when Jesus taught people using parables or stories, *He always cited real-life situations.*

For example, Jesus spoke of a prodigal son who returned home after squandering his money (Luke 15:11-32); a man who found a buried treasure in a field (Matthew 13:44); a king who put on a wedding feast for his son (Matthew 22:1-14); a slave-owner who traveled abroad and then returned home to his slaves (Matthew 25:14-30); a man who constructed a vineyard (Matthew 20:1-16); and so on. All of these were common occurrences in biblical days.

Jesus never illustrated His teaching with a fairy tale. This being the case, we must conclude that Luke 16 is real-life and should be taken as a solid evidence for conscious existence after death. Any other interpretation makes an absurdity of the text.

▶ By describing death as "falling asleep," did Jesus teach there is no conscious existence following the moment of death (John 11:11–14)?

In John 11:11–14 Jesus said that Lazarus had "fallen asleep"—meaning that he had died. This does not mean there is no conscious existence of the soul following death. Indeed, Scripture consistently teaches that the souls of both believers and unbelievers are conscious between death and the future res-urrection. Unbelievers are in conscious woe (Luke 16:22,23;

Mark 9:43-48; Revelation 19:20) while believers are in conscious bliss (Philippians 1:23; 2 Corinthians 5:8).

The term "sleep," when used in contexts of death in Scripture, always refers to *the body*, not the soul. Sleep is an appropriate figure of speech for the death of the body since the body takes on the *appearance* of sleep (see Acts 7:60; 1 Corinthians 15:20; 1 Thessalonians 4:13-18).[13]

The evidence for conscious existence following death is very strong. Consider the following:

- The rich man and Lazarus were conscious following death (Luke 16:19-31).
- Jesus' spirit went to the Father the day He died (Luke 23:46).
- Jesus promised that the repentant thief would be with Him in paradise the very day he died (Luke 23:43).
- Paul said it was far better to die and be with Christ (Philippians 1:23).
- Paul affirmed that when we are "away from the body," then "we are at home with the Lord" (2 Corinthians 5:8).
- The "souls" of those martyred during the tribulation period are conscious in heaven, singing and praying to God (Revelation 6:9).
- Jesus, in speaking about the Old Testament saints Abraham, Isaac, and Jacob, said that God "is not the God of the dead, but *of the living*" (Luke 20:38). In effect, Jesus said, "Abraham, Isaac, and Jacob, though they died many years ago, are actually living today. For God, who calls Himself the God of Abraham, Isaac, and Jacob, is not the God of the dead but of the living."

▶ Did Jesus teach that in the afterlife resurrected human beings will no longer be married (Matthew 22:30)?

In Matthew 22:30 Jesus affirmed, "At the resurrection people will neither marry nor be given in marriage; they will be like the angels in heaven." The context here indicates that once believers receive their glorified resurrection bodies, the need for procreation—one of the fundamental purposes for marriage (Genesis 1:28)—will no longer exist. We will be like the angels in the sense that we will not be married and will not procreate any longer. (We know that angels do not procreate and reproduce, for all the angels in the universe were created at one and the same time—see Psalm 148:2-5; Colossians 1:16.)

We should not think of the dissolution of marriage as a deprivation. It is important to understand that the pleasures of heaven will far exceed anything that human beings have ever known on earth. Indeed, heaven is often described as "paradise," a word that literally means "garden of pleasure" or "garden of delight" (2 Corinthians 12:4). We are told in 1 Corinthians 2:9, "No eye has seen, no ear has heard, no mind has conceived what God has prepared for those who love him."

▶ Did Jesus teach that even the wicked will one day be resurrected (John 5:28,29)?

Yes. In John 5:28,29 Jesus said, "Do not be amazed at this, for a time is coming when all who are in their graves will hear his voice and come out—those who have done good will rise to live, and those who have done evil will rise to be condemned."

Consulting the broader scope of Scripture, we learn that there are two types of resurrection—respectively referred to as the first resurrection and the second resurrection (Revelation 20:5,6, 11-15). The first resurrection is the resurrection *of Christians*, while the second resurrection is the resurrection *of the wicked*. This second resurrection will be a resurrection *unto judgment*.

The "second" resurrection will be an awful spectacle. All the unsaved of all time will be resurrected at the end of Christ's millennial kingdom, judged at the Great White Throne judgment, and then cast alive into the lake of fire (Revelation 20:11-15). They will be given bodies that will last forever, but capable of experiencing pain and suffering. *An awful spectacle indeed.*

▶ Was hell originally created for the fallen angels and not fallen man (Matthew 25:41)?

That is correct. Hell was not part of God's original creation, which He called *good* (Genesis 1:10,12,18,21). Hell was created later to accommodate the banishment of Satan and his fallen angels who rebelled against God (see Ezekiel 28:11-15 and Isaiah 14:12-20). As Jesus put it, the place called hell refers to "the eternal fire prepared for the devil and his angels" (Matthew 25:41). Human beings who reject Christ will join Satan and his fallen angels in this infernal place of suffering (Revelation 20:11-15).

▶ Is hell a place of darkness, as Jesus said, or is there light there as a result of fiery flames (Matthew 8:12)?

Jesus described hell as a place of "outer darkness" (Matthew 8:12 NASB; compare with 22:13 and 25:30). Elsewhere hell is described as a place of "fire" (Revelation 20:14) and "unquenchable flames" (Mark 9:48). But fire and flames give off light. How can hell be "dark" when there is light there?

The apparent contradiction is solved by recognizing that not all language in the Bible is literal. It may be that one or the other (or both) of the terms "fire" and "darkness" are figures of speech the biblical writers used to describe the inconceivable reality of hell. Some theologians say hell is like fire because it is a place of pain, punishment, and destruction. Other theologians suggest that fire may be a metaphorical way of expressing the great wrath of God. Scripture tells us, "The LORD your God is a consuming fire, a jealous God" (Deuteronomy 4:24). "God is a consuming fire" (Hebrews 12:29). "His wrath is poured out like fire" (Nahum 1:6). "Who can stand when he appears? For he will be like a refiner's fire" (Malachi 3:2). God said, "My wrath will break out and burn like fire because of the evil you have done—burn with no one to quench it" (Jeremiah 4:4).

Yet, despite the presence of "fire," hell is also like *outer darkness* because it is permeated by spiritual darkness and people are lost in this gloomy place forever and ever. It is said to be "outer" in the sense that it is far, far away from God and all that is good.

In view of the above, it is clear that hell is a literal place, but not every description of it should be taken literally. Theologian Norman Geisler notes that other figures of speech are used to describe the eternal destiny of the lost in Scripture that, if taken literally, would contradict each other. For example, hell is depicted as an eternal garbage dump (Mark 9:43-48), which has a bottom. But it is also portrayed as a bottomless pit (Revelation 20:3). While not to be taken literally, each figure of speech is a vivid depiction of hell as a place of everlasting punishment.[14]

▶ Does Jesus teach that anyone who lives well now will without doubt be punished in the afterlife (Luke 6:25)?

In Luke 6:25 Jesus said, "Woe to you who are well fed now, for you will go hungry. Woe to you who laugh now, for you will mourn and weep." At first glance it may appear that Jesus is saying that anyone who lives well during his or her earthly sojourn will without exception experience a reversal in the afterlife and be punished. But this is not the case.

The disciples had given up everything to follow Jesus. In contrast to them were those loaded with money and wealth, many of whom did not sense the gravity of their true situation (that is, their need of redemption in view of the sin problem). Such self-sufficient and prideful individuals would laugh at and scorn others who spoke of sin and the need for redemption.

It is these blinded individuals that Jesus spoke of in Luke 6:25. It is these individuals—who do not trust in Jesus but instead trust in their riches and the comfort that wealth brings—who will one day experience a reversal and find themselves engulfed in eternal punishment. "People who live thinking that what they have is all-sufficient, who allow material possessions to be all-in-all and who think they have no need of God, are assured *you shall hunger*."[15]

▶ Did Jesus teach the doctrine of reincarnation (Matthew 11:14; John 3:3)?

Individuals who claim Jesus taught reincarnation typically point to Matthew 11:14 and John 3:3. Let us take a brief look at both of these.

Matthew 11:14 says, "If you are willing to accept it, he [John the Baptist] is the Elijah who was to come." It is sometimes claimed that John the Baptist is a reincarnation of Elijah. However, Luke 1:17 clarifies any possible confusion on the proper interpretation of this verse by pointing out that the ministry of John the Baptist was carried out "in the spirit and power of Elijah." Nowhere does it say that John the Baptist was a reincarnation of Elijah. Reincarnation enthusiasts conveniently forget that John the Baptist, when asked whether he was Elijah, flatly answered "No!" (John 1:21).

In John 3:3 Jesus said to Nicodemus, "I tell you the truth, no one can see the kingdom of God unless he is born again." It is sometimes argued that Jesus was referring to "cyclical rebirth" in this verse. However, the context clearly shows that Jesus was referring to a *spiritual rebirth* or regeneration. In fact, the phrase "born again" carries the idea of "born from above," and can even be translated that way. Nicodemus could not have understood Jesus' statement in any other way, for Jesus clarified His meaning by affirming that "flesh gives birth to flesh, but the Spirit gives birth to spirit" (verse 6).

Beyond the above, there are many problems with the salvation-by-works doctrine of reincarnation. For example:

- We must ask, Why does one get punished (via the law of karma) for something he or she cannot remember having done in a previous life?
- If the purpose of karma is to rid humanity of its selfish desires, then why hasn't there been a noticeable improvement in human nature after all the millennia of reincarnations?
- If reincarnation and the law of karma are so beneficial on a practical level, then how do advocates of this

doctrine explain the immense and ever-worsening social and economic problems—including widespread poverty, starvation, disease, and horrible suffering—in India, where reincarnation has been systematically taught throughout its history?

There are also many biblical problems with believing in reincarnation. For example, in 2 Corinthians 5:8 the apostle Paul states, "We are confident, I say, and would prefer to be away from the body and at home with the Lord." At death, then, the Christian immediately goes into the presence of the Lord, not into another body. In keeping with this, Luke 16:19-31 tells us that unbelievers at death go to a place of suffering, not into another body.

Further, Hebrews 9:27 assures us that "man is destined to die once, and after that to face judgment." Each human being *lives once* as a mortal on earth, *dies once*, and then *faces judgment.* He does not have a second chance by reincarnating into another body.

FIFTEEN

THE DEVIL AND HELL'S ANGELS

൭ᴡᴡᴏ

▶ Did Jesus indicate that Peter was possessed by the Devil when He said to him, "Get behind me, Satan" (Mark 8:33)?

In context, Jesus had just taught His disciples that He was to be killed, but that He would rise again three days later (see Mark 8:31-38). Peter then rebuked Jesus for saying He must die. Peter may have been holding on to the popular misconception of the Messiah that involved a conquering king that would deliver Israel from Roman domination. This conception of the Messiah would be impossible if the Messiah had to die. Jesus then turned to Peter and said, "Get behind me, Satan! You do not have in mind the things of God, but the things of men" (verse 33).

Jesus recognized that Satan was behind these words of Peter. Aware of God's plan, Satan was bent on doing anything he could to prevent Jesus from going to the cross. Recall that Satan had earlier attempted to divert Jesus from going to the cross in the wilderness temptations (Mark 1:12,13). Now Satan attempted to divert Jesus through one of His closest associates, His friend and disciple Peter.

The fact that Satan spoke through Peter does not mean Peter became explicitly *possessed* of the Devil. Peter became an unwitting *spokesman* for the Devil because he had set his mind on the things of men rather than the things of God. Because his mind was set on the things of men, his mind was easily swayed by the master-tempter Satan, who has had thousands of years of experience in leading human beings astray. Jesus' public rebuke of Peter was not just a warning to Peter, but was a warning to the other disciples as well. All of them were to beware of the activity of the adversary.

It is important to understand the scriptural reasons behind my statement that Peter was not possessed of the Devil. It is my understanding of Scripture that *no* Christian can be demon-possessed. Theologian Charles Ryrie notes that demon possession involves—

> a demon residing in a person, exerting direct control and influence over that person, with certain derangement of mind and/or body. Demon possession is to be distinguished from demon influence or demon activity in relation to a person. The work of the demon in the latter is from the outside; in demon possession it is from within.[1]

According to the definition given above, a Christian cannot be possessed by a demon since he is perpetually and unceasingly indwelt by the Holy Spirit (1 Corinthians 6:19; see also 3:16). I like the way my former colleague, the late Dr. Walter Martin, once put it. He said that when the Devil knocks on the door of the Christian's heart, the Holy Spirit opens it and says, "Get lost!"

It is highly revealing that there is not a single instance in Scripture of a Christian being said to be demon-possessed. There are examples of Christians being *afflicted* by the Devil,* but not *possessed* by the Devil.

---

* Satan and his host of demons are very active in seeking to harm believers in various ways. Satan tempts believers to sin (Ephesians 2:1-3; 1 Thessalonians 3:5), to lie (Acts 5:3), and to commit sexually immoral acts (1 Corinthians 7:5). He accuses and slanders believers (Revelation 12:10), hinders their work in any way he can (1 Thessalonians 2:18), sows tares among them (Matthew 13:38,39), and incites persecutions against them (Revelation 2:10).

Satan seeks to wage war against believers (Ephesians 6:11,12), opposes them with the ferociousness of a hungry lion (1 Peter 5:8), seeks to plant doubt in their minds (Genesis 3:1-5), seeks to foster spiritual pride in their hearts (1 Timothy 3:6), and seeks to lead them away from "the simplicity and purity of devotion to Christ" (2 Corinthians 11:3 NASB).

Christians have been delivered from Satan's domain. As Colossians 1:13 puts it, Christ "has rescued us from the dominion of darkness and brought us into the kingdom of the Son he loves." Furthermore, we must remember that "the one who is in you is greater than the one who is in the world" (1 John 4:4). This statement would not make much sense if Christians could be possessed by the Devil.

To sum up, then, even though a Christian cannot be possessed, he can nevertheless be oppressed or influenced by demonic powers (see Job chapters 1 and 2). But the oppression or influence is *external* to the Christian, not internal. The demons seek to work *from outside* the Christian to hinder him; they do not work *from within* him. This is what happened to Peter. Satan worked from outside of Peter, not from within. The Devil influenced Peter's mind, but this sinister work was an external influence.

▶ Did Jesus teach that Satan must ask permission from God before tempting or attacking Christians (Luke 22:31,32)?

In Luke 22:31,32, Jesus said to the disciple Peter, "Simon, Simon, Satan has asked to sift you as wheat. But I have prayed for you, Simon, that your faith may not fail. And when you have turned back, strengthen your brothers." As a backdrop to understanding this passage, wheat in ancient times was sifted in order to remove the chaff and the dirt, as well as to eliminate the broken and withered grains. The sifting process revealed the impure elements that had to be removed from the good wheat.[2] In like manner, Satan often tempts believers with a view to revealing and emphasizing their weaknesses. This is what Satan sought to do to Peter.

Contextually, it seems clear from Luke 22:31,32 that Satan is "on a leash." He cannot go beyond what our sovereign God will allow him to do. We see this not only in Luke 22 but also in the book of Job, where Satan had to obtain permission from God before afflicting Job (see Job 1:9-12).

We should all rest secure in the fact that God is in control of the universe, and that Satan cannot simply do as he pleases in our lives. The trials and testings that come to God's people are only those which He allows.[3]

Another observation we can make is that Jesus, fully aware that Satan wanted to tempt Peter, prayed for Peter *before the temptation even began* that Peter's faith would not fail (Luke 22:32). What a wonderful Savior we have! Hebrews 7:25 tells us, "He is able to save completely those who come to God through him, because *he always lives to intercede for them*" (italics added).

▶ What did Jesus mean when He said to the disciples, "I saw Satan fall like lightning from heaven" (Luke 10:18)?

In context, Jesus had chosen and sent out 70 disciples to minister to others on His behalf (Luke 10:1-16). The 70 then returned and reported that even the demons were subject to Jesus' name (verse 17). It is at this point that Jesus said, "I saw Satan fall like lightning from heaven" (verse 18).

It is hard to say just what Jesus was referring to here. Some scholars have surmised that perhaps this is a reference to Satan being cast out of heaven following his initial fall.[4] We read of Lucifer (Satan) in Isaiah 14:12: "How you have fallen from heaven, O morning star, son of the dawn! You have been cast down to the earth, you who once laid low the nations" (see also Ezekiel 28:11-15).

Other scholars suggest that as the 70 disciples went from town to town ministering, they witnessed the defeat of their great adversary, the Devil. This defeat, to the disciples, was as sudden and unexpected as a flash of lightning. In this view, the term "from heaven" is connected not to the word *Satan* but to the word *lightning* (lightning often has the appearance of falling from the sky or the heavens). This word picture, then, would indicate that through the preaching of the gospel Satan had suffered a great defeat, and this defeat was sudden and unexpected, just like a lightning bolt from heaven.[5] The kingdom of God was thus making tremendous inroads as it pushed back the kingdom of darkness.

Still other scholars suggest that perhaps Jesus was referring to a vision He had. F. F. Bruce is an advocate of this view:

> Jesus may be describing an actual vision which he experienced during the mission of the seventy— not unlike the vision seen by John of Patmos, when, as he says, war broke out in heaven "and the great dragon was thrown down, that ancient serpent, who is called the Devil and Satan, the deceiver of the whole world" (Rev. 12:9).[6]

▶ What was Jesus' point in saying that seven evil spirits might return to possess a man who had been delivered from one demon (Matthew 12:43-45)?

In Matthew 12:43-45 Jesus said, "When an evil spirit comes out of a man, it goes through arid places seeking rest and does not find it. Then it says, 'I will return to the house I left.' When it arrives, it finds the house unoccupied, swept clean and put in order. Then it goes and takes with it seven other spirits more wicked than itself, and they go in and live there. And the final condition of that man is worse than the first. That is how it will be with this wicked generation."

Contextually, Jesus was speaking with the Pharisees, who were seeking a sign from Him (Matthew 12:38). Jesus answered by charging that they were seeking a sign for all the wrong reasons (verses 39-45). He then zeroed in on the real problem of the Pharisees: They were seeking to externally reform themselves but were without inner spiritual conversion and hence were without the power of God in their lives.

Jesus compared the Pharisees to a man who had been delivered of a demon. Following this deliverance, the man did everything he could *by natural means* to clean up his life. But the man did not truly convert to God and believe in Him; he merely engaged in practicing religion. Then seven other spirits returned and possessed the man, and the man was in much worse condition than he initially had been.

The lesson Jesus was teaching the Pharisees was that they were in danger of the same type of thing happening to them. Their human attempts at reformation—without personal conversion, without trusting in Christ, without experiencing the true power of God—would ultimately lead them to a worse condition than they were presently in.[7]

Some scholars have noted that "sevenfold" was a traditional Jewish way of expressing severe punishment.[8] For example, in Genesis 4:15 God said, "If anyone kills Cain, he will suffer vengeance seven times over." In Leviticus 26:18 God said to His people, "If after all this you will not listen to me, I will punish you for your sins seven times over." So Jesus' allusion to the seven spirits carries definite overtones of judgment, and certainly the Pharisees were ripe for such judgment.

▶ Why would Jesus not let the demons "speak because they knew who he was" (Mark 1:34)?

In Mark 1:34 we read that Jesus "drove out many demons, but he would not let the demons speak because they knew who he was." The parallel account in Luke's Gospel tells us that Jesus "rebuked them and would not allow them to speak, because they knew he was the Christ" (Luke 4:41).

There were probably several reasons as to why Jesus would not allow the demons to speak. First, Satan is called the father of lies (John 8:44; see also Genesis 3:4), and the demons who follow Satan no doubt reflect the character of their diabolic leader. Certainly Jesus would not want any testimony regarding His identity from a sinister, lying source. Moreover, one must keep in mind that some of the Jewish leaders associated Jesus with Beelzebub, "the prince of demons" (Mark 3:22). Hence, allowing testimony from lying spirits might add fuel to the fire regarding that claim.[9]

A second possible reason for Jesus silencing the demons might have been to demonstrate that He had authority over the demons. This would be in keeping with other verses in the Gospels where this authority is openly demonstrated (for example, Mark 8:33; 9:38; Luke 10:17).

A third possible reason for silencing the demons might relate to the popular misconceptions of the Messiah held by many people in first-century Judaism. The Jews were expecting the coming of a glorious conquering Messiah who would deliver the Jews from Roman domination. If a demon prematurely blurted out that Jesus was the Messiah, the Jews who were present might interpret the term "Messiah" in this mistaken sense. It might be, then, that Jesus silenced the demons from revealing His identity at this early juncture so that He could, in His own time, demonstrate by word and deed that He was the true *biblical* Messiah.[10]

Finally, we might observe that it was Jesus' purpose not to have His identity established by the testimony of lying spirits, but rather by the messianic signs (miracles) that He performed (see Matthew 11:4-6; Luke 7:21-23).[11] These miraculous signs were predicted of the Messiah in the Old Testament (see Isaiah 29:18; 35:4-6).

▶ Does Satan have a throne somewhere on the earth (Revelation 2:13)?

In Revelation 2:12-17 the risen Christ is seen giving a message to the church at Pergamum: "I know where you live—*where Satan has his throne.* Yet you remain true to my name. You did not renounce your faith in me, even in the days of Antipas, my faithful witness, who was put to death in your city—*where Satan lives*" (verse 13, italics added).

In what way did Satan have a "throne" and "live" in Pergamum? We know that Satan, a spirit-being, is not omnipresent (everywhere-present) like God is, and therefore must have *local* existence (he can be in only one place at a time). It may be that Satan, at the time Christ spoke these words, was localized in Pergamum.

Scholars have noted that Pergamum in ancient times was the official center of emperor worship in Asia.[12] In fact, Pergamum was among the first cities of Asia to build a temple to a Roman emperor.[13] Other scholars have noted that Pergamum was the city where the temple of Asclepius (a pagan god) was located.[14] The symbol of this false god was a serpent (a term also used of Satan in Scripture—see Genesis 3:1). There was also a giant altar of Zeus that overlooked Pergamum.[15] With all the false religion in this city, it is not surprising to hear Jesus say that Satan had a throne there.

The citizens who lived within the walls of this city in biblical times were expected to fully participate in the civil (pagan) religion. To fail to do this would cause one to be suspected of disloyalty to the state.[16] Christ thus commended the Christians in Pergamum for avoiding participation in such paganism and remaining committed to Him despite where they lived (Revelation 2:13).

▶ Did Jesus teach that Christians can "bind" and "loose" demons (Matthew 18:18)?

This is a common misconception. While it is true that God has given Christians all they need to have victory over the Devil (see Ephesians 6:11-18), it is also true that the New Testament verses that speak of binding and loosing have nothing to do with spiritual warfare.

In Matthew 18:18, for example, Jesus said, "Whatever you bind on earth will be bound in heaven, and whatever you loose on earth will be loosed in heaven." The terms "bind" and "loose" were Jewish idioms indicating that what is announced on earth has already been determined in heaven. To *bind* meant to forbid, refuse, or prohibit; to *loose* meant to permit or allow. We can announce the prohibition or allowance of certain things on earth because heaven (or God) has already made an announcement on these matters.

In the context of Matthew 18, Jesus was speaking expressly about church discipline. The basic idea He was communicating in this context was that those members of the church who sin and repent are to be "loosed" (that is, they are to be restored to fellowship) while those who are unrepentant are to be "bound" (that is, they are to be barred from fellowship). These ideas can be declared on earth because heaven (God) has already declared them.

There is another reference to binding and loosing in Matthew 16:19: "Whatever you bind on earth will be bound in heaven, and whatever you loose on earth will be loosed in heaven." The context of this verse relates to witnessing and evangelism by the apostles. "Binding" here refers to prohibiting entry into God's kingdom to those who reject the apostolic witness of Jesus Christ. "Loosing" refers to granting entry into God's kingdom among those who accept that witness (see John 20:23; Acts 2:38-41).[17] The apostles could prohibit entry *(bind)* or grant entry *(loose)* into God's kingdom only because heaven has already declared that entry into the kingdom hinged on accepting the apostolic witness regarding Jesus Christ.

Clearly, then, the two passages that deal with "binding" and "loosing" in the New Testament have nothing to do with spiritual warfare. That being the case, there is no scriptural precedent for the practice of binding demons. I emphasize again, though, that God has made *full* provision for our personal victory over the powers of darkness (Ephesians 6:11-18).

Sixteen

Some Puzzling Sayings of Jesus

∾✺∿

▶ Why did Jesus say He came "to bring fire on the earth" (Luke 12:49)?

In Luke 12:49 Jesus said, "I have come to bring fire on the earth, and how I wish it were already kindled!" Scholars have interpreted Jesus' words differently, and all agree that it is hard to know precisely what He had in mind here.

Some scholars point out that in Old Testament times fire often symbolized judgment. This has led some to conclude that when Jesus said, "I have come to bring fire on the earth," He was saying He would bring judgment to the earth. This would fit with John 9:39, where Jesus said, "For judgment I have come into this world."

Other scholars relate the fire to the Holy Spirit. Recall that John the Baptist had prophesied that when Jesus came He would baptize "with the Holy Spirit and with fire" (Luke 3:16). Later, when the baptism of the Holy Spirit first occurred on the Day of Pentecost, the people saw "what seemed to be tongues of fire" that came on those filled with the Spirit (see Acts 2:1-4).

Other scholars offer a similar view, but relate the fire to the power of God: "The *fire* stands for the spread of the message of the power of God, and Jesus longs that it might spread more quickly."[1]

Still other scholars relate the fire to Jesus' work on the cross. The cross was the central focus of all His activities, and all that He did during His three-year ministry pointed toward this momentous event. When Jesus said, "how I wish it were already kindled," perhaps He was expressing His yearning to bring this task to fulfillment.

And still other scholars suggest a variation of the above. They say that when Jesus said He came to bring fire on the earth, He was talking about bringing judgment—not the judgment of others but rather *His own* judgment. "It is a judgment that the Messiah will bear for others, not one He will inflict on others."[2]

My personal view is that the "fire" is probably a reference to the tremendous power of God wrought on the earth through Jesus' miraculous ministry and continued in the book of Acts through the mighty power of the Holy Spirit, which He sent to earth following His ascension into heaven (John 15:26).

▶ Are we not to call our earthly fathers "father" (Matthew 23:9)?

In Matthew 23:9 Jesus said, "Do not call anyone on earth 'father,' for you have one Father, and he is in heaven." This is definitely a puzzling saying, but it would seem from the context (which deals with the Pharisees) that Jesus was *not* talking about biological fathers. Nor was He apparently talking about spiritual fathers, for in the New Testament the apostle Paul was a spiritual father to young Timothy (1 Corinthians 4:15), and referred to Timothy as "my dear son" (2 Timothy 1:2).

As a backdrop to understanding this verse, I should note that among the ancient Jews, particularly the Pharisees, the rabbis of the time were often respectfully referred to as "Abba" or "Papa." It was a title of great honor. The former rabbis who had died were often collectively referred to as "the fathers." They were considered the source of wisdom among the Jews. The rabbis in turn would address their disciples as their children.[3] The word "father" among the ancient Jews came to denote authority, eminence, superiority, a right to command, and a claim to high respect.[4]

Jesus' point in Matthew 23:9, then, would seem to be that *only God* should be in the place of reverence and unquestioned obedience. *Only God* truly deserves the title "Father" in this exalted sense. *Only God* is truly the wise One who cares for us as His beloved children, in contrast to the Pharisees, who often led their followers into spiritual bondage.

▶ What did Jesus mean when He spoke of angels ascending and descending on the Son of Man (John 1:51)?

In John 1:51 Jesus said to Nathanael, "I tell you the truth, you shall see heaven open, and the angels of God ascending and descending on the Son of Man." The ascent and descent of angels seems to recall the vision of Jacob in Genesis 28:12, a vision that graphically illustrated *communication between heaven and earth.** This is probably the key to understanding Jesus' statement.

It appears that Jesus in John 1:51 is portraying Himself as the revelatory link between heaven and earth.[5] He is the One through whom the realities of heaven would be brought down to earth (John 6:33,38,46,51,52). Jesus went on to communicate divine revelation to people throughout the rest of this Gospel (see, for example, the Upper Room Discourse in John 14–16). We see Christ's role as divine revelator defined for us at the very beginning of this Gospel: "No one has ever seen God, but God the one and Only [Jesus Christ], who is at the Father's side, has made him known" (John 1:18).

▶ Does Jesus have His own angel (Revelation 22:16)?

In Revelation 22:16 Jesus said to the apostle John, "I, Jesus, have sent my angel to give you this testimony for the churches."

---

* Angels were often used by God to communicate divine revelation to human beings (see Job 33:23; Daniel 8:16,17; 9:21-23; Luke 1:11-19; Acts 7:53; 8:26; 27:23,24; Galatians 3:19; Hebrews 2:2,3; Revelation 1:1).

In Revelation 1:1 Jesus made a similar statement: "The revelation of Jesus Christ, which God gave him to show his servants what must soon take place. He made it known by sending his angel to his servant John."

It seems clear from these verses that indeed Christ did utilize "His" angel in conveying revelation to John. But we should be careful to note that the entire angelic realm is in submission to Jesus Christ, not just a single angel.

The apostle Paul affirmed that by Christ "all things were created: things in heaven and on earth, visible and invisible, whether thrones or powers or rulers or authorities; all things were created by him and for him" (Colossians 1:16). It is highly revealing that Paul said Christ created "thrones," "powers," "rulers," and "authorities," for in the rabbinic (Jewish) thought of the first century, these words were used to describe different orders of angels (see Romans 8:38; Ephesians 1:21; 3:10; 6:12; Colossians 2:10,15; Titus 3:1). Apparently there was a heresy flourishing in Colosse (to which church Paul wrote Colossians) that involved the worship of angels. In the process of worshiping angels, Christ had been degraded. So, to correct this grave error, Paul emphasized in Colossians 1:16 that Christ created all things—*including all the angels*—and hence He is supreme and is alone worthy to be worshiped.[6]

Paul also stated of Christ that all things were created "for him" (Colossians 1:16b). Creation is *for* Christ in the sense that He is the end for which all things exist. They are meant to serve His will, to contribute to His glory. Christ is sovereign over all creation, for it was created by Him and indeed *for* Him.

Hence, angels were created—as were all other things—to serve and glorify Christ, not to act according to their own wills or independently of God. We conclude, then, that the angel mentioned in Revelation 1:1 and 22:16 was merely one of many angels at Christ's disposal.

It is interesting to note that in the Old Testament the Lord used Gabriel to send messages to the prophet Daniel (see Daniel 8:16; 9:21,22), as well as to Mary and Zechariah in the New Testament (see Luke 1:26-31). The Lord seems to have used

Gabriel in bringing some of the greatest and most important revelations to humankind. Understandably, some scholars believe it is possible that the angel Jesus utilized in the book of Revelation was Gabriel.

▶ Did Jesus teach that Christians have a single guardian angel that stays with them throughout life (Matthew 18:10)?

In Matthew 18:10 Jesus, speaking of little children, said, "See that you do not look down on one of these little ones. For I tell you that their angels in heaven always see the face of my Father in heaven."

Based on Jesus' statement in this verse, it is certainly *possible* that each believer has a specific guardian angel assigned to him or her. Many of the early church fathers believed that every individual is under the care of a particular angel who is assigned to him or her as a guardian. Likewise, the great philosopher and theologian Thomas Aquinas said that each person has a guardian angel assigned to him or her at birth. Prior to the birth of the child, Aquinas said, the child in the womb falls under the care of the mother's guardian angel.[7]

Other theologians, however, argue that Matthew 18:10 constitutes flimsy evidence for such an idea. These theologians note that the angels of the little ones in this verse are said to be *in heaven*, not specifically with the little ones on earth. They also point out that Scripture seems to indicate that *many multitudes of angels* are always ready and willing to render help and protection to each individual Christian whenever there is a need.

For example, we read in 2 Kings 6:17 that Elisha and his servant were surrounded by many glorious angels. Luke 16:22 indicates that several angels were involved in carrying Lazarus' soul to Abraham's bosom. Jesus could have called on 12 legions of angels to rescue Him if He had wanted (Matthew 26:53). Psalm 91:9-11 tells us, "If you make the Most High your dwelling—even the LORD, who is my refuge—then no harm will befall you,

no disaster will come near your tent. For he will command his
angels concerning you to guard you in all your ways."

▶ Did Jesus teach that Christians can be doctrinally deceived
(Matthew 7:15)?

It would seem that this is indeed the case. Jesus warned
those who believed in and followed Him, "*Watch out* for false
prophets. They come to you in sheep's clothing, but inwardly
they are ferocious wolves" (Matthew 7:15, italics added). Why
would Jesus warn His followers to "watch out" if there were no
possibility that they could be deceived?

Jesus also warned His followers, "*Watch out* that no one
deceives you. For many will come in my name, claiming, 'I am
the Christ,' and will *deceive many*. . . . Many false prophets will
appear and *deceive many people*" (Matthew 24:4,5,11, italics
added). Again, why would Jesus warn *His followers* of such
deception if it were not possible that they be deceived and end
up believing a lie?

We see this same point emphasized elsewhere in Scripture.
In 2 Corinthians 11:2,3 the apostle Paul warned Christians, "I
am jealous for you with a godly jealousy. I promised you to one
husband, to Christ, so that I might present you as a pure virgin
to him. But I am afraid that *just as Eve was deceived* by the serpent's cunning, *your minds may somehow be led astray* from your
sincere and pure devotion to Christ" (italics added). Paul
clearly saw the possibility that Christians could be deceived.

In Acts 20:28-30 the elders of the Ephesian church were
warned: "*Keep watch* over yourselves and all the flock of which
the Holy Spirit has made you overseers. Be shepherds of the
church of God, which he bought with his own blood. I know
that after I leave, savage wolves will come in among you and *will
not spare the flock*. Even from your own number men will arise
and *distort the truth* in order to draw away disciples after them"
(italics added).

It seems clear, in view of such verses, that Christians can
indeed be deceived and led astray by false doctrine. The

From the Office of...
STEVE LOWE

PLEASE RETURN
when Done

THK,

STEVE

remedy? We need to saturate our minds on a daily basis with the Word of God (see 2 Timothy 3:16,17).

▶ What did Jesus mean when He said, "Whoever has will be given more; whoever does not have, even what he has will be taken from him" (Mark 4:25)?

In Mark 4:24,25 Jesus said, "Consider carefully what you hear. With the measure you use, it will be measured to you—and even more. Whoever has will be given more; whoever does not have, even what he has will be taken from him."

The context is clearly set for us with the opening statement: "Consider carefully *what you hear*." Jesus' intended meaning seems to be that those who respond positively to the truth *they hear* will be given more. Those who do not respond positively to the truth *they hear* will lose what they had. Or, as one scholar put it, "The more we appropriate truth now, the more we will receive in the future; and if we do not respond to what little truth we may know already, we will not profit even from that."[8]

I believe we see this principle illustrated in the life of Cornelius. This Gentile was obedient to the limited amount of truth he had heard—that is, he had been obedient to Old Testament revelation (Acts 10:2). But he did not have enough "revelational light" to believe in Jesus Christ as the Savior. So God sent Peter to Cornelius' house to explain the gospel, after which time Cornelius believed in Jesus and was saved (verses 44-48). ("Whoever has *will be given more*.")

▶ Why did Jesus instruct the disciples to "be as shrewd as snakes and as innocent as doves" (Matthew 10:16)?

In Matthew 10:16 Jesus instructed the disciples, "I am sending you out like sheep among wolves. Therefore be as shrewd as snakes and as innocent as doves." This instruction must be understood as part of a larger discourse in which Jesus warned the disciples about possible dangers they might face in coming days as they ministered in His name (Matthew 10:16-23). He spoke about how they would be persecuted by religious and civil authorities (verses 17,18), and even rejected by their own families (verses 21,22). Understandably, He began His discourse by telling them they should be as shrewd as serpents and innocent as doves.

In the ancient Near East the snake or serpent was considered to be a cunning creature.* So when Jesus said His followers should be as "shrewd as snakes," He was speaking in a way they would have readily understood. In the original Greek, the word "shrewd" carries the idea of "prudent." The disciples were to be circumspect, discreet, judicious, and sensible in the way they handled themselves before others. They were to seek to avoid attacks against them whenever possible.

The disciples were also to be *innocent* as doves. The Greek word for "innocent" carries the idea "without any mixture of deceit," "without falsity," "unadulterated," "harmless," "pure."[9] *Vine's Expository Dictionary of Biblical Words* tells us that in Matthew 10:16 the word implies "the simplicity of a single eye, discerning what is evil, and choosing only what glorifies God."[10]

Despite the fact that the disciples were headed for some hard times with civil and religious authorities and even their families, being shrewd and innocent in how they dealt with others would go a long way toward minimizing their conflict. This is what Jesus was communicating to the disciples in Matthew 10:16.

▶ Why did Jesus say, "Do not give dogs what is sacred; do not throw your pearls to pigs" (Matthew 7:6)?

In Matthew 7:6 Jesus said, "Do not give dogs what is sacred; do not throw your pearls to pigs. If you do, they may trample them under their feet, and then turn and tear you to pieces." The words "pigs" and "dogs" portray that which is vicious and unclean. The terms seem appropriate ways of describing the enemies of the gospel.

---

* Even in Egyptian hieroglyphics the serpent was a symbol of great wisdom.

It would seem that in Matthew 7:6 Jesus was communicating to His followers that in their relationships with enemies of the gospel, they were to be very cautious, recognizing that these enemies may turn on them and even kill them. The teaching that is given to others should always be in accordance with their spiritual capacity.

For those who have little or no spiritual capacity (enemies of the gospel), one must be cautious in what one says and not "throw your pearls to pigs." One must be cautious not to pass on the sacred to that which is profane. One should be careful not to pass on holy things to unholy people who will have nothing but disdain for the things of Christ.

An example of this would be when Jesus sent out 70 disciples to proclaim the gospel. He instructed them that if they came to a village and the people there rejected their teachings, they were to shake the dust off their feet and go elsewhere (Luke 10:10,11). The idea Jesus communicated to them was, "Don't throw your pearls before swine. Move on to another city and share your pearls there."

Even Jesus put this maxim into practice. He gave no answer to Herod Antipas when Herod "plied him with many questions" (Luke 23:9). Jesus no doubt knew it would have been useless to proclaim His message to Herod.[11]

But, do not read more into Jesus' words than is warranted. Jesus is *not* speaking against evangelism. Elsewhere in Scripture Jesus very clearly talks about the call of evangelism on our lives (Matthew 28:19,20). The point Jesus was making in Matthew 7:6 is that we must be discerning in *what* we share with *whom*. The warning is against giving the pearls of the gospel to those who have vicious scorn and hardened contempt against the gospel.

▶ Why did Jesus refer to our eyes as the "lamp of the body" (Matthew 6:22,23)?

In Matthew 6:22,23 Jesus said, "The eye is the lamp of the body. If your eyes are good, your whole body will be full of light.

But if your eyes are bad, your whole body will be full of darkness. If then the light within you is darkness, how great is that darkness!"

In context (Matthew 6:19-23) Jesus was cautioning His followers about a proper attitude toward money and material things. Jesus used the illustration of the eye to show that one's *outlook* will determine one's pattern of living. He noted that if one has clearness of purpose in serving God ("if your eyes are good") it will affect every area of one's life in a positive way (verse 22). If one lacks clearness of purpose in serving God ("if your eyes are bad"), it will affect every area of one's life in a negative way (verse 23a). If one is totally bound up in a quest for money and material things ("if the light within you is darkness"—that is, your values are reversed from what they should be), then one is really in bad shape, for this has the potential to destroy one's life (verse 23b).

Jesus' instructions about money and wealth are extremely important, for the Pharisees believed that *whom the Lord loveth, the Lord maketh rich*. In the above story, the Pharisees would be those who had bad eyes. Their eyesight was diseased and distorted. They truly lacked clearness of purpose. They wanted to serve God *and* money. That is why Jesus went on to say in verse 24, "No one can serve two masters. Either he will hate the one and love the other, or he will be devoted to the one and despise the other. You cannot serve both God and Money."

▶ Why did Jesus teach His followers to use worldly wealth to gain friends (Luke 16:9)?

In Luke 16:9 Jesus said, "I tell you, use worldly wealth to gain friends for yourselves, so that when it is gone, you will be welcomed into eternal dwellings." It would seem that Jesus was teaching that if worldly wealth is good for anything at all, it should be used for some kind of eternal benefit. Money and wealth should be used shrewdly with a view to the future, not in a selfish way that focuses only on the present.

Jesus indicates we should be ready to make use of any wealth God has given us in helping other people. Those we are able to help while on earth may one day welcome us as we enter the gates of heaven at the moment of our deaths. As Bible scholar Leon Morris put it, using money wisely "will gain us friends and it will stand us in good stead when money fails, that is, when we die and money is of no more use."[12]

▶ What is it in allegiance to Jesus that causes family breakups (Matthew 10:21,22)?

In Matthew 10:21,22 Jesus said to those who would follow Him, "Brother will betray brother to death, and a father his child; children will rebel against their parents and have them put to death. All men will hate you because of me, but he who stands firm to the end will be saved."

We find Jesus' words about family breakups in a broader discourse in which Jesus warned the 12 disciples about possible dangers they would face in their work of ministry (Matthew 10:16-23). He first warned them that they would be persecuted and would have to answer to religious and civil authorities (verses 16-18). He then warned that they would even be hated by their own families for following Him (verses 21,22). He taught that commitment to following Him would be tested by all the significant relationships in life—civil, religious, and family.

A little later in Matthew's Gospel Jesus said, "Do not suppose that I have come to bring peace to the earth. I did not come to bring peace, but a sword. For I have come to turn 'a man against his father, a daughter against her mother, a daughter-in-law against her mother-in-law—a man's enemies will be the members of his own household'" (Matthew 10:34-36).

In a Jewish culture—a culture in which the family unit was highly esteemed, honor shown to parents was of supreme importance, and families worshiped together as a unit[13]—such words from the mouth of Jesus must have sounded harsh.[14] But the point He was leading up to is a substantial one: "Anyone who loves his father or mother more than me is not worthy of me; anyone who loves his son or daughter more than me is not worthy of me" (Matthew 10:37).

Many scholars have noted that "love" in the biblical sense is much more than an emotional feeling. True love also involves subjection and obedience. Christ's point, then, was that anyone who puts family members before Him and submits to them instead of submitting to Him is not worthy of Him or His kingdom.

Certainly it is quite possible and even likely that when a person becomes a Christian, he or she will be ostracized and even persecuted by other family members. Even today, for a Jew in Israel to become a Christian, for a Muslim in an Arab country to become a Christian, for a Buddhist in China to become a Christian, or for a Shintoist in Japan to become a Christian, there will be harsh and even cruel reactions by other family members.* But Christ calls His followers to submit to Him and not to family members. *Christ must reign supreme.*

In view of the above, we should not conclude that the *object* of Jesus' coming to earth was to cause discord and contention. Rather, the context indicates that the *effect* of Christ's coming would sometimes be discord and contention among family members.[15]

▶ How could Jesus have remained in the tomb "three days and three nights" if He was crucified on Friday afternoon and rose on Sunday morning (Matthew 12:40)?

The Gospel accounts are clear in stating that Jesus was crucified and buried on Friday, sometime before sundown. (Sundown was considered the beginning of the next day for the Jews.) This means Jesus was in the grave for part of Friday, the entire Sabbath (Saturday), and part of Sunday. In other words,

---

* During the writing of this book, there were news reports of an Islamic leader who had his 15-year-old son beheaded for trusting in Christ and becoming a Christian.

He was in the tomb for two full nights, one full day, and part of two days.

How do we reconcile this with Jesus' words in Matthew 12:40, "For as Jonah was three days and three nights in the belly of a huge fish, so the Son of Man will be three days and three nights in the heart of the earth"? This is not hard to explain. In the Jewish mindset, any *part* of a day was reckoned as a *complete* day. The Talmud (a set of Jewish commentaries) tells us that "the portion of a day is as the whole of it." Hence, though Jesus was really in the tomb for part of Friday, all of Saturday, and part of Sunday, in Jewish reckoning He was in the tomb for "three days and three nights."

▶ Why did the resurrected Jesus tell Mary not to hold on to Him (John 20:17)?

In John 20:17 the resurrected Jesus said to Mary, "Do not hold on to me, for I have not yet returned to the Father." The Greek tense in this verse carries the idea "Stop holding on to me."[16] Mary was apparently so excited to see that Jesus had risen from the dead and was present with her that she grasped on to Him, not wanting to let go. But Jesus told her to stop. He indicated to her that He had not yet ascended to the Father and would in fact still be on earth for a time prior to His ascension, and hence she did not need to cling to Him. There would still be plenty of opportunity for them to see each other before He went to heaven.[17] It was more important at the present moment for Mary to go tell the disciples that He was risen.

▶ Did Jesus teach that Peter is the "rock" upon which the church is built (Matthew 16:18)?

In Matthew 16:15 Jesus asked the disciples, "Who do you say I am?" Simon Peter answered, "You are the Christ, the Son of the living God" (verse 16). Jesus then replied to Peter, "Blessed are you, Simon son of Jonah, for this was not revealed to you by man, but by my Father in heaven. And I tell you that you are Peter, and on this rock I will build my church, and the gates of Hades will not overcome it" (verses 17,18).

There are several factors in the Greek text of this passage that argue against the idea that Peter is the rock upon which the church is built. First, whenever Peter is referred to in this passage (Matthew 16), it is in the second person ("you"), but "this rock" is in the third person (verse 18). Moreover, "Peter" (*petros*) is a masculine singular term and "rock" (*petra*) is a feminine singular term. Hence, they do not have the same referent. What is more, the same authority Jesus gave to Peter (Matthew 16:18) is later given to all the apostles (Matthew 18:18). So Peter is not unique. It would seem that in Matthew 16:18 Jesus was praising Peter for his accurate statement about Him ("You are the Christ"), and was introducing His work of building the church on *Himself* as the capstone (see 1 Corinthians 3:11).

Ephesians 2:20 affirms that the church is "built on the foundation of the apostles and prophets, with Christ Jesus himself as the chief cornerstone." Two things are clear from this: first, that *all* the apostles, not just Peter, are the foundation of the church; second, that the only One who was given a place of uniqueness or prominence was Christ, the capstone. Indeed, Peter himself referred to Christ as "the capstone" of the church (1 Peter 2:7) and the rest of believers as "living stones" (verse 5) in the superstructure of the church.

BIBLIOGRAPHY

ᏀᎥᎥᎥᎥᎾ

General Works

Bible Knowledge Commentary: New Testament. Edited by John F. Walvoord and Roy B. Zuck. Wheaton: Victor Books, 1983.

Bible Knowledge Commentary: Old Testament. Edited by John F. Walvoord and Roy B. Zuck. Wheaton: Victor Books, 1985.

Concise Evangelical Dictionary of Theology. Edited by Walter A. Elwell. Grand Rapids: Baker Book House, 1991.

Evangelical Commentary on the Bible. Edited by Walter A. Elwell. Grand Rapids: Baker Book House, 1989.

International Bible Commentary. Edited by F.F. Bruce. Grand Rapids: Zondervan Publishing House, 1986.

Nelson's New Illustrated Bible Dictionary. Edited by Ronald Youngblood. Nashville: Thomas Nelson Publishers, 1995.

New Bible Commentary. Edited by R.T. France, D.A. Carson, J.A. Moyer, and G.J. Wenham. Downers Grove, IL: InterVarsity Press, 1994.

NIV Study Bible. Edited by Kenneth Barker. Grand Rapids: Zondervan Publishing House, 1985.

Quest Study Bible. Edited by *Leadership* and *Christianity Today.* Grand Rapids: Zondervan Publishing House, 1994.

Ryrie Study Bible. Edited by Charles Caldwell Ryrie. Chicago: Moody Press, 1994.

Vine's Expository Dictionary of Biblical Words. Edited by Merrill F. Unger, W.E. Vine, and William White. Nashville: Thomas Nelson Publishers, 1985.

Wycliffe Bible Commentary. Edited by Everett F. Harrison and Charles F. Pfeiffer. Chicago: Moody Press, 1974.

Zondervan NIV Bible Commentary: New Testament. Edited by Kenneth L. Barker and John Kohlenberger III. Vol. 2. Grand Rapids: Zondervan Publishing House, 1994.

Zondervan NIV Bible Commentary: Old Testament. Edited by Kenneth L. Barker and John Kohlenberger III. Vol. 1. Grand Rapids: Zondervan Publishing House, 1994.

Books by Individual Authors

Archer, Gleason. "Alleged Errors and Discrepancies in the Original Manuscripts of the Bible." In *Inerrancy*, edited by Norman Geisler. Grand Rapids: Zondervan Publishing House, 1980.

———. *Encyclopedia of Bible Difficulties.* Grand Rapids: Zondervan Publishing House, 1982.

Arndt, William. *Bible Difficulties and Seeming Contradictions.* St. Louis: Concordia Publishing House, 1987.

Arndt, William, and Wilbur Gingrich. *A Greek-English Lexicon of the New Testament and Other Early Christian Literature.* Chicago: The University of Chicago Press, 1957.

Barnes, Albert. *Notes on the New Testament.* Grand Rapids: Baker Book House, 1996.

Bowman, Robert M. *Understanding Jehovah's Witnesses.* Grand Rapids: Baker Book House, 1991.

———. *Why You Should Believe in the Trinity.* Grand Rapids: Baker Book House, 1989.

Boyd, Gregory. *Oneness Pentecostals and the Trinity.* Grand Rapids: Zondervan Publishing House, 1992.

Bruce, F.F. *The Gospel of John.* London: Pickering & Inglis Ltd., 1983.

———. *The Hard Sayings of Jesus.* Downers Grove, IL: InterVarsity Press, 1983.

Davids, Peter. *More Hard Sayings of the New Testament.* Downers Grove, IL: InterVarsity Press, 1991.

Douty, Norman F. *The Death of Christ.* Swengel, PA: Reiner, 1972.

Edersheim, Alfred. *The Life and Times of Jesus the Messiah.* Grand Rapids: Eerdmans, 1971.

Erickson, Millard J. *Christian Theology.* Grand Rapids: Baker Book House, 1987.

Fitzmyer, Joseph A. *The Gospel According to Luke (I-IX).* New York: Doubleday & Company, 1983.

Geisler, Norman, and Ronald Brooks. *When Skeptics Ask.* Wheaton: Victor Books, 1990.

Geisler, Norman, and Thomas Howe. *When Critics Ask: A Popular Handbook on Bible Difficulties.* Wheaton: Victor Books, 1992.

Geisler, Norman, and William Nix. *A General Introduction to the Bible.* Chicago: Moody Press, 1978.

Geisler, Norman, and Ron Rhodes. *When Cultists Ask.* Grand Rapids: Baker Book House, 1997.

Geisler, Norman L., and Jeff Amano. *The Infiltration of the New Age.* Wheaton: Tyndale House Publishers, 1990.

Gomes, Alan W. *Unmasking the Cults.* Edited by Alan W. Gomes. Grand Rapids: Zondervan Publishing House, 1995.

Hodges, Zane C. *The Gospel Under Siege.* Dallas: Redencion Viva, 1981.

Hoekema, Anthony A. *The Four Major Cults.* Grand Rapids: Eerdmans Publishing Company, 1978.

Hoyt, Herman A. *The End Times.* Chicago: Moody Press, 1969.

Hunt, Dave. *In Defense of the Faith: Biblical Answers to Challenging Questions.* Eugene: Harvest House Publishers, 1996.

Lane, William L. *The Gospel According to Mark.* Grand Rapids: Eerdmans Publishing Company, 1974.

Marshall, I. Howard. *The Gospel of Luke.* Grand Rapids: Eerdmans Publishing Company, 1978.

McDowell, Josh. *The Resurrection Factor.* San Bernardino, CA: Here's Life Publishers, 1981.

McDowell, Josh, and Don Stewart. *Answers to Tough Questions Skeptics Ask About the Christian Faith.* Wheaton: Tyndale House Publishers, 1988.

———. *Reasons Skeptics Should Consider Christianity.* Wheaton: Tyndale House Publishers, 1988.

Morris, Leon. *Luke.* Grand Rapids: Eerdmans Publishing Company, 1983.

———. *The Gospel According to John.* Grand Rapids: Eerdmans Publishing Company, 1987.

O'Brien, David. *Today's Handbook for Solving Bible Difficulties.* Minneapolis: Bethany House Publishers, 1990.

Pentecost, J. Dwight. *The Parables of Jesus.* Grand Rapids: Zondervan Publishing House, 1982.

———. *The Words and Works of Jesus Christ.* Grand Rapids: Zondervan Publishing House, 1981.

Reed, David. *Jehovah's Witnesses Answered Verse by Verse.* Grand Rapids: Baker Book House, 1992.

Reymond, Robert L. *Jesus, Divine Messiah: The New Testament Witness.* Phillipsburg, NJ: Presbyterian and Reformed, 1990.

Rhodes, Ron. *Angels Among Us: Separating Truth from Fiction.* Eugene: Harvest House Publishers, 1994.

———. *Christ Before the Manger: The Life and Times of the Preincarnate Christ.* Grand Rapids: Baker Book House, 1992.

———. *The Complete Book of Bible Answers.* Eugene: Harvest House Publishers, 1997.

———. *The Counterfeit Christ of the New Age Movement.* Grand Rapids: Baker Book House, 1990.

———. *The Culting of America: The Shocking Implications for Every Concerned Christian.* Eugene: Harvest House Publishers, 1994.

————. *The Heart of Christianity: What It Means to Believe in Jesus.* Eugene: Harvest House Publishers, 1996.

————. *Heaven: The Undiscovered Country — Exploring the Wonder of the Afterlife.* Eugene: Harvest House Publishers, 1996.

————. *The New Age Movement.* Grand Rapids: Zondervan Publishing House, 1995.

————. *Reasoning from the Scriptures with the Jehovah's Witnesses.* Eugene: Harvest House Publishers, 1993.

Rhodes, Ron, and Marian Bodine. *Reasoning from the Scriptures with the Mormons.* Eugene: Harvest House Publishers, 1995.

Ryrie, Charles Caldwell. *The Holy Spirit.* Chicago: Moody Press, 1980.

————. *You Mean the Bible Teaches That?* Chicago: Moody Press, 1974.

Sire, James. *Scripture Twisting: 20 Ways the Cults Misread the Bible.* Downers Grove, IL: InterVarsity Press, 1980.

Sproul, R.C. *Now, That's a Good Question.* Wheaton: Tyndale House Publishers, 1996.

Stein, Robert. *Difficult Passages in the New Testament.* Grand Rapids: Baker Book House, 1990.

Story, Dan. *Defending Your Faith: How to Answer the Tough Questions.* Nashville: Thomas Nelson Publishers, 1992.

Toussaint, Stanley D. *Behold the King: A Study of Matthew.* Portland: Multnomah Press, 1980.

Vincent, Marvin R. *Word Studies in the New Testament.* Grand Rapids: Eerdmans Publishing Company, 1975.

Walvoord, John F. *Jesus Christ Our Lord.* Chicago: Moody Press, 1969.

————. *The Prophecy Knowledge Handbook.* Wheaton: Victor Books, 1990.

————. *The Rapture Question.* Grand Rapids: Zondervan Publishing House, 1979.

NOTES

"Truly I Say to You"

1. F. F. Bruce, *The Hard Sayings of Jesus* (Downers Grove, IL: InterVarsity Press, 1983), p. 16.

2. Bernard Ramm, *Protestant Biblical Interpretation* (Grand Rapids: Baker Book House, 1978), pp. 156-57.

3. J. Dwight Pentecost, *The Parables of Jesus* (Grand Rapids: Zondervan Publishing House, 1982), p. 14.

4. Ramm, *Protestant*, p. 276.

5. Pentecost, *Parables*, p. 12.

6. Ibid., p. 12. See also Ron Rhodes, *Christ Before the Manger: The Life and Times of the Preincarnate Christ* (Grand Rapids: Baker Book House, 1992), pp. 118-23.

7. Pentecost, *Parables*, p. 12. See also *Theological Dictionary of the New Testament*, ed. Geoffrey Bromiley (Grand Rapids: Eerdmans, 1985), p. 302.

8. Pentecost, *Parables*, p. 12.

9. Ramm, *Protestant*, p. 282. I recommend that you consult Alfred Edersheim, *The Life and Times of Jesus the Messiah* (Grand Rapids: Eerdmans, 1971).

10. Ramm, *Protestant*, p. 282. See also *Nelson's New Illustrated Bible Dictionary*, ed. Ronald Youngblood (Nashville: Nelson, 1996), p. 943.

11. Pentecost, *Parables*, p. 20. A great resource for this is *Nelson's New Illustrated Bible Dictionary*.

12. Pentecost, *Parables*, p. 19.

13. J. I. Packer, *"Fundamentalism" and the Word of God* (Grand Rapids: Eerdmans, 1958), p. 102.

14. Consider the parable in Luke 8:5-8:

A farmer went out to sow his seed. As he was scattering the seed, some fell along the path; it was trampled on, and the birds of the air ate it up. Some fell on rock, and when it came up, the plants withered because they had no moisture. Other seed fell among thorns, which grew up with it and choked the plants. Still other seed fell on good soil. It came up and yielded a crop, a hundred times more than was sown.

After speaking this parable, Jesus proceeded to provide the correct interpretation of it in verses 11-15. He indicated that the *seed* is the Word of God. Then He taught:

- The seed that fell along the path refers to those who hear the Word of God, but the Devil comes along and takes it away from their hearts so they cannot believe and be saved.
- The seed that fell on the rock refers to people who initially receive the Word of God with joy when they hear it, but the seed does not take root; the people believe for a little while but they fall away during the time of testing.
- The seed that fell among the thorns represents people who hear the message but get carried away by the worries, riches, and pleasures of this world.
- The seed that fell on good soil represents people who hear the Word of God and believe it, and end up serving the Lord.

This parable and its interpretation serves as a model for interpreting the other parables.

(A special thanks to my 10-year-old son David for researching this aspect of the parables in preparation for this chapter.)

Chapter One—Jesus' Claims About Himself

1. Benjamin B. Warfield, *The Person and Work of Christ* (Philadelphia: Presbyterian and Reformed Publishing, 1950), p. 56.
2. James Oliver Buswell, *A Systematic Theology of the Christian Religion* (Grand Rapids: Zondervan Publishing House, 1979), 1:105.
3. Norman Geisler and Ron Rhodes, *When Cultists Ask* (Grand Rapids: Baker Book House, 1997), p. 105.
4. Ibid.
5. Marvin R. Vincent, *Word Studies in the New Testament* (Grand Rapids, MI: Eerdmans Publishing Company, 1975), II:197.
6. Geisler and Rhodes, *Cultists*, p. 176.
7. Leon Morris, *The Gospel According to John* (Grand Rapids: Wm. B. Eerdmans Publishing Co., 1971), p. 658.

8. Robert M. Bowman, *Why You Should Believe in the Trinity* (Grand Rapids: Baker Book House, 1989), pp. 14-15.

9. Albert Barnes, "John," in *Notes on the New Testament* (Grand Rapids: Baker Book House, 1996), p. 334.

10. *The IVP Bible Background Commentary*, New Testament, electronic version, Logos Software.

11. Barnes, "John," in *Notes*, p. 230.

12. Morris, *John*, p. 313.

13. Ibid.

14. Robert P. Lightner, *The God of the Bible* (Grand Rapids: Baker Book House, 1978), p. 55.

15. John Gill, *The Online Bible* (electronic media), version 2.5.2.

16. Ibid.

17. Ibid.

18. See Barnes, "John," in *Notes*, p. 353.

19. Ibid.

20. Barnes, "Mark," in *Notes*: "He had a human nature. He grew as a man in knowledge. As a man his knowledge must be finite" (p. 379).

21. Robert L. Reymond, *Jesus, Divine Messiah: The New Testament Witness* (Phillipsburg, NJ: Presbyterian and Reformed, 1990), p. 80.

22. Geisler and Rhodes, *Cultists*, p. 139.

23. Bowman, *Trinity*, p. 72; see also Morris, *John*, p. 842.

24. Geisler and Rhodes, *Cultists*, p. 121.

25. Ibid.

26. William L. Lane, *The Gospel According to Mark* (Grand Rapids: Eerdmans Publishing Company, 1974), p. 94.

27. For more on this, see my book *Christ Before the Manger: The Life and Times of the Preincarnate Christ* (Grand Rapids: Baker Book House, 1994).

28. Millard J. Erickson, *Christian Theology* (Grand Rapids: Baker Book House, 1987), p. 434.

29. The fulfillment of this "seed" promise is a major theme of both the Old and New Testament Scriptures. The promise given originally to Abraham (Genesis 12:1-3) was narrowed to his son Isaac (Genesis 26:2-4), then further narrowed to Jacob and his sons (Genesis 28:13-15). Other sons of Abraham were eliminated as inheritors of the promise as was Esau, Jacob's older twin.

Chapter Two—The Miracles of Jesus

1. William L. Lane, *The Gospel According to Mark* (Grand Rapids: Eerdmans Publishing Company, 1974), p. 204.

2. Leon Morris, *Luke* (Grand Rapids: Eerdmans Publishing Company, 1983), p. 159.

3. *The Wycliffe Bible Commentary*, ed. Everett F. Harrison and Charles F. Pfeiffer (Chicago: Moody Press, 1974), p. 1048.

4. Peter H. Davids, *More Hard Sayings of the New Testament* (Downers Grove, IL: InterVarsity Press, 1991), p. 26.

5. Alfred Edersheim, cited in J. Dwight Pentecost, *The Words and Works of Jesus Christ* (Grand Rapids: Zondervan Publishing House, 1981), p. 148.

6. *The Bible Knowledge Commentary: New Testament*, ed. John F. Walvoord and Roy B. Zuck (Wheaton: Victor Books, 1983), electronic edition, Parson's Library.

7. Leon Morris, *The Gospel According to John* (Grand Rapids: Eerdmans Publishing Company, 1987), p. 646.

8. *The IVP Bible Background Commentary*, New Testament, electronic version, Logos Software.

9. *The Wycliffe Bible Commentary*, p. 1005.

Chapter Three—The Kingdom of God

1. See William L. Lane, *The Gospel According to Mark* (Grand Rapids: Eerdmans Publishing Company, 1974), p. 360.

2. Leon Morris, *Luke* (Grand Rapids: Eerdmans Publishing Company, 1983), p. 180.

3. William Arndt, cited in J. Dwight Pentecost, *The Words and Works of Jesus Christ* (Grand Rapids: Zondervan Publishing House, 1981), p. 272.

4. Gleason Archer, "Alleged Errors and Discrepancies in the Original Manuscripts of the Bible," in *Inerrancy*, ed. Norman Geisler (Grand Rapids: Zondervan Publishing House, 1980), p. 324.

5. *The IVP Bible Background Commentary*, New Testament, electronic version, Logos Software.

6. Joseph A. Fitzmyer, *The Gospel According to Luke (I-IX)* (New York: Doubleday & Company, 1983), p. 837.

7. Arndt in Pentecost, *Words and Works*, p. 272.

8. Stanley D. Toussaint, *Behold the King: A Study of Matthew* (Portland: Multnomah Press, 1980), p. 152.

9. Marvin R. Vincent, *Word Studies in the New Testament* (Grand Rapids: Eerdmans Publishing Company, 1975), I:64.

10. *Zondervan NIV Bible Commentary: New Testament*, ed. Kenneth L. Barker and John Kohlenberger III, Vol. 2 (Grand Rapids: Zondervan Publishing House, 1994), p. 56.

11. *Zondervan NIV Bible Commentary: New Testament*, p. 56.

12. See F. F. Bruce, *The Hard Sayings of Jesus* (Downers Grove, IL: InterVarsity Press, 1983), p. 64.

13. See J. Dwight Pentecost, *The Parables of Jesus* (Grand Rapids: Zondervan Publishing House, 1982), p. 53.

14. Edersheim, in Pentecost, *Words and Works*, p. 217.

15. Pentecost, *Words and Works*, p. 257.
16. Ibid., p. 256.

Chapter Four—The Jews and Judaism

1. See J. Dwight Pentecost, *The Parables of Jesus* (Grand Rapids: Zondervan Publishing House, 1982), p. 27.
2. *The Bible Knowledge Commentary: New Testament*, ed. John F. Walvoord and Roy B. Zuck (Wheaton: Victor Books, 1983), electronic edition, Parson's Technology.
3. See Norman Geisler and Thomas Howe, *When Critics Ask: A Popular Handbook on Bible Difficulties* (Wheaton: Victor Books, 1992), p. 330.
4. F. F. Bruce, *The Hard Sayings of Jesus* (Downers Grove: InterVarsity Press, 1983), p. 32.
5. *The NIV Study Bible*, ed. Kenneth Barker (Grand Rapids: Zondervan Publishing House, 1985), MacBible software, Zondervan.
6. *The NIV Study Bible*, MacBible software.
7. *The Wycliffe Bible Commentary*, ed. Everett F. Harrison and Charles F. Pfeiffer (Chicago: Moody Press, 1974), p. 993.
8. *Evangelical Commentary on the Bible*, ed. Walter A. Elwell (Grand Rapids: Baker Book House, 1989), p. 771.
9. David A. Reed and John R. Farkas, *Mormons Answered Verse by Verse* (Grand Rapids: Baker Book House, 1993), p. 68.
10. *The Bible Knowledge Commentary*.
11. William L. Lane, *The Gospel According to Mark* (Grand Rapids: Eerdmans Publishing Company, 1974), p. 280.
12. *The Bible Knowledge Commentary*.
13. *The IVP Bible Background Commentary*, electronic version, Logos Software.
14. Ibid.

Chapter Five—Sense and Nonsense About God

1. *The IVP Bible Background Commentary*, electronic version, Logos Software.
2. *The Bible Knowledge Commentary: New Testament*, ed. John F. Walvoord and Roy B. Zuck (Wheaton: Victor Books, 1983), electronic edition, Parson's Technology.
3. Benjamin B. Warfield, *The Person and Work of Christ* (Philadelphia: Presbyterian and Reformed Publishing Co., 1950), p. 66.
4. Ibid.
5. Norman Geisler and Ron Rhodes, *When Cultists Ask* (Grand Rapids: Baker Book House, 1997), pp. 41, 77, 94, 130, 231, 247, 299.
6. *The NIV Study Bible*, ed. Kenneth Barker (Grand Rapids: Zondervan Publishing House, 1985), MacBible software, Zondervan.

Chapter Six—The Holy Spirit

1. Robert M. Bowman, *Why You Should Believe in the Trinity* (Grand Rapids: Baker Book House, 1989), p. 116.

2. Ibid., p. 117.

3. Albert Barnes, "John," in *Notes on the New Testament* (Grand Rapids: Baker Book House, 1996), p. 346.

4. *The Wycliffe Bible Commentary*, ed. Everett F. Harrison and Charles F. Pfeiffer (Chicago: Moody Press, 1974), p. 1109.

5. *The NIV Study Bible*, ed. Kenneth Barker (Grand Rapids: Zondervan Publishing House, 1985), MacBible software, Zondervan.

6. *The International Bible Commentary* notes: "There is no reason for assuming that the Holy Spirit was not fully imparted at this moment. . . . That they were quickened here is beyond question" (*The International Bible Commentary*, ed. F. F. Bruce [Grand Rapids: Zondervan Publishing House, 1986], p. 1262).

7. See *New Bible Commentary*, ed. R. T. France, D. A. Carson, J. A. Moyer, and G. J. Wenham (Downers Grove, IL: InterVarsity Press, 1994), p. 1064.

8. *The Bible Knowledge Commentary: New Testament*, ed. John F. Walvoord and Roy B. Zuck (Wheaton: Victor Books, 1983), electronic edition, Parson's Technology.

9. The *NIV Bible Commentary* suggests: "Surely what Jesus is speaking of here is not an isolated act but a settled condition of the soul—the result of a long history of repeated and willful acts of sin through hardness of heart (cf. [Mark] 3:5)" (*Zondervan NIV Bible Commentary: New Testament*, ed. Kenneth L. Barker and John Kohlenberger III, vol. 2 [Grand Rapids: Zondervan Publishing House, 1994], p. 151).

10. *The IVP Bible Background Commentary*, New Testament, electronic version, Logos Software.

11. See *Wycliffe Bible Commentary*, p. 950.

12. *NIV Bible Commentary*, p. 151.

13. Ibid., p. 321.

Chapter Seven—The Reality of Human Sin

1. William L. Lane, *The Gospel According to Mark* (Grand Rapids: Eerdmans Publishing Company, 1974), p. 105.

2. Quoted in Ron Rhodes, *The Heart of Christianity: What It Means to Believe in Jesus* (Eugene: Harvest House Publishers, 1996), p. 106.

3. *The Bible Knowledge Commentary: New Testament*, ed. John F. Walvoord and Roy B. Zuck (Wheaton: Victor Books, 1983), electronic edition, Parson's Technology.

4. Norman Geisler and Ron Rhodes, *When Cultists Ask* (Grand Rapids: Baker Book House, 1997), p. 175.

5. Alfred Edersheim, quoted in J. Dwight Pentecost, *The Words and Works of Jesus Christ* (Grand Rapids: Zondervan Publishing House, 1981), p. 289.

6. *Zondervan NIV Bible Commentary: New Testament*, ed. Kenneth L. Barker and John Kohlenberger III, Vol. 2 (Grand Rapids: Zondervan Publishing House, 1994), p. 327.

7. *The NIV Study Bible*, ed. Kenneth Barker (Grand Rapids: Zondervan Publishing House, 1985), p. 1637.

8. *Bible Knowledge Commentary*, p. 343.

9. Robert Stein, *Difficult Passages in the New Testament* (Grand Rapids: Baker Book House, 1990), p. 83.

Chapter Eight—Jesus' Redemptive Sufferings

1. Albert Barnes, "Luke," in *Notes on the New Testament* (Grand Rapids: Baker Book House, 1996), p. 85.

2. *The Wycliffe Bible Commentary*, ed. Everett F. Harrison and Charles F. Pfeiffer (Chicago: Moody Press, 1974), p. 1024.

3. *The Wycliffe Bible Commentary*, p. 1024.

4. *The Bible Knowledge Commentary: New Testament*, ed. John F. Walvoord and Roy B. Zuck (Wheaton: Victor Books, 1983), electronic edition, Parson's Technology.

5. William L. Lane, *The Gospel According to Mark* (Grand Rapids: Eerdmans Publishing Company, 1974), p. 573.

6. *The Bible Knowledge Commentary*.

7. *The Quest Study Bible*, ed. *Leadership* and *Christianity Today* (Grand Rapids: Zondervan Publishing House, 1994), p. 1408.

8. *The Quest Study Bible*, p. 1408.

9. Barnes, "John," in *Notes*, p. 372.

10. Wilbur Gingrich William Arndt, *A Greek-English Lexicon of the New Testament and Other Early Christian Literature* (Chicago: The University of Chicago Press, 1957), pp. 681-83.

11. Anthony A. Hoekema, *The Four Major Cults* (Grand Rapids: Eerdmans Publishing Company, 1978), p. 349.

12. John Calvin, *Commentary on John's Gospel* (Grand Rapids: Baker Book House, 1949), Vol. 1, p. 64.

13. Millard J. Erickson, *Christian Theology* (Grand Rapids: Baker Book House, 1985), p. 834.

14. John Calvin, *Commentary on Romans* (Grand Rapids: Baker Book House, 1949), p. 211.

15. Cited in Norman F. Douty, *The Death of Christ* (Swengel, PA: Reiner, 1972), p. 15.

16. Calvin, *Commentary on John's Gospel*, Vol. 1, p. 126.

17. Walter Elwell, "Atonement, Extent of the," in *Evangelical Dictionary of Theology* (Grand Rapids: Baker Book House, 1984), p. 99.

Chapter Nine—The Salvation of Humankind

1. Norman Geisler and Ron Rhodes, When *Cultists Ask* (Grand Rapids: Baker Book House, 1997), p. 151.
2. Ibid.
3. Leon Morris, *The Gospel According to John* (Grand Rapids: Eerdmans Publishing Company, 1987), pp. 321-22.
4. *The NIV Study Bible*, ed. Kenneth Barker (Grand Rapids: Zondervan Publishing House, 1985), MacBible software, Zondervan.
5. William L. Lane, *The Gospel According to Mark* (Grand Rapids: Eerdmans Publishing Company, 1974), p. 307.
6. *The Bible Knowledge Commentary: New Testament*, ed. John F. Walvoord and Roy B. Zuck (Wheaton: Victor Books, 1983), p. 32, emphasis added.
7. *The IVP Bible Background Commentary*, New Testament, electronic version, Logos Software.
8. Leon Morris, *Luke* (Grand Rapids: Eerdmans Publishing Company, 1983), p. 128.
9. *The Quest Study Bible*, ed. *Leadership* and *Christianity Today* (Grand Rapids: Zondervan Publishing House, 1994), p. 1426.
10. *The Wycliffe Bible Commentary*, eds. Charles F. Pfeiffer and Everett F. Harrison (Chicago: Moody Press, 1974), p. 1078.
11. J. Dwight Pentecost, *The Words and Works of Jesus Christ* (Grand Rapids: Zondervan Publishing House, 1982), p. 125.
12. *Ryrie Study Bible*, ed. Charles Caldwell Ryrie (Chicago: Moody Press, 1994), p. 1500.
13. Albert Barnes, "John," in *Notes on the New Testament* (Grand Rapids: Baker Book House, 1996), p. 248.
14. F. F. Bruce, *The Hard Sayings of Jesus* (Downers Grove, IL: InterVarsity Press, 1983), p. 24.
15. Pentecost, *Words and Works*, p. 238.
16. John Blanchard, *Whatever Happened to Hell?* (Durham, England: Evangelical Press, 1993), p. 11.

Chapter Ten—Can Salvation Be Lost?

1. *The Bible Knowledge Commentary: New Testament*, ed. John F. Walvoord and Roy B. Zuck (Wheaton: Victor Books, 1983), electronic edition, Parson's Technology.
2. See *The Wycliffe Bible Commentary*, ed. Everett F. Harrison and Charles F. Pfeiffer (Chicago: Moody Press, 1974), p. 947.

3. See *Ryrie Study Bible*, ed. Charles Caldwell Ryrie (Chicago: Moody Press, 1994), p. 1649.

4. *Zondervan NIV Bible Commentary: New Testament*, ed. Kenneth L. Barker and John Kohlenberger III, Vol. 2 (Grand Rapids: Zondervan Publishing House, 1994), p. 350.

5. *The Bible Knowledge Commentary*, Parsons Technology.

6. J. Dwight Pentecost, *The Words and Works of Jesus Christ* (Grand Rapids: Zondervan Publishing House, 1981), p. 441.

7. *The NIV Study Bible*, ed. Kenneth Barker (Grand Rapids: Zondervan Publishing House, 1985), MacBible software, Zondervan.

8. *The Bible Knowledge Commentary*, electronic edition, Parsons Technology.

9. Zane C. Hodges, *The Gospel Under Siege* (Dallas: Redencion Viva, 1981), p. 42.

10. Pentecost, *Words and Works*, p. 442.

11. *The Bible Knowledge Commentary*, electronic edition, Parsons Technology.

12. See Albert Barnes, "Matthew," in *Notes on the New Testament* (Grand Rapids: Baker Book House, 1996).

13. John Wesley, *The Nature of Salvation* (Minneapolis: Bethany House Publishers, 1987), p. 134.

14. John Blanchard, *Whatever Happened to Hell?* (Durham, England: Evangelical Press, 1993), p. 116.

15. Wesley, *Nature*, p. 130.

Chapter Eleven—Treating Others Kindly

1. *The Wycliffe Bible Commentary*, ed. Everett F. Harrison and Charles F. Pfeiffer (Chicago: Moody Press, 1974), p. 1013.

2. *The Bible Knowledge Commentary: New Testament*, ed. John F. Walvoord and Roy B. Zuck (Wheaton: Victor Books, 1983), electronic edition, Parson's Technology.

3. Joseph A. Fitzmyer, *The Gospel According to Luke (I-IX)* (New York: Doubleday & Company, 1983), p. 641.

4. Fitzmyer, *Luke*, p. 641.

Chapter Twelve—Living Ethically

1. John Howard Yoder, *The Politics of Jesus* (Grand Rapids: Eerdmans, 1972), chs. 2, 5, 8.

2. *The Quest Study Bible*, ed. *Leadership* and *Christianity Today* (Grand Rapids: Zondervan Publishing House, 1994), p. 1459. Robert Stein says that "any literal interpretation of the passage is incorrect" (Robert Stein, *Difficult Passages in the New Testament* [Grand Rapids: Baker Book House, 1990], p. 93).

3. R. C. Sproul, *Now, That's a Good Question* (Grand Rapids: Tyndale Publishing House, 1996), p. 523.

4. Myrtle Langley, *The New International Dictionary of New Testament Theology*, ed. Colin Brown (Grand Rapids: Zondervan, 1978), 3:978.

5. J. P. Moreland and Norman Geisler, *The Life and Death Debate: Moral Issues of Our Time* (New York: Praeger, 1990), p. 135.

6. Leon Morris, *Luke* (Grand Rapids: Eerdmans Publishing Company, 1983), p. 245.

7. *The Bible Knowledge Commentary: New Testament*, ed. John F. Walvoord and Roy B. Zuck (Wheaton: Victor Books, 1983), electronic edition, Parson's Technology.

8. Stein, *Difficult*, p. 91.

9. Ibid., p. 81.

10. See Albert Barnes, "Luke," in *Notes on the New Testament* (Grand Rapids: Baker Book House, 1996), p. 99.

11. The *Bible Knowledge Commentary*.

12. J. Dwight Pentecost, *The Parables of Jesus* (Grand Rapids: Zondervan Publishing House, 1982), p. 96.

13. Stein, *Difficutt*, p. 72.

14. Ibid.

15. J. Dwight Pentecost, *The Words and Works of Jesus Christ* (Grand Rapids: Zondervan Publishing House, 1981), p. 180.

16. *The Wycliffe Bible Commentary*, ed. Everett F. Harrison and Charles F. Pfeiffer (Chicago: Moody Press, 1974), p. 938.

17. F. F. Bruce, *The Hard Sayings of Jesus* (Downers Grove, IL: InterVarsity Press, 1983), p. 67.

Chapter Thirteen—Prayer and Faith

1. *Evangelical Commentary on the Bible*, ed. Walter A. Elwell (Grand Rapids: Baker Book House, 1989), p. 820.

2. Leon Morris, *Luke* (Grand Rapids: Eerdmans Publishing Company, 1983), p. 195.

3. *Evangelical Commentary on the Bible*, p. 821.

4. Marvin R. Vincent, *Word Studies in the New Testament* (Grand Rapids: Eerdmans Publishing Company, 1975), II:260.

5. See *Zondervan NIV Bible Commentary: New Testament*, p. 31.

6. *The Bible Knowledge Commentary: New Testament*, ed. John F. Walvoord and Roy B. Zuck (Wheaton: Victor Books, 1983), electronic edition, Parson's Technology.

7. Ibid.

8. Ibid.

9. F. F. Bruce, *The Hard Sayings of Jesus* (Downers Grove, IL: InterVarsity Press, 1983), p. 111.

10. David O'Brien, *Today's Handbook for Solving Bible Difficulties* (Minneapolis: Bethany House Publishers, 1990), p. 139.

11. Norman Geisler and Ron Rhodes, *When Cultists Ask* (Grand Rapids: Baker Book House, 1997), p. 137.

12. Ibid.

Chapter Fourteen—The Prophetic Future and the Afterlife

1. *The Wycliffe Bible Commentary*, ed. Everett F. Harrison and Charles F. Pfeiffer (Chicago: Moody Press, 1974), p. 1525.

2. *The Bible Knowledge Commentary: New Testament*, ed. John F. Walvoord and Roy B. Zuck (Wheaton: Victor Books, 1983), electronic edition, Parson's Technology.

3. *The IVP Bible Background Commentary*, New Testament, electronic version, Logos Software.

4. *The Bible Knowledge Commentary*.

5. Leon Morris, *Luke* (Grand Rapids: Eerdmans Publishing Company, 1983), p. 264.

6. *The IVP Bible Background Commentary*.

7. Ibid.

8. *Zondervan NIV Bible Commentary: New Testament*, ed. Kenneth L. Barker and John Kohlenberger III, Vol. 2 (Grand Rapids: Zondervan Publishing House, 1994), p. 23.

9. Anthony A. Hoekema, *The Bible and the Future* (Grand Rapids: William B. Eerdmans, 1984), p. 280.

10. Merrill F. Unger, *Beyond the Crystal Ball* (Chicago: Moody Press, 1973), p. 167.

11. Hoekema, *Bible and Future*, p. 285.

12. Leon Morris notes: "Many see it as an adaptation of a popular folk-tale, perhaps originating in Egypt, which contrasted the eternal fates of a bad rich man and a virtuous poor man. If Jesus had taken over a popular tale, He has given it a stamp of His own" (*Luke*, p. 252).

13. *The NIV Study Bible*, ed. Kenneth Barker (Grand Rapids: Zondervan Publishing House, 1985), MacBible software, Zondervan.

14. Norman Geisler and Ron Rhodes, *When Cultists Ask: A Popular Handbook on Cultic Misinterpretation* (Grand Rapids: Baker Book House, 1997), p. 104.

15. Morris, *Luke*, p. 128.

Chapter Fifteen—The Devil and Hell's Angels

1. Charles C. Ryrie, cited in Paul Enns, *The Moody Handbook of Theology* (Chicago: Moody Press, 1989), p. 298.

2. *The Wycliffe Bible Commentary*, ed. Everett F. Harrison and Charles F.

Pfeiffer (Chicago: Moody Press, 1974), p. 1064.

3. Leon Morris, *Luke* (Grand Rapids: Eerdmans Publishing Company, 1983), p. 309.

4. Ibid., p. 185.

5. Ibid.

6. F. F. Bruce, *The Hard Sayings of Jesus* (Downers Grove, IL: InterVarsity Press, 1983), p. 134.

7. *The Bible Knowledge Commentary: New Testament*, ed. John F. Walvoord and Roy B. Zuck (Wheaton: Victor Books, 1983), electronic edition, Parson's Technology.

8. *The IVP Bible Background Commentary*, New Testament, electronic version, Logos Software.

9. Peter H. Davids, *More Hard Sayings of the New Testament* (Downers Grove, IL: InterVarsity Press, 1991), p. 27.

10. *The NIV Study Bible*, ed. Kenneth Barker (Grand Rapids: Zondervan Publishing House, 1985), MacBible software, Zondervan.

11. Davids, *Hard Sayings*, p. 27.

12. *The NIV Study Bible*, p. 1928.

13. *The IVP Bible Background Commentary*.

14. *The Bible Knowledge Commentary*.

15. *The IVP Bible Background Commentary*.

16. Ibid.

17. See *Evangelical Commentary on the Bible*, ed. Walter A. Elwell (Grand Rapids: Baker Book House, 1989), p. 742.

Chapter 16—Some Puzzling Sayings of Jesus

1. *New Bible Commentary*, ed. R. T. France, D. A. Carson, J. A. Moyer, and G. J. Wenham (Downers Grove, IL: InterVarsity Press, 1994), p. 1002.

2. Leon Morris, *Luke* (Grand Rapids: Eerdmans Publishing Company, 1983), p. 219.

3. *The IVP Bible Background Commentary*, New Testament, electronic version, Logos Software.

4. Albert Barnes, "Matthew," in *Notes on the New Testament* (Grand Rapids: Baker Book House, 1996), p. 242.

5. See *New Bible Commentary*, p. 1029.

6. See Marvin R. Vincent, *Word Studies in the New Testament*, Vol. 3 (Grand Rapids: Eerdmans, 1975), pp. 469-70; Kenneth S. Wuest, *Wuest's Word Studies*, Vol. 1 (Grand Rapids: Eerdmans, 1973), p. 184.

7. *Millard J. Erickson, Christian Theology* (Grand Rapids: Baker Book House, 1987), p. 435.

8. *The NIV Study Bible*, ed. Kenneth Barker (Grand Rapids: Zondervan Publishing House, 1985), p. 1500.

9. Vincent, *Word Studies*, I:60.

10. *Vine's Expository Dictionary of Biblical Words*, ed. Merrill F. Unger, W. E. Vine, and William White (Nashville: Thomas Nelson Publishers, 1985), p. 291.

11. F. F. Bruce, *The Hard Sayings of Jesus* (Downers Grove, IL: InterVarsity Press, 1983), p. 87.

12. Morris, *Luke*, p. 249.

13. *The Wycliffe Bible Commentary*, ed. Everett F. Harrison and Charles F. Pfeiffer (Chicago: Moody Press, 1974), p. 1051.

14. *The IVP Bible Background Commentary*.

15. Barnes, "Matthew," in *Notes*, p. 115.

16. Vincent, *Word Studies*, II:293.

17. Barnes, "John," in *Notes*, p. 376.

Primary
Verse Index

Subject
Index

⟨≈⟩

Reasoning from the Scriptures Ministries is a discipleship ministry that exists to help you grow strong in the Word of God and equip you to become knowledgeable in the application of biblical wisdom.

We publish a free newsletter and offer numerous materials (many free) on a variety of relevant issues.

If you would like to be on our mailing list, or if we can be of service to you in any way, please do not hesitate to write.

Ron Rhodes
Reasoning from the Scriptures Ministries
P.O. Box 80087
Rancho Santa Margarita, CA 92688

We also have a free Internet newsletter that goes out to thousands of Christians in over 40 countries. If you would like to subscribe, send an e-mail to ronrhodes@earthlink.net and put "Subscribe" in the body of your e-mail.

⟨≈⟩